# Out in the Cold

Travels North:
Svalbard, The Faroe Islands, Iceland,
Greenland & Atlantic Canada

**Also by Bill Murray**

**Common Sense and Whiskey:**
**Modest Adventures Far from Home**

**Visiting Chernobyl,**
**A Considered Guide for Travelers:**
**What You'll See and What to Know**

# Out in the Cold

### Travels North: Adventures in Svalbard, the Faroe Islands, Iceland, Greenland, & Canada

## Bill Murray

EarthPhotos Books · Georgia USA

**Out in the Cold**
**Travels North: Svalbard, the Faroe Islands,**
**Iceland, Greenland & Atlantic Canada**

Because of the dynamic nature of the internet, some of the web sites mentioned in this book may have changed or no longer be valid. They were accurate on the original publication date.

Photographs in this book are available for purchase or download from, and appear in color on, the website EarthPhotos.com.

Set in PT Serif font and printed in the United States of America.

ISBN-13: 978-1541039841
ISBN-10: 154103984X

Cover Photograph: The Faroe Islands

Visit these associated websites:
CommonSenseAndWhiskey.com
EarthPhotos.com

Portions of Part Four: Greenland appeared in the book
*Common Sense and Whiskey*

EarthPhotos Books
Young Harris, Georgia, USA

**Neophyte Publishing**
**2017**

For my mother, Jean E. Murray

# CONTENTS

Preface

1 Svalbard                                          1
2 The Faroe Islands                                57
3 Iceland                                         105
4 Greenland                                       167
5 Canada, and a Bit of France in North America    221

Acknowledgements                                  303
References and Further Reading                    319
About the Author                                  323

**A NOTE ABOUT NUMBERS:**

This book assumes a basic knowledge of both the metric and imperial systems of measuring distance and temperature. Judging that a conversion in parenthesis in each instance, for example, "Lava shot 1.4 kilometers (0.86992 miles) into the sky," would detract from both flow and impact, I have used both systems, depending on which seems more appropriate.

If you are entirely unfamiliar with one system or the other, do not fret. Some simple rules of thumb will hold you in good stead:

- 1 meter is a little more than a yard (1.09), and thus
- 1 yard is a little less than a meter (.91)
- 1 kilometer is a little more than half a mile (0.62), and
- 1 mile is about a kilometer and a half (1.6)

Some reference points for temperature:

minus 20C = -4 F
minus 10C = 14 F
zero C = 32 F
10 C = 50 F
20 C = 68 F, and it won't get much warmer than that where we are going.

## PREFACE

I'm pretty sure the discovery of America started with a bar fight and I believe I can persuade you that it is so. The chain of events that brought Norse ships to Newfoundland began when a court in Norway found Thorvald Erickson guilty of murder and tossed him out of the country.

The Saga of Eirik the Red, Thorvald's son, doesn't say exactly what his old man got up to that night, just that he was exiled "because of some killings," so Thorvald and the clan loaded up the truck and they moved to northwest Iceland.

Eirik grew up and married a local girl. When Thorvald died they moved south where before long the local sheriff found Eirik guilty of murder just like his old man, and Eirik was banished from Iceland. Thorvald's bar fight led to Iceland, Greenland and the New World. We will visit the settlement his grandson built in Newfoundland.

But this is not about the Vikings, although they are here. This is a collection of northern tales from the frozen-tight Svalbard archipelago, 800 miles from the North Pole, the Faroe Islands, Iceland, Greenland and Atlantic-facing Canada.

•••••

A daiquiri on your cruise ship balcony may imply that you are on vacation, but it does not mean that you are traveling. Crowding people together on "fun ships" to share viruses for several days holds up as well as socks from Wal-Mart.

Once, in the Himalayas, in a place called Sikkim, whose very geography required vocational derringdo, a mad driver told me "Man didn't evolve from apes to act like sheep." He meant that you must engage.

Your free time is as surely an asset as your home or your car. I say, get out there and put some of it to good use. If the unexamined life isn't worth living (Socrates), get to examining. Compare and contrast your experiences to those of others.

In these pages we will meet an artisan carver of narwhal bones in Greenland. We'll cruise the streets of Reykjavik with an ebullient Icelandic author, hike with a part-time tour guide in Labrador who cannot imagine why you'd want to be anywhere other than on the tundra, and spend time with others whose lives, objectively, are nothing like your own.

We will shake hands with the President of Iceland and stand naked and alone on the side of the glacier Vatnajokull (separately from the president). We will drop in on the last French outpost in North America, talk shop with a diplomat and eat wind dried sheep in the Faroe Islands, dine with strangers alongside icebergs at a lighthouse north of Newfoundland, and find Greenland so beguiling, we will visit twice.

•••••

Who ever thinks they are finally and fully grown up? Not me, not in my 20s, or 30s or even 40s. I still think people who wear adult clothes and enjoy it, skirt and blazer, suit and tie, selling investments or copiers or conjuring income from intangibles like air time or web space - those people are grown up, or at least grown up in a way I'm not, in the western businessy way.

I will never be a winning jockey in the Great American Corporate Advancement Derby. I don't enjoy yard work or the NBA and I don't know anything about grown-up stuff like the American Automobile Association or why you should be a member. Or what those ads for active traders are talking about, when you be honest.

I don't buy clothing with the logo of its manufacturer or shop on Black Friday. That others do, that's real nice. I just don't have their motivation. But I think I've got one thing on them: I'm pretty sure the flame burns brighter in my magic adventure lamp.

Let us all think of a place that sounds exciting, take ourselves there and see what happens, minding Nelson Mandela's words: May our choices reflect our hopes and not our fears.

•••••

Imagine a range of actions: At one extreme, you never leave your house, and at the other you drive into Somalia honking your horn and waving an American flag. I like it just inside the go-too-far side of that tent, poking on the fabric with a dull knife, trying not quite hard enough to cut through.

Within reason, mind you. Cut through the fabric and you end up kidnapped in Niamey, blasted in two in Helmand or beheaded in the new Caliphate. So let us stick with adventure reasonably achievable. In this case, starting 800 miles shy of the North Pole, chasing a total eclipse.

- Bill Murray, Young Harris, Georgia, March 2017

# PART ONE: SVALBARD

*Bill Murray*

# GETTING READY

Two hours before totality, 61 minutes before first contact. I have checked, packed and repacked my gear a dozen times since dawn. It's going to get hot in all this Arctic padding. Time to get moving.

We've chosen a spot along the shore of the fjord called Isfjorden opposite the triple glaciers Wahlenberg, Bore and Hansen, down at the base of Longyearbyen on the island of Spitsbergen in the archipelago of Svalbard. It's about a twenty-minute walk.

Eighteen scant degrees above the horizon. The sun will rise no higher today, so not everywhere in town has an unrestricted view, because mountains ring Longyearbyen on all sides except down by the fjord.

Long before first contact I have two tripods up, Nikons tested, mounted and ready, and only then, more than an hour before totality, do I realize I am standing on a plain of ice, the temperature is minus 16 and neither can I leave my cameras nor do I have a thing to do.

So I jump up and down in place to keep warm. I run little circles around the tripods. I march one way and then the opposite, commanding blood to the extremities. I visualize my heart pumping blood from my chest, the rhythm of warmth radiating through narrowing arteries out to the end of the line, to my double-glove-protected fingertips.

Not much of a crowd. Incredible, but through my wide angle lens, right now I count only eighteen people on the Isfjorden plain. And while I feel foolish doing clown runs around the cameras, no need. Everybody else is finding their own ways to stay warm.

The lady in front of me does a slide-hop-kick clapping thing, side to side. People walk left to right then right to left and their breath clouds toot up into the sky.

3

My wife Mirja bounds into view across the snow, invigorated by the hike and ready for the big excitement. We stand together under an utterly clear sky, in place with time to spare for our third total eclipse. Awe me, we say.

We bounce around like flash-frozen, chattering little Michelin men while the moon's umbral shadow screams up from the Faroe Islands, Tórshavn to Longyearbyen in thirty minutes and nine seconds.

## ARRIVALS

Only the bare conjecture of dawn hints at a horizon. Lights wink along shore off Keflavik and the NATO base closed in 2006 that then and now doubles as Iceland's international airport.

There is just a confectioner's glaze of snow, far less than in Boston, where exhausted mounds of ice sulked beside the taxiways wanting to melt. Icelandic snow resists the shade of industrial grunge.

Passengers, cashiers, all of us stumble dull through the terminal and shake off remnants of sleep. The cashiers, older women, tend to plastic-wrapped sandwiches and coffee and they tender kroner from the till.

"It's not worth much." They shake their heads.

Scandinavia has a style all its own and the Keflavik airport mimics trendiest Södermalm. Blonde wood, boxy shapes, lots of space in the public space. From the air you could see the faintest prospect of day but from inside sludgy twilight perseveres.

We fiddle with our paper cups, ponder our personal desynchronoses and listen to the security admonishment not to let our bags out of our sight. Here, a good spin of the earth from every terror acronym, everybody is named -son or -dottir.

4

Sunday morning March 15th. The hashtag #tse2015 exults about the fair skies forecast over Longyearbyen in five days for Total Solar Eclipse 2015.

•••••

**NORWAY**

"Hello."

"Hello. The eclipse?" The man behind the glass peers over his reading glasses.

"Yes sir."

"Svalbard?" He already knows it.

"Svalbard." We confirm it.

He stands canted just forward, august, with airs kindlier than American passport clerks who welcome you with home and hearth warmth that says "look at me wrong and you will find yourself in a room down the hall until Thursday."

Not guarding a contentious entrepôt. None of the not-so-veiled menace. Not the suggestion of intrigue of the former Soviet apparat, and certainly not the rapacity of the wiry west African man with the stamp pad who can't even see you until your bags are under his syndicate's care.

This man, on his feet, in his dignity and his years, leaning forward in his blazer, confides, "I think Svalbard may sink. Hundreds of you have come today." They stamp everybody through, rows of clerks do, and we flood the Gardermoen arrivals hall.

A cabbie from Baidoa drives with the all the finesse of a Somali villager. It's ten degrees in the mist and a long ride into town.

Snow in the fields.

Driving underground makes sense in Oslo. Buses and cars branded as Nissan Qashqais, Renault Zoes and Hyundai Tucsons zip underground and weather free through the tunnels Smestad, Festningstunnelen and Granfoss, Bryn, Tåsen and Ekeberg, Svartdal and Vålereng and Hammersborg and Vaterland, to name ten.

In 2015 the Oslo City Council banned cars from 2019, replacing them with 60 kilometers of bicycle lanes and expanded public transportation. Helsinki has similar plans by 2050.

•••••

There is a thumping through the window. I pull back the curtain on fog and rain and yes it is, the oompa of brass and drums, a marching band. Before long a platoon of uniformed musicians comes a marching, determined, soggy, disheveled, squishing in their boots. They stomp into an urban copse that obscures the Parliament building. They disappear and reappear, squishing and banging and blowing their horns, off and on, here and there. What do they celebrate with a parade in Oslo the day after St. Patrick's Day?

Oslo doesn't seethe, or even put on a modest bustle. Urban angst is vanishingly small. The crisp tension of Anne Holt, the craven terror of Jo Nesbo? Invisible to me.

There is a sign in the window of a bank down by Big Brown City Hall: "We do not change money and we are not tourist information. Have a nice day."

I think, "Right! I'd love to come in!"

A woman jumps to her feet as I push open the glass. Once hands have been wrung and pearls clutched, she is kind enough to tell me where to find the Forex bank.

Norway's per capita GDP is more than $100,000, second in Europe to Luxembourg and sixth in the world. Its pension fund, Norges Bank Investment Management, is the world's largest sovereign wealth fund. Norway imports garbage to fuel its incinerators. Above and beyond its North Sea oil wealth, hydropower provides 99 percent of Norway's energy.

Its five million people live in Europe's fifth-largest country by area if you don't count Russia. The pilot Mark Vanhoenacker, in his book *Skyfaring*, considers countries by the time it takes to fly across them. Belgium is a fifteen-minute country, he says, while Norway is a full two hours south to north.

The flip side of Norway's surfeit of land, energy and riches is the second highest cost of living in the world behind Switzerland. Even so, tourists come because Norway is gorgeous.

The collapse of Iceland's krona boosted tourism there in 2008 but despite the strong Norwegian krone, both air and cruise arrivals are at records, says Visit Norway, the tourism board.

•••••

A man from New Delhi I know says power in his part of the world is all about setting up two sides to fight and then standing back. This strikes me as the opposite of Norwegian inclusion, by which even Anders Behring Breivik is technically scheduled to be let back into society in 2033.

Breivik, the product of an ill-fated liaison between a diplomat and a nurse who met in the laundry room of their block of flats, shot up the government quarter and the island of Utøya in 2011, killing many. That evil day has beat on these people, hammered them, because they are but a small tribe, alone up here by themselves, just trying to live with each other, in the rain.

Every so often you see fawning news reports about the Norwegian corrections system, about its 71 detainees per 100,000 versus 698 in the United States. It's not just Norway. In Denmark prisoners wear their own clothes, cook their own food and may have private family visits up to once a week in an effort to lower recidivism.

On immigration, too, Scandinavia's well-meant efforts get a lot of press, or at least they used to. Prior to 2015's confusing and record breaking year of asylum seeking, nearly one percent of Norway's population were refugees. There were 119 Norwegians per refugee, versus these numbers in nearby states: Sweden,107, Denmark 412, Finland 582, Iceland 5504.

Not that the best intentions don't draw criticism. An Oslo professor named Unni Wikan argues that Norway is creating a culture of welfare dependence that attracts immigrants in a dangerous way. Wikan's tough-love campaign has brought charges of racism.

Rubbish, she says. She just wants all these good Norwegian country folk to wake up. After a spate of rapes involving immigrants she called Norwegian women "blind and naive" towards non-Western immigrants.

Her book *Generous Betrayal* argued that social benefits and good intentions actually stood in the way of more meaningful integration, resulting in an immigrant underclass. Public opinion is racing to catch up with *Generous Betrayal,* which was published way back in 2001.

As migration speeds up, entirely different cultural and religious traditions swarm all the northern lands. A would be immigrant to

Norway named Abdu Osman Kelifa, from Eritrea, told *The New York Times* in December 2015 that where he comes from, "if someone wants a lady he can just take her and he will not be punished," and that "men have weaknesses and when they see someone smiling it is difficult to control." The idea of justified rape is novel in Norway.

With "immigrants" morphing seamlessly into "refugees" all across Europe, Norway runs education programs at asylum centers cross the country, schooling men from Eritrea and Sudan, men in flight from the wars of the Arab Spring and even men in search of a life better than they had in the Balkans.

The course manual teaches asylum seekers that "to force someone into sex is not permitted in Norway, even when you are married to that person." The courses explain that it is "not religion that sets the laws" and ask asylum seekers, "is it O.K. to 'soften someone up' with alcohol?"

At the same time Norway's national police press ahead with an idea unthinkable in the United States, announcing in early 2016 it will disarm the cop on the beat "as soon as possible," or at least require him/her not to wear weapons in holsters but rather to leave them in their patrol cars.

In 2014 Norwegian police fired their weapons twice the entire year, causing no injury. For the previous dozen years the police had killed two. In the U.S. over 1,000 were killed by police in 2015.

"As things stand now," said Odd Reidar Humlegard, the national police commissioner, "our laws do not allow for systematic arming."

And thus in steps forward and back, a small, culturally pure group comes to terms with multi-culturalism in a process that has produced, in extremis, self-deluded cultural protectors like Breivik.

# STEREOTYPES

Finland, Sweden, Norway, Denmark, Iceland. Before the recent migration challenges each had homogenous, similarly isolated and relatively small populations. Scandinavians are country folks at heart, whose Norse ancestors' sailing adventures made them inadvertent people of the world by opening up trade routes across the Atlantic, the Baltic, even across Russia to the Black Sea.

Not that there aren't differences between them. The stereotypes run like this:

The Finns are the hopeless exiles, caught out for too long in their own top right corner of Europe, their language unrelated to the Scandinavians on one side or the Russians on the other, unallied, with not even cold comfort from their Russian border.

The Swedes are arrogant and wealthy, the Icelanders too far away. The Danes are decadent pleasure-seekers. The whole region drinks too much but somehow the Danes pull it off as hedonists, carefree, while the Finns are seen as alcoholic and depressed.

And Norway? They're pointy bearded fishermen in flannel and hip boots. Outdoorsmen. Country people. The butt of "stupid" jokes clear across Scandinavia:

- Andreas wore both of his winter jackets when he painted his house last July. The directions on the can said "put on two coats."

- Ole and Håkon brought bananas on their first train ride. As they began to peel them, the train entered a long, dark tunnel. "Have you eaten your banana yet?" Ole asked. "No," replied Håkon. "Vell don't touch it den," Ole exclaimed. "I yust took vun bite and vent blind!"

- A neighbor asked Eirik why the Norwegian government doesn't draft men until age 45. Eirik explained, "Dey vant to get dem right otta of high school."

## CHASING SHADOWS

Let's get one thing straight at the beginning. A lunar eclipse simply will not do. You may have seen a partial solar eclipse, but neither will that do. The sun is such a monster that until a few minutes before totality the light from the sun blasts right around the disk of the moon and the Earth is little changed.

Annie Dillard wrote that the difference between a partial eclipse and a total one is the difference between kissing a man and marrying him.

Just so. So people search out totality, no matter how remote the spot.

The illuminati of the eclipse world are here. There's Miloslav Druckmueller from Brno University of Technology, Czech Republic, the undisputed king of eclipse photographers. He's out by the airport, part of a research team that calls itself the Solar Wind Sherpas, here on their twelfth eclipse excursion led by Dr. Shadia Habbal of the Institute for Astronomy at the University of Hawaii.

The Sherpas have split into two groups to maximize the chances that one gets clear skies. They're using imaging and spectroscopy to learn why the sun's corona is hotter than its surface, far hotter, as much as a million degrees or more.

These researchers join those at the world's northernmost higher education facility, The University Centre here in Longyearbyen, who study the aurora and the ionosphere, among other topics (courses include Radar Diagnostics of Space Plasma, Polar Magnetospheric Substorms and Geological Constraints of $CO_2$ Sequestration).

11

*Bill Murray*

And now, wielding more kroner to spend then expertise to lend, here come the rest of us. The umbraphilic trickle becomes a deluge with six planeloads arriving in Svalbard in one day, the most ever, 737s full of para-astronomers and armchair scientists, some bearded with thick glasses, others post-adolescent with knock knees, all poking at devices glimmering and electronic.

We ride up in the Norwegian Air Shuttle, main cabin. Unkempt hair, dandruff, and too-short slacks prevail; men with organized, step-by-step minds mingle in the aisle with all the agitated, giggling aplomb of engineers at a prom.

Some among us are young and some are not; some of the not so young have resigned themselves to the Sansabelt approach to fashion, waistbands spreading under polo shirts of dubious style. Anticipation crackles between scientist and civilian.

You don't get this vibe flying to Florida to meet a cruise ship. No hedonism here. Slide rules, had they still existed. Discomfort readily endured in search of two minutes twenty eight seconds of perfection.

"What precise time is totality?" "Where is the place to see it best?"

Everyone swaps their eclipse greatest hits:

"I saw THAT one from Turkey...." (29 March, 2006. We saw that one from Turkey, too. From Cappadocia.)

"The Libyans turned us away at the border!" (Same eclipse, different place. But there's another chance at seeing a total solar eclipse in Libya in 2027.)

"...it was so beautiful and Victoria Falls was grand ...." (the solstice eclipse in Zimbabwe, June 2001.)

"...made plans THREE YEARS in advance!" This was Lime Green Polo, and he could have been talking about any eclipse.

For the 2006 eclipse we reserved our hotel before it occurred to the management to raise prices. For this eclipse the only chain hotel in Longyearbyen was bulk-booked by a travel outfit - all of the rooms - even before you could buy airline tickets.

• • • • •

Around 18:45 two days before the eclipse, the sun touches the horizon at 78 degrees north latitude as we deplane in Svalbard. You can tell the minute you step outside that two hours forty minutes flying north from Oslo is a long way north.

"Six planes today!" The airport bus lady shakes her head. Normally SAS comes in twice a day and Norwegian once on Mondays, Wednesdays and Fridays.

Six times today this procession of 737-800s packed six across delivers 186 or 189 people into a tundra settlement of two thousand, all of us carrying every gadget and recording contraption, each of us hoping for nothing more than a fair morning on Friday.

A retired NASA scientist named Fred "Mr. Eclipse" Espinak signs his emails wishing you "Clear Skies, Fred." We all concur.

Mr. Eclipse is the only star in the eclipse firmament who is missing. Fred Espinak is taking in his 27th eclipse down in the Faroe Islands.

• • • • •

## LONGYEARBYEN

People apparently will live anywhere on this Earth. Even in Svalbard, this cold-hammered raft of ice 800 miles from the North Pole, people pursue careers, raise families and form a tight, thriving community of 2,667 people in July 2015, albeit one with the approximate diversity of an Appalachian city hall.

They conduct scientific research. They fall in love. They buy lip balm in bulk just because a bunch of it comes in. They handle the everyday and the mundane, like clearing snow or driving a bus or standing behind the counter at the apotek or providing airport security.

A few of them raise families. Mostly very young families. 2015 statistics show 124 children up to age 12, but only 31 of high school age. There are two kindergartens but only one other school, covering all grades through high school. Young adults come to live in Svalbard, graduate students, contract workers. They come for a fixed assignment and then most of them go home.

Longyearbyen reaps the benefits of being part of modern, advanced Norway in a way that the nearby Russian settlement does not (it's called Barentsburg, and we will visit shortly). Longyearbyen has almost as many snowmobiles as people (2,163 v. 2,667) and 95.7 percent household penetration of broadband. Statistics for Barentsburg are not available. The average income for working people in Svalbard is higher than on the mainland because Svalbard is largely tax free and prices are lower.

The high Arctic comes with its peril. The weather presents sometimes fatal challenges; just before Christmas 2015 a storm with hurricane force winds caused an avalanche that killed two people who were buried right in their homes.

Because of polar bears firearms are mandatory outside Longyearbyen town, though it must be said that after all the public warnings, if you come face to face with a polar bear something has already gone horribly wrong. Above all, Longyearbyen is cold, with average air temperatures ranging from -8C/17.6F in February to 8/46.4 in high summer. People in Longyearbyen spend a great deal of time trying to stay warm.

Peoples' teeth chatter, we shiver, we get goosebumps, and all of that is good, our natural defenses at work. With origins on the savanna, we humans are just not designed to live in a place like Svalbard.

Our hairs that stand up to cause goosebumps, (a process called "horripilation,") are an evolutionary vestige of our ancestral furriness, but a weak mimicking of the natural ability of your dog or cat, who will appear larger as her fur stands up when the temperature dips below freezing. Check it out.

Other animals use fat to stay warm, sometimes several inches of it. A poor heat conductor, fat keeps the core warm. This is the polar bear's trick, so much more effective than layered clothing.

The body's core temperature is 37C and things can go badly wrong with even small deviations. At 38C you have a fever and at 36C you begin to shiver.

The agent here is a gland in the brain called the hypothalamus. It is a driven little bastard whose job is to maintain homeostasis, the status quo, across all the body's systems.

•••••

"I may have faults but being wrong ain't one of them," Jimmy Hoffa declared.

The hypothalamus is like Jimmy Hoffa. It has no second thoughts. It is genial as a tomcat in a bathtub. It has no compassion and it does not fool around. In extreme cold it will sacrifice your extremities to maintain warmth in your core.

Have you ever used one hand to prise the other hand's fingers away from, say, a snow shovel you have kept in a tight grip on a cold day? If you have, you have seen the hypothalamus in action. Your fingers needed blood to warm them, but that would have sent more cooled blood than usual back to your body's core, a course that could ultimately lead to hypothermia. So your hypothalamus refused.

To keep warm blood in your core it constricted blood flow to the extremities, actually making your blood vessels physically smaller. And

16

it was willing to keep it up all the way to frostbite, which can freeze not just your skin, but the muscles and tissue beneath it.

Your corneas can freeze, too. Not with short exposure because the salinity of tears will lower the freezing temperature. But because the cornea is ninety percent water it is fragile and at risk, and so when skiing or snowmobiling, which can produce a mighty chill wind, goggles are mandatory. People have dropped out of cross-Arctic races because of freezing-eye problems.

Cold weather problems are not equal opportunity. Non-white elderly men are most susceptible, young white women least. The temperature gradient from skin to core is greater in women than men, which both helps women maintain a more stable core temperature, and explains why women's hands are always cold.

Who doesn't enjoy hearty stews more in winter than in summer? Heavier foods don't give us layers of fat like polar bears have, but your body yearns for them in the service of staying warm and it will lead you to find them.

Once, in the Tibetan village of Tinggri near the Nepalese border, downright frigid in winter at 4,300 meters (14,107 feet), an irresistibly delicious aroma lured us up a ladder to a sort of restaurant where the only food on offer was deep fried yak fat. When in Tibet....

•••••

**BARENTSBURG**

A little group gathers this morning down by the fjord at the edge of town. The day before the eclipse has dawned clear. Our luck is holding.

We are utterly out of our element, tourists through and through. Today holds the promise of hours of pounding across the tundra, a snowmobile trip to the Russian settlement at Barentsburg.

We are all curious about our Arctic wear. We paw through different sizes and splay ourselves out across the room pulling ourselves into one-piece snowmobile suits.

The other day I watched a woman walk down to the waterfront in tight blue jeans and no head cover. Stylish as she found herself, you just can't do that kind of thing here and the snowmobile people can't be responsible for your hypothermia, so you strap yourself into their suit, boots, helmet, goggles and today, double balaclavas because it is cold cold, one of the guides, Hans Peter says. One man opts out of the trip rather than surrender his medical shoes for mandatory fur boots.

The suits work. They keep you if not warm, then not cold. The danger is the contact points between goggles and balaclava because if you expose skin there, while moving at 35 or 50 kilometers per hour, wind chill will cause frostbite in short order.

When we are all strapped into our thermals, wool undergarments, ski pants, gloves and heavy outer mittens, double balaclavas, helmets and goggles, everybody looks like everybody else. We are so anonymous that later inside the dining hall at Barentsburg and stripped of our outerwear the guides ask around, "are you with us?"

Anonymity serves as metaphor for the dark season in Longyearbyen, where the sun set 25 October and only rose again (for an hour) on 15 February. In winter, with the tourists gone and Longyearbyen's population shrunk to maybe 1,500, are people drawn into a more tightly knit community?

I conjure visions of ruddy cheeks and hot chocolate at a toasty warm community center, cozy people playing chess and discussing books and quilting. Hans Peter says no, it's not that way, not really. Community develops reluctantly among anonymous bundles hurrying up the foot paths in the cold and the dark.

They suit us up and put 22 strangers through our paces on how to drive a snowmobile. It is only a five-minute lesson because there really isn't much to learn. Push this to start the engine, pull that to go, wiggle your body with the curves. And supervision is close at hand.

This outfit is all about moving along, sportsters through and through. They run us through novice moves, herding us in a tentative straight line. We ease out along a coastal plain, the Isfjorden to our left, just a little ice bobbing in the water, shuttered and abandoned coal mines on our right, busy with the pylons of old coal-carrying cableways, stacked up along the hill that hems in Longyearbyen to the east. Just minutes, the buildings along the Longyearbyen waterfront still visible, a shakedown cruise, then we stop for final questions.

The propriety of handing unfamiliar go-fast machines to anybody who shows up, I'm not sure about that, but I'm glad. Over the course of the day I race up to 70 kph briefly and it is a pure thrill.

Now we are firing across capacious plains ringed by snow-laden hills. From here to Barentsberg we run for forty, fifty minutes between stops. We buckle in, adjust our balaclavas and goggles to cover our faces and plunge into an extended run the length of Adventdalen, the valley behind the ridge east of Longyearbyen.

Clean, dry and bitterly cold, the beauty of the route utterly unmediated by man save for snowmobile tracks. Beauty no one sees. Bits of moisture not quite snow, not hail or rain, evanescent, suspended, rise as often as they fall in the monochrome. The air is alive but the earth is stone still.

*Bill Murray*

Somewhere along the way we come upon the most unexpected spectacle - the launch of a hot air balloon. A team from the Connecticut-based Slooh "community observatory" is practicing for their video coverage of the eclipse from the air. When the balloon disappears behind a fell, one snowmobile towing another sets out to follow it and pick up the crew wherever they land.

It tickles me, the grim military bearing the leaders wield like a club to bring all these unsteady novices to a stop. Up front Hans Peter leans forward and opens up a little space between him and the pack so that he can hop off his mount and guide us all in for a rest stop, forming up in rows four or five abreast. He moves to each spot and rotates his forearm down from the elbow with a stiff wrist flick and I imagine a scowl of doom behind his helmet.

We stop on a low rise called a pingo for a random geology lesson. Dome shaped mounds like mini-volcanoes, pingos form in permafrost when artesian groundwater forces its way up, freezes under the ground and rises under pressure from the water below. Pingos grow vanishingly slowly and take decades or longer to form, often at the base of fells (fell, "fjall" is the Old Norse word for mountain), as has the one on whose summit we sit frozen to our seats this morning, between two ridges.

Interesting in a textbook maybe, but you don't read textbooks on a lump of frozen tundra that shows all the vitality of a mound scraped off the runway at Boston Logan. It is not unlike the landscape as far as the eye can see. With the temperature firmly, stubbornly below zero, I use Hans Peter's lecture as an opportunity to dab ineffectually at my nose and balaclavas with my mittens, and readjust my goggles.

In short order I have run into the indelicate problem of a very runny nose under my double balaclavas. I have reassured myself since that I was not alone with deficient hygiene.

Your nose is meant to prep the outside air to meet your nice warm, moist lungs. Cold air is usually dry, so when you breathe in your nose is preauthorized to add moisture, and will automatically produce more fluid. Then when you exhale, the outside air can't hold all the moisture in the nice warm air inside you, so it condenses right there on the tip of your nose. Cold air gets you coming and going.

There may be an avoidance technique the accomplished snowmobiler knows but I have no idea. In long stretches of snowmobiling there is no opportunity to clean your balaclava, so the problem ... accumulates. At occasional stops, wearing mittens with only thumbs, it is a challenge to, ah, clean yourself up, especially in the midst of your 21 new best friends. At least we are anonymous. I hope all those standard issue balaclavas they handed out in duplicate came from the island's best laundry.

•••••

My fingers have formed to the shape of the handlebar grip, my shoulders are frozen high and tight to my neck. Blood sinking toward my center, I think. Careful. We thunder into Grøndalen, green valley, that leads to Grønfjorden, "Green Fjord," a liquid icicle intruding perhaps fifteen kilometers inland from the larger Isfjorden. A track along its eastern shore provides our entrée to Barentsburg. The top of the ridge on the far side of Gronfjord provides visual drama, dipping in and out of cloud.

Driving conditions into Barentsburg village are good because late-in-the-season snow is compacted, not too fresh, and snowmobiles work best on compacted paths, where their tracks find and naturally slide into the grooves made by those who came before.

Opening the snowmobile up to modest speed for a sport snowmobiler feels secretly heroic for those of us with more timid ambition. Blazing along at seventy kilometers per hour I find myself grinning under all that headwear, holding on tight, very, very tight.

•••••

If, as Sylvain Tesson suggests, the art of civilization is combining the most delicate pleasures with the constant presence of danger, then Norway has not civilized the archipelago, but only the little settlement at Longyearbyen.

For outside of Longyearbyen, on the other side of those Beware of Polar Bears signs, there is only ice. None of the perpendiculars of carpentry, no angular form fashioned by man. Just snow, ice, a horizon that undulates, and sky. No sound but snowmobile engines and the wind in your helmet.

No evidence of life extends beyond us and the sound of our engines. No animals, no birds, no roads or road signs, no cables carrying power or pipes pumping water. An entirely inanimate place, or at least one whose only animation, the glacial movement of ice, evades our perception.

•••••

Stephen J. Pyne, who spent months as a member of a party of twelve near the center of Antarctica, writes "... the self can only exist — can only be felt and known — in contrast to an Other." In much of the polar regions there is no Other, only a constricted, inanimate, frozen world. And that is a challenge for mental hygiene.

Admiral Richard E. Byrd tried to spend an Antarctic winter alone in 1934. Byrd had parlayed a respected naval career into $150,000 in cash contributions (during the Great Depression!) for his expedition. Among other things Byrd's team of 56 men meant to build a meteorological base where a team of three would record the weather conditions daily. (Also on this expedition was an American named Paul Siple, who developed the "wind chill factor.")

Construction of the weather hut began too late in the fall, on 22 March, amid appalling conditions in temperatures as low as -60F. Water condensed and froze in the fuel lines of the tractors. The dog sled teams pulled out after three days and the tractors after three more. After just six days of camp construction, Admiral Byrd remained alone inside the 9x13, eight-foot-tall prefabricated building. When the last tractor left the hut was already buried, with only the radio antennae and the instrument shelter visible.

The sun set for the winter on 19 April. Byrd maintained regular weather and aurora observations and a three-times-a-week schedule of radio communications until he fell ill on 31 May. His erratic manner on the radio eventually prompted a rescue - after two failed attempts - as three men reached Byrd's hut by tractor on 10 August. Byrd was too ill to leave the hut until finally spring weather allowed a flight in on 12 October.

The conventional explanation for Byrd's illness is carbon monoxide poisoning caused by poor ventilation in the hut. Water froze in the ventilator and stove pipes and the exhaust pipe of the engine that drove the generator.

Stephen Pyne has a different theory: "The truer answer might be the folly of trying to simplify existence amid what was already so simple as to belong on a moon of Saturn."

Pyne isn't surprised things went awry for Admiral Byrd.

"Freedom is relative: it requires coercion of various sorts in order to have meaning," he says. But in his stay in Antarctica "there was nothing to rebel against. You could do whatever you wished. The catch was, there was almost nothing to do .... There is not enough on site to generate the contrasts that allow ideas to arc between them."

The pilot and author Ernest K. Gann got round to the same idea in a different way. In the context of flying through cloud, he put it like this: "It would be better if there were something to relate to something else and so provide a focus for the mind."

•••••

To the great Norwegian explorer Roald Amundsen, adventure was just bad planning, but to the poor lady in our improbable little Arctic tribe who inexplicably just suddenly drives off alone, so deep into uncompacted snow that her snowmobile finally judders to a halt in a bank she tosses up higher than she, snowmobiling is no adventure.

There is no reason why. It just happens. Our convoy pulls up to wait while they fish our errant snowmobiler out of the snowbank just below Barentsburg town. She is shaken and insists on riding pillion from now on. They tow her snowmobile.

While we wait the sun bursts through the clouds onto the opposite shore, just so gorgeous, so pristine, all the Earth silent but for our snowmobiles. We are thirty five miles of coastline toward the Greenland Sea from Longyearbyen and we might as well be alone in the world.

We leave our snowmobiles in a big jumble in the middle of town - happy not to be vibrating to the motor and bouncing on the snow - and fan out along Main Street. A Lenin statue, the kindergarten and housing blocks, a brewery. The Orthodox church perches lonely at the far end of town, toward the water. The only modern-looking building, the Russian consulate, sits way at the back of town, behind the blocks of flats.

Lenin in Barentsburg

A scant posse of three mottled reindeer regards us down there. They might come to eat a biscuit from our hand if we have one but we don't. Their ancestors walked here during the last ice age, alongside Svalbard's only other land mammal, the Arctic fox. It is illegal to disturb wildlife, but today they present as forlorn, dependent on humans, begging for scraps.

Walking one end of town to the other and back takes scarcely ten minutes. It takes a half hour for all of us to climb out of our gear, find our own place on the floor to make a pile of it and assemble in the dining hall, and another half hour to repeat the process in reverse when it is time to go.

Outpost Barenstburg's Sovietness may be a day trip from Longyearbyen by snowmobile but it is decades - and one Cold War - away in style. Even this far from the Motherland it has what the young

*Bill Murray*

Croatian writer Sara Nović calls the "Eastern Bloc aura - the posturing with size and cement."

Could life in Norilsk be like this? Could the unrelenting sting of some godforsaken terminus way up on the River Lena feel like Barentsburg? It must be even more bleak out there in Siberia.

This must be cleaner, even though coal dust falls across the snow when the wind is just so. If the eastern shore of Gronfjorden is this bereft of succor, Norlisk, where life expectancy doesn't even touch fifty because nickel rots your lungs, must be a not very virtual hell.

•••••

Arktikugol, the mining company and only employer, has been pulling coal out of the ground in Barentsburg since 1932. Since 1989 forty workers have died beneath this ground.

Arktikugol bought the operation from a Dutch company which named the place Barentsberg after Willem Barentz, the Dutchman who discovered Svalbard in 1596. Barentsburg was shelled to the ground by the German battleship Tirpitz during World War Two after its Soviet citizenry had been evacuated to Arkangelsk.

Most of today's workers are Donbass Ukrainian. Léo Delafontaine, a French photographer who has made three trips to document Barentsburg (and whose expertise helps inform my impressions of Barentsburg) tells me the conflict in eastern Ukraine bubbles not far underneath the surface:

"You can find in Barentsburg pro-Russians, pro-Ukrainians, pro Donbass Republic. In my opinion, pro-Russians are more willing to express their opinion. And the pro-Ukraininans are more discreet. But everybody knows in the town on which side you are. They just don't

26

talk about it in order to avoid conflicts. Barentsburg is very small, and it's better like this."

Life in the mine may be dangerous as the civil war back home and above ground may be cold, but you won't be sniped dead from the rooftop across the way. The pay, around $1,000 a month, runs triple what they might get back home, even if it is in rubles. Which is okay with most of these workers, who after all come from the Russian-speaking east of Ukraine.

Most are here on two year deals. A few come from farther corners of the former Soviet space. The Tajiks and Armenians do the less skilled work. Armenians tend to work in construction so they mostly live in Barentsburg in summer. Tajiks clear the snow. While the Russians and Ukrainians have their own kitchens and bathrooms in proper apartments, the couple dozen Tajiks and Armenians sleep in dormitories or shared flats.

There is no cash money in Barentsburg. Those rubles are paid to a magnetic card issued when the worker signs up with Arktikugol. There is a canteen and a supermarket with prices in rubles.

But this is Norway, after all, and so the hotel bar takes Norwegian kroner. Much better for the hotel, also owned by Arktikugol, but not so great for workers. All they can afford is Russian canned food from the company store.

Tourists can't buy things for workers because the supermarket only takes rubles. Between the language and monetary borders, workers and tourists can't really mix at all.

•••••

It is a fair question how much post-Soviet life has improved. The despair of getting your pay in scrip in Russian money you can't spend anywhere but the company store. The baleful hopelessness of trudging to your frozen dormitory after mining coal grim and underground, regarding the bulging muscles of the heroic workers on the murals, knowing their time - like the Lenin statue's - is firmly past.

Out front of your door a rusty monument mocks you: "Our Goal - Communism!" With an exclamation mark. (There are prettier murals, of fishies and flowers, children and walruses and whales).

The 70s and 80s concrete Soviet Brutalist buildings. Still! in 2016! That's the ones that aren't wooden and falling in on themselves. The grime. The soot.

If you feel you must grasp for superlatives, let's see, you can say "Barentsburg is the second-largest settlement in Svalbard," which is true, but besides Barentsburg and Longyearbyen there are only Ny-Ålesund, a research station with a population of 35 this time of year, two Norwegian meteorological outposts with populations of ten and four, and a Polish science station with a population under a dozen.

In the good old days fellow Russians lived in the mining community of Pyramiden, over a thousand of them, just across the fjord, but they abandoned that operation in 1998 (leaving behind the "bottle house," a drinking establishment lined with 5,308 empty glass bottles).

But wait just a minute, what? Russians and Poles, you're asking? What are they doing in Norway in the first place?

Svalbard started out like Antarctica, as a territory not owned by any nation, but that became untenable once mineral wealth was discovered. As part of the Versailles negotiations following the Great War nine countries signed the Svalbard Treaty making the archipelago part of the Kingdom of Norway, but guaranteeing all the signatories the right to carry out commercial activity here (the list has grown to 42 today including Afghanistan and North Korea). Russia keeps

Barentsburg no more for coal than as a foothold way up here in the Arctic.

During the most frigid part of the Cold War workers sought out the Barentsburg cold. There was a sports palace and a cultural center. There was a cow house and a greenhouse and food from the mainland, and all of the food was free. Everything was free. No unemployment. A worker's paradise.

Like many Soviet cities, Barentsburg was organized around its principal industry. It was a self-contained mini-city, the mining business supporting the cinema, the apartments, day care. The collapse of the Soviet Union in the 1990s was as tough on Barentsburg as it was on Russia.

Barentsburg's population fell from over 1,300 to about 350 today. Back home, the union was shorn of its republics in 1991 and decay proceeded apace. The army occupied the Russian White House in Moscow in 1993. In 1994, the first Chechen War. And in 1996 an Arktikugol-chartered flight carrying 141 workers and their families slammed into the mountain Operafjell on approach to Longyearbyen.

There were no survivors. The crash so devastated the Russian community that it precipitated the closure of Pyramiden. Since then four more Russian helicopters have crashed.

There is a small museum and a sports center with pool, a Russian staple. In Chernobyl we saw the Olympic-sized pool they built for the leading Soviet scientists who came to live in that model city. I didn't see the pool in Barentsburg but I learned that it is about half Olympic size.

There is a textile factory that clothes the miners and a Norwegian company uses the factory's low prices to produce traditional Norwegian costumes. Fifty kids live here, or twenty. The numbers

29

change year to year. There is a kindergarten and a primary school. The murals of children at play and flowers and fishies are pretty but not entirely accurate. Children must play inside in the winter.

There is no movie theatre but since reliable and widespread internet came a couple of years back, maybe that's not so bad.

The Russians have a lingering Soviet knack, a certain way against warmth. We all sit in rows of tables warmed by the set meal and we are grateful and it is good, but the scene reminds me, almost to individual curtains, of the same meal at the end of a long day once in Chernobyl.

•••••

Now a half day from Longyearbyen, we are only a few hours away from a much anticipated lecture at UNIS, where scientists will gather those interested for a lecture on tomorrow's eclipse. We are fairly confident that the bus will be here soon to take us back. A friend in Finland once came here by the boat that ties up 140 steps down to the harbor. That'll work, too.

But there is no bus and the boat doesn't sail between February and May. The only way back is the way we came. Suit up and go.

•••••

Heading home, I am very much alive. Kudos to those who live here and love it. From time to time we drive through ferocious bursts of snow, reducing all visual cues to one - the tail light on the snowmobile in front of you. Damn it Hans Peter, slow the hell down up there before my last connection with color in the whole wide world disappears.

But he does not so I'm by god speeding up. I'm not going to lose sight of that tail light. I will not become lost in the Arctic.

It may have been a wee bit irresponsible for them to load up twenty two-odd first timers and then take us to trounce across the tundra at fifty kph and more. At long last, as we are about to gun it over the glacier and back into Longyearbyen, an attempt that take two tries because some of our fellows miss the approach, Sigrid, the trailing guide, comes around to each of our snowmobiles to make sure we engage "sport mode."

"We like sports here," she explains.

It shows. She doesn't need to be drawn to boast of her project for the coming summer - filming the eastern fjords by kayak.

•••••

**GUNS!**

As the clouds of the American Civil War gathered, Sen. James Hammonds of South Carolina described the mood in the U.S. Congress in 1860: "The only persons who do not have a revolver and a knife are those who have two revolvers." He generally described the legal mandate for a tundra tour in Svalbard. These groups leave well armed.

The guides at each end of our snowmobile train carry kit aimed at preventing a polar bear attack. In case of snow squalls they bring tents for an emergency overnight stop. They are equipped with flares, maps and compasses and a whole load of gear towed on sleds behind both the lead and trailing snowmobile, plus towing equipment, used today to bring back the snowmobile of the lady who lost her nerve somewhere in a snowbank.

For camping, the University Centre recommends a .308 Win or higher caliber rifle, devices to drive off polar bears like flare guns or emergency signal flare pens with crack cartridges, a first aid kit, wind-proof personal survival kits, a groundsheet, maps and compass, a GPS device, trip wires (preferably at two heights, 30 and 70 centimeters above the ground) with flares to protect camps, emergency food and liquid, additional mittens, gloves and caps, an emergency beacon, another means of communication (VHF radio, cell phone, satellite phone), matches in waterproof container, burner and cooking fuel, pots, a tent and sleeping bag, 20 meters of rope for hauling or rescue, a survival suit and during winter, an avalanche transceiver, avalanche search rod, head torch with extra battery, ice spikes for personal rescue, snow shovel and candle.

When setting up camp, "the use of tripwire is recommended. Test your weapon, the flare gun/pen and pyrotechnical gear prior to, and, by all means, also during your expedition," according to the University Centre's field safety guide.

Walking around Longyearbyen town proper without such protection is okay, but carrying a rifle is mandated by law outside of the center, and on the airport road just at the base of town stands a sign that warns, Polar Bears!

So this headline comes as no surprise:

> **Polar Bear Mauls Svalbard Tourist**
> Last-minute eclipse seekers had been warned
> *By: The Editors*
>
> Czech tourist Jakub Moravec was camping on the Norwegian archipelago of Svalbard for the solar eclipse when he was dragged from his tent and mauled by a polar bear. He was treated at a local hospital for superficial claw wounds to his back.
>
> "It was going for my head. I used my hands to protect my head," Jakub Moravec told the AP.

Moravec had been part of a group of six tourists on the remote island archipelago. They were camping north of Longyearbyen, Svalbard's main town, which thousands of tourists have been visiting recently to view the solar eclipse. Lodging was sold out for years in advance of the event.

It's certainly not the first time a tourist on Svalbard has been attacked by a polar bear. The animals live on the islands and have frequent interactions with people.

Tourists had been warned in advance about the dangers of the island, especially when camping out. "I think there's been a tendency, even before the eclipse, that a lot of people come here and they don't know where they're going," Aksel Bilicz, manager of Longyearbyen Hospital, told the AP. "Both the weather conditions and the bears can be very dangerous."

## BEARS!

"Animals are routinely superhuman in one way or another. They outstrip us in this or that perceptual or physical ability, and we think nothing of it."

It would be nice if, as Amit Majmudar hopes in *The Brains of Animals*, we would "cease to regard animals as inferior, preliminary iterations of the human—with the human thought of as the pinnacle of evolution so far—and instead regard all forms of life as fugue-like elaborations of a single musical theme."

The polar bear's theme would be variations on solitude.

The world's largest land carnivore hunts the margins of the ice, the surface of the water and the continental shore. He slips into the sea without a splash and soundlessly breaks the surface on his return. He may tread water twenty miles from shore.

"In winter," writes Barry Lopez in *Arctic Dreams*, "while the grizzly hibernates, the polar bear is out on the sea ice, hunting. In summer his tracks turn up a hundred miles inland, where he has feasted on crowberries and blueberries." The polar bear is called ice bear ("isbjorn") in Norwegian and Icelandic. Individuals are known from tagging to range from here in Svalbard all the way to Greenland, via the ice.

Polar bear fur is unique to mammals, and not terribly protective in water. Beaver fur traps a layer of air between skin and water. Bear fur, by contrast, loses 90% of its insulative value in water. Mother bears are reluctant to swim with young cubs in the spring: the cubs don't have enough fat (bear cubs are so small at birth, weighing scarcely more than a pound, that a mother can hide one in the rolled toes of her front paw). As long as they don't have to go into water, dry fur keeps little cubs warm at very cold spring temperatures.

Instead of fur, polar bears, like whales, rely on a layer of blubber, measuring as much as 4.5 inches thick, to keep them warm in water. Outside the water their winter pelage is adequate for temps as low as -40F with a 15 mph headwind.

The conservationist and Sierra Club founder John Muir said bears move "as if the country had belonged to him always," a bear metaphor that fits the current Russian leadership.

The San, the bushmen of southern Africa, are said to be such expert trackers that infidelity is practically non-existent, in part because everyone recognizes everyone else's footprints. In the same vein, Lopez says, the Inuit "make a fine distinction between male and female (bear) tracks, not merely on the basis of size - a male's paw may be 13 inches long and 9 wide - but because of faint marks left by longer

34

hairs around a male's foot and because of the female's slightly more pigeon-toed track."

Polar bears eat seals (adult males need to kill 50 - 75 per year). Native tales say polar bears push blocks of ice ahead of them as shields when stalking seals, wounded bears will stanch the flow of blood with snow, and that bears will throw rocks at walruses to distract them in order to snatch an unprotected calf.

And one more thing, according to Lopez: "If one must leap in desperation from a charging bear it should be to the bear's right." Most polar bears are left-pawed.

•••••

The smallish island of Kongsøya to the east, a low and frozen place surrounded by skerries, has the highest known density of bear dens in the world. Because of nearly catastrophic over-trapping in the last century the Norwegian government has prohibited human activity there without approval.

Norway has blown hot and cold on interdicting polar bear trafficking. After over 900 bears a year were killed in Svalbard in the 1920s, Norway had, by 1927, prohibited use of poison and twelve years later had closed denning areas to hunting.

Still, in the 1950s hunters chartered boats, airplanes and helicopters to shoot the bears. From 1952 tourist hunters could cruise with a sealing ship to the pack ice and shoot one bear each. By the 1960s the Norwegian Travel Service declared bear hunting in Svalbard to be "one of the finest big game hunts in the world ... hunting them in the pack ice is an experience a hunter can never forget."

By 1970 scientists estimated there were no more than 1,000 bears in the archipelago, and that the population was endangered. A 1973 international agreement regulated hunting and today researchers believe the population is in healthy recovery. As a result, by one count there were twelve dens per square kilometer on Kongsøya, and authorities counted 168 bears on the island in the 1980s.

Today, poaching is the greatest direct human threat to polar bears - but not the only threat, especially in Russia. Indirectly people threaten polar bears, and whales, as we will see in the Faroe Islands, with pollution. Bears and whales are at particular risk because they rest at the summit of the food chain where they consume prey that have progressively accumulated toxins from farther down the chain.

•••••

We never see a polar bear on our visit. A 2004 census counted more bears than people in the survey area, which comprised the archipelago and Russian parts of the Barents Sea, the bears' natural migratory area. The most recent count came in fall 2015, and according to a report by the Norwegian Polar Institute, "as the Russians did not take part this time, the results are uncertain," though it suggests the total number of bears in the Norwegian part of the survey area has increased.

March is not when the bears are most numerous in inhabited areas. Most confrontations occur in December. From the end of summer until then scant ice has formed in the fjords around Longyearbyen, and so the bears may wander closer to town for food and surprise people with their first appearance of the season.

Two or three bears are killed most years in self defense and any bear shot in defense of self or property becomes property of the state. The shooting of any bear anywhere in the archipelago is referred to police. Several years ago a trapper protecting his dog food shot two bears. The shootings were ruled unnecessary and the trapper fined.

## ANTICIPATION

What an extraordinary run of fine weather! A woman in the grocery grabs my arm to emphasize how lucky this all is. It has almost always been cloudy "since I came up in February" (now it's late March) - except this string of four or five fine days. The skies, the snow, the light all shine with a high latitude clarity. And it need only hold for one more day.

We are elated. If we pull this one off, we will be three for three viewing total solar eclipses, having blundered from Budapest down to Lake Balaton in a minibus in August, 1999 and then grilled kebabs out of a van on the plains wast of Nevsehir in Cappadocia, Turkey in March 2006. Almost exactly nine years later the last minute forecast is for fine weather. But it wasn't a given that we'd be here.

Norwegian Air Shuttle pilots went on strike three weeks ago. They were our ride from Oslo to Svalbard and there was simply no question of getting here another way. The other airline flying there, SAS, was sold out when we tried to buy tickets two days after they went on sale.

It's the damnedest thing, isn't it? Everything works fine until it doesn't. You plan as if your good money, paid in good faith, assures your progress around the globe, but sometimes forces of nature or the parochial affairs of men get in the way. In this case the pilots thought they could make a better living working for the parent company rather than the Balkanized series of subsidiaries that write their paychecks in the various countries Norwegian's flights serves.

Some 700 pilots were striking and 800 cabin crew were sent home without pay. Tension rose on one particular horse farm in the southern United States. As we packed, the airline's spokesperson, Anne-Sissel Skånvik, was less than hopeful.

*Bill Murray*

"We struggle to see how we can get to a solution," she told Norway's TV2.

There was some hope. An article in the Svalbard English language newspaper Icepeople reported that after missing two scheduled flights, the third, the Monday flight from Oslo, operated despite the strike. Norwegian flies the route on Mondays, Wednesdays and Fridays. Surely they would find a way to fly despite the strike.

In the end pilots and management hammered out an agreement a few days before the eclipse. Still, the strike exposed the perils of flying to an island at the end of the Earth. No backup.

•••••

**MYTH**

A great chariot carried the sun across the ancient Norse sky, and two wolves gave chase. Suppose they caught it? Some said that was when an eclipse occurred. In old French and German there are expressions like "God protect the moon from wolves."

To Transylvanians, human failing caused the sun to shudder and turn away in disgust, covering herself with darkness. Putrid fogs gathered, poisonous dew fell from the sky and ghosts swarmed the earth. After an eclipse water and produce were thought contaminated and unsafe, even for livestock. The poisonous dew might bring plague.

Native Alaskans too believed eclipses sent something vile descending to earth. Whatever it was could cause sickness if it settled on cooking tools so women turned over their pots and hid the spoons underneath.

Into the nineteenth century humans would huddle indoors. If they had to go out they would cover their mouths and noses. All across the

Carpathian mountains the more superstitious would even destroy clothing they'd left drying outdoors.

In the Faroe Islands 1954 eclipse "a woman named Erla Kirstin Viberg recalled her mother telling her to bring in the sheets from the clothesline so that they wouldn't burn. 'People were talking about total destruction,'" wrote Lavinia Greenlaw in *The New Yorker*.

Since they were accustomed to the sun disappearing for long stretches during the winter, it's hard to say just how alarmed northern people became at the loss of the sun, but elsewhere people clanged and pounded on pots and pans, screamed, shouted and cried out to scare away whatever evil spirit had descended. The Chippewa shot fiery arrows into the sky hoping to rekindle the sun.

And whoever they were and whatever they did, in time the people were always successful. The demon always left the sun.

•••••

An often quoted statistic by laymen like we in Longyearbyen is the wonder-filled fact that total eclipses are possible only because the sun's diameter is about 400 times that of the moon, while the moon is about 400 times closer to earth, allowing for the moon's disk to just cover the sun's. Consider the serendipity.

Further, we just happen to be here at the right moment in the cosmos. The moon's orbit drifts about four centimeters a year away from earth. Scientists have measured its retreat using tools left on the moon by the Apollo program. A billion years ago all eclipses entirely blotted out the sun, and in just fifty million years the moon will be too small when viewed from Earth to ever cover the sun. Even now it barely does. If the moon's diameter were just 169 miles smaller total eclipses would be impossible.

*Bill Murray*

Suppose that next Tuesday you wake up on the equator. Swinging in a hammock on the beach and turning with the earth, you will travel 24,901 miles that day, not counting the swinging.

Pull your calculator from your bathing suit, divide 24,901 by the length of a day, 23 hours, 56 minutes and four seconds, and you find that you and your hammock have been traveling 1,040 miles per hour.

Up here, more than the beachwear is different. At Longyearbyen the Earth's circumference is just 5,101 miles. At 78 degrees north the Earth turns at a leisurely 215 miles per hour. The Central European time zone at Svalbard stretches just 212 miles. With the fastest car and a good road you could just about drive across the time zone before an hour was up and go back in time.

•••••

A legendary Welsh shepherd named Guto Nyth Bran was so fast that he could blow out a candle and be tucked into bed before the light faded. Like the shadow of the moon, he traveled faster than the fastest commercial jet. Except the Concorde.

The speed of the moon's umbral shadow - the thing that causes totality - varies with the latitude at which it crosses Earth. It can move as slowly as 1,710 kilometers per hour, and Concorde's maximum cruising speed was 2,200 kilometers per hour, which got scientists thinking. In 1973 a team aboard Corcorde flight 001 chased the moon's shadow for an incredible 74 minutes of totality across Africa, besting by nearly ten times the maximum earthbound length of totality, which is about 7-1/2 minutes.

The Concorde didn't go into passenger service until 1976, but in 1973 was in in-flight testing. Packed with gear from a British team headed by Dr. John Beckman with the Astrophysics Group at Queen Mary College, London, flight number 001 rose into the air for a rendezvous.

The pilot, André Turcat, and a crew of four were joined by seven astronomers, two assistants and a photographer for a mach 2.05, hour and fourteen minute totality like no other.

•••••

At the beginning of each lunar month we call the moon "new." The sun, moon and Earth line up like you did in grade school, one behind the other. Out in space this happens every 29.5 days. Here on Earth the Gregorian calendar rules the business and legal world but the rhythm of the moon regulates more soulful realms like the Chinese and Vietnamese New Years, the Hindu Diwali festival, and the Islamic holy month of Ramadan.

At new moon the moon is between the Earth and the sun, so the sun shines on the side of the moon facing away from the Earth, and the moon is invisible to us, beginning its monthly cycle. The scientific word for this is syzygy, more a word I might connect with human reproduction, or questionable hygiene.

Eclipses occur in clusters. A bit of celestial mechanics shows why. The orbit of the moon is tilted about five degrees from the Earth's orbit around the sun, so the plane of the moon's path crosses the Earth's twice a year on opposite sides of its orbit (called nodes), once ascending and once descending, in intervals of 30 to 37 days. This is when you see eclipses.

(Worthy digression: The moon doesn't really orbit the Earth. They centrifugally pull each other around a common center of gravity roughly 3000 miles from the Earth's center).

The orbits of the sun, Earth and moon don't all sync up, so the sun crosses one of the moon's nodes and returns to it every 346.62 days, not quite a year. As a result eclipse "seasons" march slightly backward across our Gregorian calendar, as does Ramadan, calculated by the 354 day lunar calendar.

Either the Chaldeans of Babylon were incredibly smart people, or there wasn't much to do in Mesopotamia hundreds of years BCE. Studying the heavens, the Chaldeans determined that every 6,585.3 days the yearly cycle of the moon around the Earth around the sun repeats, and so every eighteen years ten days and eight hours (or 18 years 11 days eight hours, depending on some dense math about leap years) there occurs a very similar eclipse.

This discovery led to eclipses being grouped into families, each called a *saros*. Today there are 40 different saros series in progress. Our Svalbard eclipse belongs to saros 120.

For any two eclipses separated by one saros, the moon is nearly at the same position with respect to its node (that point at which the moon's orbit crosses Earth's orbit) and is also at almost the same distance from Earth. Not only that, the eclipse occurs at virtually the same time of year.

Saros series are not equal to a whole number of days (eighteen years ten days and *eight hours*). In those eight hours the earth rotates, so later eclipses are viewed by people a third of the globe away. The path for each successive eclipse in a saros series shifts about 120 degrees westward. Make your reservations for eighteen years from now accordingly.

•••••

**FIGURING OUT ECLIPSES**

Besides being tiny bits of land surrounded by oceans, Svalbard and the west African island of Principe share vanishingly little, but just like the Solar Wind Sherpas are doing on Svalbard this week, a hardy team of

British scientists set out a hundred years ago to made eclipse history on Principe.

On 8 March, 1919 Sir Arthur Stanley Eddington and his party sailed from Liverpool bound for the equator, and just north of there, on 23 April, landed in the Gulf of Guinea on a small, humid, buggy island around a hundred twenty miles west of the African coast.

Albert Einstein's audacious 1915 theory of general relativity sorely needed testing. If it were proven right it would mean that space and time are pliable as the surface of a trampoline, twisting and bending all over the place.

Relativity predicted that light need not always travel straight, but rather should warp as it passes the gravitational field of an object in space, like the sun. But how to measure such a thing?

If light from stars *behind the sun* were bent by the sun's gravitational field, those stars' apparent position might be distorted so that they became visible. Their apparent position should be different from their position in the sky at night, when the sun is far away on the other side of the Earth.

But how to see behind the blinding light of the sun? Perhaps with the help of the moon, during an eclipse.

Two years after publication of Einstein's theory, the British Astronomer Royal Sir Frank Watson Dyson worked out that during the eclipse of 29 May, 1919, the sun would cross the Hyades, a cluster of stars near enough that there would be a number of stars bright enough to see through a telescope, and that the island of Principe would be a fine place to watch it.

Dyson sent Eddington to test Einstein's theory.

Scientific cooperation between countries waxes and wanes as surely as celestial bodies. Freed from Soviet restrictions, in the 1990s Russian scientists rushed to collaborate with their counterparts, eager to compare their science with the West. Some of that collegiality has since lessened.

Similarly, by 1919 the Great War had severed lines of scientific communication. A Russian mathematician knew of Einstein's work but couldn't participate from behind the walls of a German prison. A German astronomer couldn't test the theory from his perch at a Russian prison camp. A naval blockade kept German scientific journals from crossing the English Channel. To Eddington that was plain wrong.

Eddington learned of Einstein's work through a middleman mathematician in neutral Holland, whom Einstein could visit.

A British scientist's aggressive work on the theories of a German physicist kicked up controversy, especially as Eddington, a Quaker, claimed conscientious objector status and needed the help of Dyson, his boss the Astronomer Royal, to stay out of jail. Packing Eddington off to do science on a remote island for several months was just the thing.

•••••

Eddington: "The baggage was brought ... mainly by tram, but with a break of about a kilometer, where it had to be transported through the wood by native carriers."

The party set up their viewing station at latitude one degree forty minutes north, using "freely" the "ample resources of labour and material" available locally.

Eddington noted that "Near the center" of this tiny six-by-ten mile island, "mountains rise to a height of 2,500 feet, which generally attract heavy masses of cloud."

And so they did. "The days preceding the eclipse were very cloudy. On the morning of May 29 (eclipse day) there was a very heavy thunderstorm...."

But "about half-an-hour before totality the crescent sun (partial eclipse) was glimpsed occasionally."

It would have been an awfully long trip to have come back empty, but in the end "16 (photographic) plates were obtained ... by moving a cardboard screen unconnected with the instrument."

Eddington compared a set of "true" positions of the stars - photos he had taken of the same patch of sky when the sun was nowhere around - with the set of photos he took during the eclipse. He could confirm Einstein's theory.

•••••

The day after Eddington announced his findings, the New York Times of 10 November, 1919, ran these headlines:

## LIGHTS ALL ASKEW IN THE HEAVENS
Men of Science More or Less
Agog Over Results of Eclipse
Observations.

––––––––––

### EINSTEIN THEORY TRIUMPHS

––––––––––

Stars Not Where They Seemed
or Were Calculated to be,
but Nobody Need Worry.

•••••

Politics will forever hover over science. But in this case, right in the middle of the Great War, Arthur Eddington brought down barriers to advance the scientific standard, to explain Einstein's theory and to spark the imagination of an otherwise war-distracted public.

As a bonus, the Eddington team saw the largest solar prominence to be seen at a total eclipse since. It extended some 100,000 kilometers beyond the surface of the sun.

•••••

**WONDER**

I can think of only one phenomenon that compares with totality, and like this particular eclipse, it too is a product of high latitude extremes.

The northern lights, like a solar eclipse, get to something elusive in their essence, an elemental and spiritual thing. In each there is balance. The eclipse pulses raw, brute, human-diminishing power.

"Behind that moon is the SUN!"

Physical forces heave massive objects across the heavens, yet our awe derives from the delicacy of the thing, the wispy fit of the moon over the sun, the elegance of the ballet, the notion that this is impossible, but it is happening!

The eclipse is fiery anger. The aurora is fragile delight. It fills the sky. It is utterly spellbinding. It scales your body to tiny, but broadens your soul and calls you up into the sky. There is no brute here. The aurora is delicate, its airiness calling forth humility and awe. You fall mute in its silence, for if you shout you might break it.

It swells across the firmament and you feel small as a church mouse. A Cal Berkeley psychology professor named Dacher Keltner has demonstrated that awe makes people feel physically smaller than they really are. Nicolai Ceausescu and a long line of Communist architects intuited that. As did the builders of any of Europe's grand cathedrals.

The Northern Lights' grand size casts off human scale entirely. Awe. Wonder. Emotions from childhood. Innocent, wholesome, affirming. Wonder works outside what the philosopher Jesse Prinz calls the "drab world of appearances."

The gods invite wonder. Prinz says we recruit the gods, and monsters, to explain the unknown. Wonder happens when something is utterly unique, when past experience doesn't help. Wonder comes in the absence of any frame of reference. When the totality of a solar eclipse puts up its spectacle we are rightly and truly mystified. We are awed.

The moon moves silent through all its nights and days but at the actual moment, when my jaw is agape and all of the rules of this world are suspended and we are playing by the gods' own rule book, I feel the moon rubbing across the sky and I think it should make a sound like twisting a balloon.

*Bill Murray*

Right up until the moment of totality, the Earth is not dark.

Until the moment, .....

Until the moment, ............

The moment we've been waiting for

The daytime sun gives warmth even in the Arctic, 800 miles from the North Pole. The eclipsed sun gives nothing. It is cold, and more, it is chilling, an alien body performing raw, clinical, huge-scale mathematical astronomics, throwing off flaming evidence of its anger, prominences seen only then, mighty violence on fleeting display. Once it is revealed you are frightened to have seen that it is so.

You have registered somewhere deep under the skin another alien, raw thing; the comforting life-giving sun was just five minutes ago an orange ring of flame surrounded by darkness, a fanged personality, no tulips and honeybees.

After the sharp escalation of sheer anticipation, a week of anxiety about the weather and the fusillade of emotion during the event, the diamond ring pops onto the disc of the moon and the thing is over. You remain quiet for a time, failing to quite absorb what you have seen, but more than seen, you have *perceived*.

And then you pack up and go, long before the moon has cleared the sun. The last half of an eclipse, between the third and fourth contacts, that is underrated. And under-attended.

I've always felt the clearing after a storm, a real tempest of a storm, is melancholy. The settling of atmospheric accounts that returns sunshine is the sort of thing better sorted out by the weather gods after dark than during the day.

The same after an eclipse. It takes some time for the Earth to settle back down from all that rambunctiousness.

Yet totality's fleeting brevity demands that you return to see if you really saw what you thought you saw in those hurry-up! no slow down! seconds. So we will be back. In 2017 the shadow falls right across our farm back in the U.S.A.
Mirja and I stood on an icy fjord and saw vivid prominences at 11 and 9 o'clock, and the corona, even just the idea of the corona, sent chills. It always does. Then there were the literal chills. Retired meteorologist Jay Anderson, who runs an eclipse web site and watched the eclipse in Svalbard, measured a temperature drop from minus 16C to minus 22C at totality.

• • • • •

The Faroes didn't fare so well. Anyone who has spent a day in Tórshavn will understand that it would depend on where you stood. Hamferð, a doom metal band, recorded a music video above the seaside village of Kvívík on which totality was clear. At the airport on

*Bill Murray*

Vagar, not ten miles from Kvívík, a man named Paul Deans told *Sky and Telescope* magazine, "the diamond ring through cloud (with iridescence) was amazing, and the prominences and corona were stunning." Except that clouds rolled in before third contact, and five minutes later it was raining.

But from the air! The pilot of EasyJet flight 6747 from Belfast to Keflavik found himself north of Scotland and south of the Faroes at totality, and did four impromptu circles in the middle of the north Atlantic so delighted passengers on both sides of his Airbus could see totality.

More than a dozen charters jockeyed for the centerline, and by flying along with the umbra, pilots could stretch totality for their passengers. Pilots found their planes stacked 1,000 feet apart vertically by Iceland's air traffic control, who had a more challenging than usual day, managing regular trans-Atlantic traffic at the same time.

•••••

**MEANWHILE DOWN BELOW**

As the eclipse approached Svalbard began to fret:

### Svalbard eclipse prompts warnings

January 22, 2015

Authorities on Norway's Arctic archipelago of Svalbard are bracing for an onslaught of tourists in connection with the solar eclipse on March 20. That's prompted them to issue warnings to the public, in an effort to avoid over-capacity.

"Since Longyearbyen (the main settlement on Svalbard) is a small town, we can have problems when so many people gather," the local sheriff wrote in the warning posted on Svalbard's public sector website.

Tourism agency VisitSvalbard reported that all hotels and other forms of lodging have been fully booked for several years on and around March 20. Now authorities are warning that there also is limited capacity in Longyearbyen's few local restaurants and cafés, that no warming tents will be available to ward off the chill of the Arctic night, and that anyone venturing outside the city limits of Longyearbyen must have protection against polar bears.

So worried were the authorities that the hospital didn't schedule appointments in the days around the eclipse. The town laid in extra food supplies and with characteristic Norwegian efficiency, the Red Cross had tents up and ready.

All hotels sold out a year before and they reckoned island population would swell to 3,500 or 4,000, or maybe more if you account for those who rented vacation homes or friends who came to stay with friends.

On eclipse day a dozen charter and private flights flew in for the eclipse and then out the same day, and authorities worried that a weather change could prevent those same-day visitors from departing when the whole town was already full.

In the event, the weather didn't change and Longyearbyen handled things with good humor. We all tramped up and down their normally sovereign daily paths, most people wearing appropriate gear, and I think, just five weeks since the first sunrise of the year, the clerks and barkeeps were mostly happy to see all the strangers.

Until the eclipse actually crossed the sky it seemed as if local people downplayed its significance. Maybe they just didn't think about it much, mainly marveling at the arrival of visitors from far away. I think they thought we were nuts.

Some said they hadn't planned anything special, or hadn't given it much thought. Maybe they thought they already lived in a place of wonder. Mostly, I think, the few who stayed at work wished they had taken a day off.

•••••

**HOW DID WE DO?**

I go back to around to visit people I had seen before. Two of them tell me they felt they held a privileged position in that they didn't have to get here, and maybe that was why they hadn't thought about it much, but it turned out it was something they never expected.

A lady selling wool sweaters in a tourist shop says she thought it would be darker. I suggest the majesty, noting that the width of the moon's shadow is usually only about 160 kilometers (267 km at most), so isn't it incredible that across the whole of the Earth, you should happen to find yourself exactly underneath it? And she nods, but still, to her it should have got darker.

The lady at the Apotek calls it unbelievable and magical. "And more than the eclipse, the light on the ground, everything."

The airport lady: "Amazing. I didn't think so much about it before."

Longyearbyen is fast emptying out when I walk into the tourist office the day after, deserted but for two young women with expectant smiles. Might they help me?

I want to know if the tourist office feels we all behaved ourselves on their island and they think we did. The day before the eclipse there was a snowmobile accident. There had been some frostbite (but that was always). There was that one polar bear thing. It is illegal to shoot a polar bear. Shooting a polar bear who wants to eat your son is a better idea than obeying the law, obviously, but every incident requires "full ... what? ... research ... investigation" as Sigrid, the snowmobile guide, put it.

Downtown Longyearbyen

Mark Sabbatini, editor of the local English language newspaper, tells me, "We had an arsonist which was the first time I'd ever seen that happen. I think it was last night or yesterday over on 222. All the streets here have numbers and 222 is a kinda busy residential area ... there's a whole bunch of homes, it's kind of like suburban central ... somebody went along there trying to start fires."

In other European cities you can always try to stay warm in the train station. Maybe some didn't think it through that there is no transport hub here to hide.

*Bill Murray*

"We had a rash of people who came in Thursday night on the late flight, stayed up all night at pubs, didn't have a place to stay. Pubs close down here about three or four at the latest, god knows what they did after that to stay warm until the sun came up, so they had folks going door to door basically knocking and begging to sleep on floors or hoping there was someone left their house unlocked and wasn't home, just a bunch of folks came up here to prey upon the kindness of strangers. But nobody died...."

A lady from Greece tells me she paid $150 to sleep on a travel agency office floor the first night ("They threw down skins for us to sleep on") and then $800 for a room without private bath on the night before the eclipse. We booked a year and a half out, but even then the Radisson SAS hotel (it's a small Radisson) was bulk booked by a tour company. The rumor was that it had been booked in its entirety eight years out.

You mustn't let the sunshine fool you. Days since our arrival have been sunny and if you can call -12 or -16C mild, then, mild, but the meteorological tide turns the day after the eclipse and with the sun obscured, in an Arctic, all blue way that makes the way people ambled up the main walkway the day before like leisure country rambles.

Today is all anonymity and purpose, heads wrapped, strides long and purposeful. Suddenly you see how, impossible as it seems, the last few days, with the hard frozen footpaths and the snowmobiles parked on the two-foot snowbank outside the window, were springtime for Svalbarders, a time to enjoy walking without mufflers wrapped up to their ear hats.

And it really must feel like some strange springtime, because at such a latitude as this, just in the time of our visit the length of the day increased from 11:54 to 13:10 - an extra hour and sixteen minutes of daylight in five days.

Which comports with the strangest single realization about this latitude, namely that scarcely five weeks since the first sunrise of the year (until 16 February the sun had been beneath the horizon, yet in the very first day that it rose, it didn't just peep and retreat but stayed up for a full hour and forty minutes), already it never gets totally dark at night. Instead the sun skims a shallow enough path below the horizon to give the sky a twilight glow all night, ahead of - less than a month from now - 19 April, when the sun will stay up all day.

With the weather even better than way down in Oslo, we lull ourselves into believing Svalbard is just like home, it's just way up north. Until the day after the eclipse. Snow falls all day long. Wind pounds the windows when they aren't rattled by sleet. We wake with no agenda and ponder the standard inventory of kitchen utensils at the Svalbard Lodge, which includes among other things,

- 7 glasses
- 7 wine glasses
- 7 coffee cups (mugs from Ikea)
- 7 schnapps glasses
- 7 cognac glasses

Seven.

Svalbard Lodge doesn't do coziness, the sense of well-being expressed by the German gemütlich or the Danish hyggeligt, but it has one mighty heater, and today that goes a long way. We toast to eclipse success using two-sevenths of our supply of cognac glasses.

*Bill Murray*

# PART TWO:
# THE FAROE ISLANDS

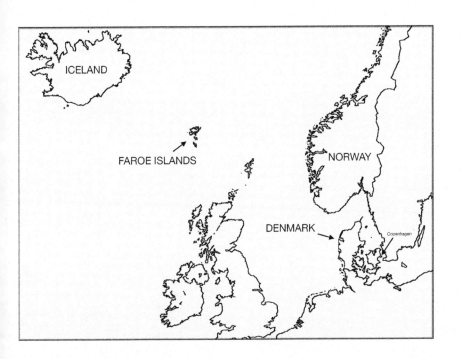

*Bill Murray*

# GÁSADALUR

They built a tunnel to Gásadalur to keep the village from dying. They blasted it right through the rock and under the Atlantic Ocean in 2004. Up to then, Dagfinnur confessed, he had never seen Gásadalur's famous waterfall to the sea.

And Gásadalur is beguiling, a captivating wind-carved plateau of ten houses beside the waterfall overlooking the Mykinesfjøröur, with views across to five basalt peaks, watchmen in the sea off Mykines, the westernmost Faroe island.

Walk to the viewpoint. Slosh down the ruts in front of Dagfinnur's taxi. Breath air that slices like daggers. Sleet stings your cheeks. Biting whips of wind, nettles against your chest. The sun shines at the same time.

Like phonetics and Gaelic, weather and the Faroes don't play by everybody else's rules.

Stand at the viewpoint. Wind stirs the waterfall to a broad gauze, an aurora dancing between the peaks dusted white and the roiling seacaps. Past Mykines out there on the sea, it's next stop, Iceland. Stand right here and you can just grasp that you are - almost - still in Europe.

It's just beyond reach, Mykines is, and you can sail over to see the puffins and the kittiwakes and the king of all the Faroese birds, the gannett, on the ferry that runs from May through August as long as the weather cooperates, but lots of times it doesn't. You should never sail to Mykines the day before you leave the Faroes because you may not be able to sail back.

Only a scattered few live over there now. Between the world wars 170 people lived on Mykines, but now it's the same as Gásadalur. Young people won't stay. Houses and a couple dozen turf-roof sheds make like a village but only a few people stay year-round. There is just no way to earn a living.

Mountains fend off the world from Gásadalur, each with its own snow chapeau. Before the tunnel you had to climb the postman's walk over them, and they are some of the tallest in the Faroes (Behind Gásadalur, Árnafjall reaches up 722 meters), or arrive by sea, and peering down at the landing brings a jolt like jarring awake from the edge of sleep. Way down where sea smashes rocks, a handrail, rusted and twisting, leads up water-slick stones, a forlorn legacy of British occupation.

Gásadalur had a population of 18 the last Dagfinnur knew. The tunnel was meant to save it, or at least stall its dying.

The postman died three years ago. Before the tunnel he walked over the mountain three times a week, winter and summer. A man who knew him told me the postman had no neck. The postman was short and compact and carried the mail in a sack strapped around his head that over his career made his neck disappear.

The waterfall at Gásadalur

Dagfinnur leads us to the viewpoint and no one is there because it hasn't occurred to anyone to go there on a day like today and on the way, in grass slick as whale oil, the three of us make a mess of our shoes. When the sun isn't shining, sleet gouges our faces.

Dagfinnur points down at the old British stairs over the edge (careful there!), hovers a moment in his city shoes, petitions for retreat and I can see him there now in his proper taxi vest, pushing hair back from his face, shirtsleeves flapping, doing a little keep-warm dance, just not flouncy enough to squish mud on his shoes. He waits using the taxi as a windbreak, smoking.

It is worth musing on the economics of a tunnel through rock to serve eighteen, but what are they going to do? You simply can't have every single person up and move to Torshavn.

There are three new houses since that they built that tunnel.

The waterfall to the sea is magnificent.

●●●●●

## MAY, 1612

Gásadalur likely means goose valley, simple as that, but there is a legend besides. The village of Kirkjubøur, on the southernmost tip of Streymoy island, was home to the Catholic diocese of the Faroes from the eleventh century until the bracing grip of the Reformation.

The bishops' radiated piety made Kirkjubøur an unfortunate birthplace for a certain woman named Gæsa. Instead of fasting for Lent she ate meat - what was she thinking - and the church confiscated her property, and the legend says that the place to which she fled, on the island of Vagar, now bears her name.

Stories, like sheep, outnumber people on an archipelago where legends reach into opaque and distant mists. It is unusual to pin down any legend's precise origin, but I believe we know the exact time, date and circumstance of one particular myth:

Down on the island of Suðuroy maybe seventy kilometers from Torshavn, down beyond the dunes of Sandoy and the lighthouse island of Stóra Dímon, population seven, down in Suðuroy's southernmost village called Sumba, four brothers strong and brave quarreled day after day. They even threatened to kill one another.

Tending sheep one spring morning the brothers were terrified to witness the Earth plunged into darkness, and they offered the Lord a deal. If the Lord would let them survive they would become better men.

A torturous eternity later the sun returned and they danced in exultant circles, they hugged each other and their sheep and they never quarreled again for all of the rest of their days.

I think what happened was the total solar eclipse that fell across Sudoroy at 11:25 on that enfabled morning of 30 May, 1612. Just like it did last week.

•••••

An old Faroese native, the proprietor of a basic, no frills inn, told me the 1954 eclipse was better than last week's, maybe because he saw that one, and much of Tórshavn was cloudy last week. In those days, in 1954, they didn't have the fancy glasses we have nowadays. The kids watched the sun through beer bottles.

Most of all he remembered the hens. When the moon crossed in front of the sun they set about tilting this way and that, madly running to get inside, just as they do at night. And then they ran right back out again minutes later. It was a new day.

This time, he thought it should have got darker. We heard the same in Svalbard.

To everybody who said that, I would explain how the umbra, the inner shadow of the moon, only measures about a hundred miles across, so there is only a very short time when you can't see beyond it on one horizon or the other. Eventually I realized they didn't mean the darkness during totality, but in the two hours between first contact and totality, and between third contact and the end of the eclipse.

The sun is such a blast furnace that its light roars right around the moon except during totality. This is the Annie Dillard idea that a partial eclipse simply will not do.

Before the eclipse people tried out hopeful words like "amazing" and "unreal." Some talked about how they felt privileged for living in totality's path, and how they hadn't given the actual event a whole lot of thought until a mild amazement that their obscure islands turned into camps for a crazy club of eclipse chasers.

Once the moment came and the thing happened, they understood. They realized that whatever words they reached for (the more literate remarked that there were no words), and whatever they had been expecting, the thing was totally different from that.

There won't be another total solar eclipse across the Faroe islands until 26 May, 2245. We can predict events two centuries away, but on the day before we can't be sure if it will be cloudy.

People down by the sea in Tórshavn saw the fiery ring as the moon crossed in front of the sun. It was more chancy up the hill. The clouds parted where Dagfinnur stood, in a field near the airport on the next door island of Vagar. The band Hamferð recorded a video on a Vagar mountaintop with totality as a background, exhibiting iron discipline in facing the camera and not the sun.

One man showed us his cell phone video, and the extinguishing and then re-ignition of roiling, gray-bottomed clouds, was exactly the stuff of a gothic thriller.

**GETTING THERE**

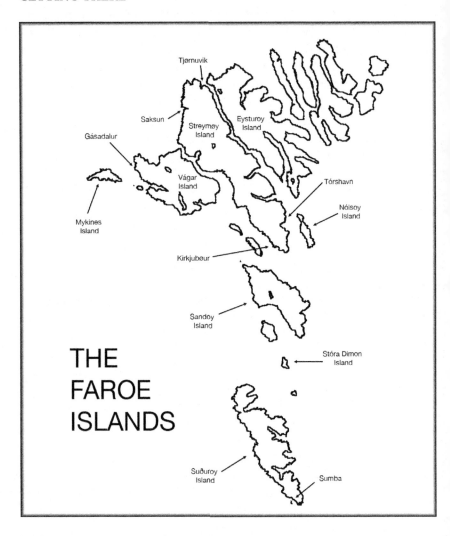

Clearing the Jutland peninsula, cruising over England, Scotland and the Shetland Islands and flying still an hour more, the dreary urban air of Copenhagen recedes. But will it last? Only seven of March's 31 days are sunny in Torshavn and today's forecast is consistent with that.

The Faroes' tiny airline, Atlantic Airways, welcomes me with a Morgenavisan Jyllansposten draped over one armrest and a coffee-stained seatback tray. Only here have I seen this; the back of the seat reads, "For your front passenger comfort please do not use the headrest as an aid when you leave your seat." Don't push forward or jerk back the guy in front of you. That's agreeable.

Another first: Atlantic Airways serves individual packets of sliced ginger, to go along with sushi and the local brew, Föroya bjór.

It is fun to glean what you can about your destination from the people on the plane. Everybody aboard has open, honest faces; there is a fair share of bohemian dress, with precious few in business attire. Local folks pop out of their seats to visit with each other at the first opportunity, and linger.

This old Airbus comprises one third of Atlantic Airways' fleet. When they put the first one into service in 2012 they had to build more runway.

Finally comes a mighty buffeting, land below flashing in and out of clouds, caught in half-second snippets. The island of Vagar. The pilot keeps the wings level, mostly, and we are on the ground in the Faroe Islands.

•••••

**HISTORY VAGUE AND DISTANT**

Fifteen hundred years ago the islands and peninsulas of northern Europe stretched open and wild, movement unimpeded for any who came. From fjord to marsh, archipelago to lake, settlers found room to spread out, breathing room, just one person for every forty or fifty today. People settled at crossroads, in valleys or along streams. They proclaimed their farmstead anywhere they might summon from the earth a way of life.

A settlement that grew into a village had no name. It didn't need a name because to the villagers, everybody in the world lived there. It was the village. There were no maps or calendars or clocks. Time divided no more precisely than by the day and the season for working the earth.

Northern people had only one name. Villages with no name at all were made up of Hakon and Garth and Canute and Canute's son or Magnus's daughter.

Only once a concentration of people required an identity might a town adopt the surname of the local lord, or individuals take on a second name indicating vocation or eccentricity, like Magnus (the) Cooper, Johann Longnose or the king who consolidated Norway, Harald Fairhair.

After the Roman withdrawal from Britain, the Angles and Saxons crossed the North Sea from the Danish peninsula now known as Jutland (roughly Jutes at the top, Angles in the middle, Saxons in the south) to populate the British Isles. From Blåvands Point in Jutland to England's Flamborough Head they sailed just under 300 nautical miles.

Languages on both sides of the sea borrowed so liberally back and forth that today the one hundred most frequently used English ("Angle-ish") words are all of Anglo-Saxon origin. In Denmark, Viking place names mixed with Anglo-Saxon names like Bramming and Grindstad, side-by-side farming villages near the coast where people have worked the earth as long as records have been kept.

Ribe, the oldest town in Denmark, sits scarcely fifteen miles south from Bramming and Grinstad, down what a millennium ago must have been just a modest horse trail. A low-slung coastal town with a cathedral-dominated medieval center, Ribe (which today offers its visitors oyster safaris) faces England on the peninsula's west.

In the eighth century Ribe found a counterpart and willing trading partner across the narrow southern neck of Jutland in the village of Hedeby (now Schleswig, in Germany), on the Schlei, a marshy east-facing inlet on the Baltic Sea. Between Ribe and Hedeby a trade route developed between the North and Baltic Seas, a way to avoid sailing all the way around Jutland. To defend the link between the two seas an earthen wall came to be known as Danevirke, or Dane's work, and by this we know that Denmark, by 750, was an organized state.

• • • • •

Even in the time of the Danevirke nearly thirteen centuries ago, days away in sailing time from Ribe and Hedeby and far out to sea, Denmark's future colony, the little Faroe Islands, was stirring.

Irish monks were probably the first to visit the Faroes, two hundred fifty or more years before the Northmen ventured out of sight of Norwegian shores. The Irishmen used the Faroes as a hermitage, but since they were celibate, their communities did not sustain themselves. Pollen analysis shows that oats have been grown on the Faroe islands of Mykines and Streymoy since about 625.

Legend says St. Brendan (c. 484-578), an Irish monk and patriarch of almost three thousand of his fellows, sailed past the islands in the sixth century. Archeological excavations suggest Brendan and his friars, in search of the promised land, visited the Faroes two or three times between about 512 and 530.

If he did visit even Brendan may not have been the first, for he saw islands "all pure white, so numerous as to hide the face of the land." He dubbed them "The Islands of the Sheep and the Paradise of Birds." Someone must have brought the sheep.

Stories said the islands of the sheep lay "situated several days" sailing distance from Scotland. Dicuil, a later Irish monk, wrote in 825 about a place that sounds exactly like the Faroes:

"There are many other islands in the ocean to the north of Britain which can be reached from the northernmost British Isles in two days' and nights' sailing, with full sails and an undropping wind. A certain holy man informed me that in two summer days and the night in between, sailing in a little boat of two thwarts, he came to land on one of them. Some of these islands are very small; nearly all of them are separated from one another by narrow sounds. On these islands hermits who have sailed from our Scotia (Ireland) have lived for roughly a hundred years."

Dicuil said the islands were "full of innumerable sheep."

Dicuil, at the court of Charlemagne, became a geographer of the world's wild places. He remarked in wonder that on nights near the summer solstice in these northern lands "the setting sun hides itself at the evening hour as if behind a little hill," so that enough light remained to pick lice from the settlers' shirts at midnight. The antiquities collection at the Oslo Historical Museum corroborates the lice problem, with its room after room of ancient fine-toothed combs.

•••••

In time, sacking and pillaging Northmen would sail in longships made of oak, high of prow and sometimes a hundred feet bow to stern. St. Brendan and his perhaps sixty men, by contrast, set out in audacious leather boats, mere ox hide stitched together and formed over a wooden frame. These boats, known as curraghs, are little more than pointed wooden baskets covered in hide, and they are still in use on Ireland's west coast, canvas substituted for the ox or cow skin.

Now to me, this idea that thirty-odd fellows would gather themselves up in ox-hide tubs at the dawn of the sixth century and sail over the horizon into the unknown, this is utter nonsense, or at best some kind of medieval batshit madness. But students of the period more thoughtful than me point out that the Irishmen would have been familiar with the migration patterns of geese and watching the directions from which they set out and returned, would have judged land lay to the west. And that as these were monks with a mission to spread God's word, journeys into the unknown were a certain matter of faith.

An arcane phenomenon of atmospheric optics may have aided their journeys. Barry Lopez writes (in *Arctic Dreams*) that mirages are not uncommon in polar conditions when warm air lies over a body of cold water. "Light rays that under other conditions might travel straight off into space are bent, or refracted, back earthward in a series of small steps as they pass through layers of air at different temperatures."

These images "are commonly seen at sea in the Arctic in summer, especially late in the afternoon of a clear day. Distant islands, ships, coastlines, and icebergs lying beyond the real horizon all appear to be closer than they are, the sea itself appears slightly concave, and the horizon seems unusually far off."

Lopez thinks that Iceland occasionally appeared to the people in the Faroe Islands "as a great looming mirage" and there is evidence we will explore later that this phenomenon may have aided in the discovery of Greenland.

• • • • •

Brendan set out from the wind-beaten Dingle peninsula below Galway in southwestern Ireland, along the Irish and then Scottish coasts, on a route of stepping stones, on to the Hebrides and across open water, arriving at the Faroes, the story goes, at the strait between Mykines and Vagar, the westernmost of the Faroes' eighteen islands. He very nearly missed them entirely.

Brendan seems to have anticipated trouble with the hides. According to the medieval *Navigatio Sanctis Brendani Abbatis* that tells Brendan's tale, his band of monks traveled with spare skins and ox fat to seal the seams.

When the explorer Tim Severin set out to replicate St. Brendan's voyage forty years ago, he sought expert opinion on the sagacity of sailing in leather. Expert:

"Oxhide is very high in protein. It resembles a piece of steak, if you like. It will decompose in the same way, either quickly or slowly, depending on various factors such as the temperature, how well it has been tanned to turn it into leather, and the amount of stress imposed upon it."

"And what happens in the end?" Severin asked.

"Just the same as if you left a piece of steak out in the air on a saucer. In time it will turn into a nasty, evil-smelling blob of jelly. Just like a rotting piece of oxhide."

(Severin's replica boat made of 49 ox hides sailed Brendan's route to Iceland then beyond, to Greenland and Newfoundland, a tale told in his book *Brendan Voyage*. Separately the Inuit, with far more austere resources in the far north, developed the same floating technology with their umiaqs, and we'll talk more about them too, in Greenland.)

We know that the permanent settlement of Iceland dates from around 860 or 870. An archipelago off Iceland's coast is called Vestmannaeyjar, or "Irishmen's islands." In the parlance of the time, "Ostmen" (eastmen) were from Norway, and "Westmen" Irish.

The fairly certain knowledge that the first men ashore in Iceland were Irish religious figures suggests the same was true in the Faroes, but there were no remaining Irishmen by the arrival of the first Norsemen, of whom we know little - except for one man named Grim Cambán. The "Færeyinga Saga," tells us that Grim Cambán "settled the Faeries" at a place called Funningur ("the find") during the rule of Harald the Fairhair, Norwegian king around 872 to 930, and Grim Cambán may have arrived in flight from the king, "for before the king's overbearing many men fled in those days."

We will consider Grim Cambán shortly and the overbearing King Harald later, but the badness quotient among leaders is a relative thing. If you stack all the leaders who have ever acted strangely end to end, they might stretch from the Faroes clear back to Norway.

•••••

## SPEAKING OF THE FAROES

Faroese is a storytelling language. One thing it isn't, along with Gaelic, is phonetic, so be prepared to mispronounce everything and sound like an uninitiated rube. Gjogv, for example, on the island of Eysturoy, sounds approximately like "Jake."

Before the Faroes were well settled a linguistic furrow opened between Norse as spoken in Sweden and Denmark ("East Norse") and Norway, the Faroes and Iceland ("West Norse"). Today Faroese, as spoken by the 50,000 islanders (and 20,000 more abroad), bears the strongest resemblance to Icelandic, though in its isolation Faroese has its own character. A standard written Faroese was only developed around 1850.

In the quiet bars down at the harbor grizzled old men, backs bent by age and the sea, hunch over their beers to hold court in an incomprehensible cackle and a cadence impossibly romantic. With the entrance of a visitor, heads turn without curiosity, one beat ... two ... three ... then turn back to their storytelling.

Gunnar Holm-Jacobsen, a diplomat and director of the Faroese Foreign Service, confirms that today's Faroese leans more toward Icelandic than the Scandinavian languages.

Sharing an afternoon at the Kaffeehuset on Torshavn's harbor, and then with his wife Sigga at the larger Hvonn brasserie, Gunnar explains that while Faroese is spoken from birth, "We have learned Danish since elementary school. When I was in school we started from third grade."

"If you are native Faroese, can you understand enough Danish? Are they similar enough, or do you have to actually learn it?"

"No, you have to learn it. Same norse roots like Norwegian and Swedish..... Faroese is closer to Icelandic to understand than to Danish. You can pick up some words though."

And another thing, says Gunnar, "There is a big cultural difference between Faroe Islands and Denmark. One of the reasons is we are living very closer to nature. We have lost a lot of fishermen on the sea."

**FISHERMEN AND WHALERS: TO THE TOP OF STREYMOY**

We set out for the upper reaches of Streymoy island with 64-year-old Kemm Poulson. Kemm, a native, comes well recommended as an expert islands-explorer and calls guiding his great interest, his real, driving mission. He arrives standing erect and wearing a taxi uniform jacket.

We drive straight into a gale and blinding snow on a highway above Tórshavn originally built to get to a NATO DEWS outpost, one of 61 Distant Early Warning System radar sites set up to detect Soviet intercontinental ballistic missiles during the Cold War. I get out of the car and it shudders with the snow bank I let in.

There is no great call for milliners on these islands despite the mighty attraction of the vocabulary of northern headwear. In the same way it has introduced a blizzard to our back seat, the wind would snare your snood or whip away your wimple.

Right from the start Kemm is muttering "What a pity."

In 1961, when engineers planned the road, Kemm says they became sufficiently alarmed at the prospect of disturbing a particular rock where elves were known to dwell that they moved the road. He shows us the rock.

Kemm was born in a red house down on Tinganes, born right there on the Parliament jetty in Torshavn, and his six decades on these islands make him an agreeable, shuffling, day-long raconteur, stories long, hair thinning, face smudged by a life long lived. He wears his life right there on his face and you can stand back and look and see it has been as trouble-filled as any, but it has been good, or at least he is reconciled.

The mark on his right cheek raises suspicions of a knife fight. As a young man in the '70s he worked his own fishing boat off Seydisfjordur harbor in Iceland. By himself. His fishing mates called him the Mad Faroese. At least that is what they called him with an elbow in his ribs, to his face.

•••••

Kemm turns off the road onto a steep drop toward the water, toward the remnant of the old whaling station at við Áir, where a YouTube video has made famous the gross explosion of a whale carcass.

As intertwined as the fates of whales and the Faroes seem today (as we will see), the whaling trade only arrived after the Norwegians had overfished the whaling grounds along their coast.

They struck out for Iceland knowing it well and, finding the whaling there fine, they realized whaling in the Faroes ought to be as good, and half as far, and they found that it was so.

A whaler named Albert Grøn from the northernmost Norwegian county of Finnmark built the Faroes' first whaling station just across this tiny sound - Streymoy here, Eysturoy over there - in 1893. With lunar gravity I think I could throw a rock over there. The seventh and last whaling station stood right on this spot, built in 1906.

At its bursting-at-the-seams mightiest in 1909 við Áir slaughtered and rendered 773 whales and harvested 13,850 barrels of oil. Dockhands lassoed and winched harpooned whales onto a ramp to be flensed and butchered for their meat. They were quartered right there on the ramp, the remnants drawn up to grinders. Adjacent tanks held the blubber, used in the manufacture of soaps and cosmetics and burned in oil lamps.

History whispers across these corrugated remnants. Whalers in the gritty, workmanlike tedium of their trade. The grim reality of their work - and their lives. The slashing of the whales' rubbery skin, carving out the innards (Damn! I sliced open my bloody thumb, too), separating the blubber (all of this is smelly), that over there, this over here, salvaging the oil, the pelting of the sleet, your world putrid, wet, near frozen. Wiping away snot and willing away the stiffness the cold brings right through your gloves, drawn by the scent of peat fires that mean home, fires that remain outside your frostbitten grasp until your work is done.

Right up through the 1960s the við Áir station put Streymoy men to work. Today machines streaked by rust list on the grass, shoved up against the outside walls, machines with rivets and pipes, gears and chains and dials. It looks as if someone started in on a paint job around the shed windows and then thought, what the hell for?

The building shrugs in preliminary decay; a window may have given out here or there but there is nothing structurally wrong. It still has more pride than to fall in, so it sits still and rusting, almost content, between two "rivers" that hardly deserve the name. (við Áir means 'by the rivers.')

Minister of Culture Jógvan á Lakjuni appointed a committee that in 2007 tabled a proposal to make the við Áir station a museum. You can read their proposal online, with sketches of happy tourists enjoying restaurants, boat rentals and camping, but the 990,000 Danish kroner funding request did not meet with government approval.

•••••

## THE GRINDADRÁP

"Good luck" in Icelandic is hvelreki, with an idea something like "may a whole whale wash up on your beach." The Faroese don't wait for luck to produce whales. They sail out and find them.

In *The Old Man and His Sons,* Heðin Brú (1901-1987), a bespectacled gentleman with a fatherly air and one of the Faroes' most important novelists, describes life in the village of Sørvágur, now adjacent to the airport on Vagar. Set vaguely in the first third of the twentieth century in subsistence era Faroes, it describes the generational strains on a rural society dragged into modernity.

Central to the tale is the whale slaughter, the grindadráp ("the grind" for short), and its importance in feeding the islanders in an era when the við Áir whaling station was at its busiest. In 1928 the Faroese county medical officer wrote, "...it cannot be emphasised enough how important this [pilot whale meat] is for the population, for whom the meat, be it fresh, dried or salted, is virtually their only source of meat."

A tinge of the exotic attaches to the grindadráp today, a summoning of vestigial heritage, a suggestion that these quiet, unassuming people fall into some bloodlust frenzy wild and savage, like Viking wildmen in helmets with horns.

Once the grindadráp was a quirky cultural asset, but not anymore. Today the grind, more than any other single thing, pits the world against the Faroes.

•••••

When a fishing boat or a ferry spies a pod of whales, a call goes out and word races through the village. Even in the middle of a work day people drop what they are doing and muster. Employers accede. Fishing boats form up in a half circle behind the whales and, banging on the sides of the boats and trailing lines weighted with stones, press the whales into a shallow bay.

Townspeople wait on the beach with hooks and knives. Mandated under new regulations, two devices, a round-ended hook and a device called a spinal lance are designed to kill the whales more quickly and thus more humanely.

The hunter plunges the hook attached to a rope into the whale's blowhole. Men line up tug of war style to pull the whale onto the beach. It takes a line of men to haul them out, for pilot whales may weigh 2,500 pounds.

The purportedly humane spinal lance severs the spinal column and the main blood vessel to the brain causing loss of consciousness in seconds. Critics maintain this works only when the whale is on the beach, not in the water, the site of the initial struggle, and so the spinal lance can only be used at the end of the torturous trauma of the drive.

•••••

The grizzled fisherman, the mayor, the citified insurance salesman - all the townspeople find common cause, shoulder-to-shoulder at the shore, harvesting the whales and dividing the spoils.

The harvest is distributed evenly, for communal benefit. This is real, retail, hands-on constituent services for the mayor, who works out what size the shares should be and hands out tickets. People go to stand beside the whale indicated on their ticket. Those sharing each whale butcher it together, right there, right then. The municipality is mandated to clear the remains within 24 hours.

The animal is cut and pieces laid on the ground skin down, blubber up. Then the meat is cut from the whale and laid atop the blubber, the whole take is divided, and the shareholders gather up their haul and carry it home. There is no industrial processing.

Even today whale accounts for a quarter of all the meat consumption on the islands. Custom and tradition tip the scales against the advice of the Faroes' Chief Medical Officer Dr. Høgni Debes Joensen, who declared in 2008 that no one ought to eat whale meat anymore because of the presence of DDT derivatives, PCBs and mercury in the meat.

The Faroese live in a society modern in every way, right down to attempts to figure out more humane ways to kill the whales, and whale meat is no longer required for the diet as it was in the days of Heðin Brú. The subsistence era was a different time. So the question arises why, if the meat is unhealthy, the tradition must continue.

Photos of a grind, the sea bright red with blood, are frightening, revolting even, and the idea of slaughtering one of the world's most intelligent creatures is unsettling. But it must also be said that the pilot whale is not endangered. The North Atlantic Marine Mammal Conservation Organization reckons the annual Faroese slaughter takes less than 0.1 percent of the pilot whale population. Gunnar Holm-Jacobsen, the diplomat, stresses that "We don't sail out and find whales. We only hunt schools of whales that are incidentally spotted from land or from a boat."

Proponents call the grind a combination of sport, tradition and a way of obtaining cheap food. It is also a direct link to the islanders' past. Opponents assert that none of these justifications hold up in the twenty-first century. Yet in a place not very accommodating to agriculture, livestock, fishing - and pilot whales - have always been central to the Faroese diet.

You can be sure that the collective personality of an isolated people will mix resourcefulness with resistance to change. Pride, too. Pride in the ability to live and flourish in an outpost. Pride in the traditions that make the place unique.

When your community has repeatedly been to the brink of starvation, when you live on a spot of land as precarious as these slippery cliffs of obstinate basalt, when you have a storied heritage dating all the way back to Odin and Thor, when you have come through all this and more and today you thrive, you may be forgiven for having the stout view that your culture is worth preservation.

Elin Brimheim Heinesen, a Faroese musician, sharpens the point: "What is completely natural for people in the Faroes, seems so alien to other people, who have never lived here – or in similar places – so they can't possibly understand the Faroese way of life. And thus many of the aspects of this life provokes them. People are often provoked or disgusted by what they don't understand."

She wants the casual visitor to understand that life still is really different on this small archipelago in a vast ocean, "that it is necessary

77

to interrupt your daily work when the time is ripe to bring the sheep home and slaughter them, or go bird-catching, or go hare-hunting – or participate in pilot whaling – and, additionally, to prepare and store the food you have provided for yourself and your family. This food constitutes a large part of the total food consumption and is completely indispensable for most families – especially for the 12 percent in the Faroe Islands who live at or below the poverty line."

Activists battle the grind and the Faroes' legislature battles back. The Parliament, called the Løgting, briefly voted in 2014 to ban members of the marine wildlife conservation organization Sea Shepherd from sending protesters. That legislation was dropped when Denmark determined it would likely be illegal.

But try, try again; a 2016 proposal to keep anti-whaling activists out equates actively protesting for an organization with work, for which foreigners require a work permit.

Hapag-Lloyd and AIDA, two big German cruise lines, have suspended or lessened arrivals in the Faroes to protest the grind. (This may be devastating to waterfront vendors but it has its appeal for those of us who believe there is a special place in hell for the inventor of the mega-cruise ship.)

The Faroese point out that the grind is an opportunistic hunt, not commercial, the meat is not exported and is shared across the entire community. The distribution of the spoils generally happens without money, and on the spot.

In the conservative British magazine *The Spectator*, Heri Joensen, the lead singer of the Faroese band Tyr writes, "In the Faroes, it is not uncommon to kill your own dinner — be it sheep, fish, bird or hare. I have slaughtered many more sheep than I have cut up whales and no one seems to care. I find that strange. Why the double standards? Because whales are endangered? The ones we eat aren't. There are an estimated 780,000 long-finned pilot whales in the Atlantic. In the Faroe Islands, we kill about 800 a year on average — or 0.1 percent of the population. An annual harvest of 2 percent is considered sustainable: compare that with the billions of animals bred for slaughter."

Joensen says that buying the same amount of beef he got in a grindadráp would have cost more than £800.

Proponents argue that the urban lifestyle of protestors is what leads to mercury poison in the whales, after all. Trouble is, the double standards defense will always be outnumbered. So, for that matter, will any other defense.

The Faroese complain that most of their critics eat meat and the animals those critics eat suffer every bit as much as a grindadráp whale. Factory farming, they say, is an industrial scale horror for profit, while the grind has no financial motive. How, they ask, can those who live entirely apart from the source of their food pass judgement on small islands, far away?

•••••

## WHALE BAY, TJØRNUVIK AND THE PECULIAR PLEASURES OF SKERPIKJØT

In the village of Hvalvík ("Whale Bay") we walk around a church - locked tight and deserted on a Sunday - made from timber from a shipwreck up at Saksun. These islands grow no trees, so they salvaged timber from that wreck to build the church.

It's a hybrid affair, the Hvalvík church, with a pulpit that originated in 1609 at a different church in Torshavn. Part of that pulpit was defaced, they say, by the swords of French pirates who besieged Tórshavn in 1677.

In the pirate period, when a ship would appear on the horizon, perhaps from France or Scotland or Ireland, Kemm says people would flee to the hills lest they be seized as slaves. Same as the Mangarevans did when Spanish slavers came to call on nearly antipodal Rapa Nui.

*Bill Murray*

A newly renovated house in Hvalvík, with a fine little garden and fence, begs for your attention, and your kroner. It could yours for just over a million, something like $150,000.

At a fresh water salmon lake beyond Hvalvík we watch red-beaked Oyster Catchers, the national bird, dive over waterfalls too many to count. Kemm says the grass is so green in summertime people disbelieve the photos, convinced they must be Photoshopped.

Outside the picture postcard village of Tjørnuvik ("Chew-new-wick") at the far end of Streymoy, we pile out for a walk along shore. Waves lap at pebbles. The sand is nearly black. Mirja gets way out in front of Kemm and me, examining tiny shells.

Perhaps Brendan and his friars stood on this shore. Evidence of a settlement dating to 600 - 650 was uncovered here back in the '70s. That wasn't long after Brendan's time, and Tjørnuvik is one of two sites where pollen analysis suggests Irish oats once grew.

Every year in spring they drive a few rams up into these hills to roam wild. On a Saturday as autumn approaches, men from all over the island, out for a bit of tradition and a day of drinking and capering about, carry spiked wooden poles into the mountains, find the rams and use the poles to make a pen to confine them.

To fanfare, commotion, camaraderie and traditional song, they herd the rams back into Tjørnuvik for slaughter and auction. Call it the Faroese equivalent of tailgating on a college football Saturday.

The Stakksdagur festival ushers in the season to prepare the Faroes' other distinctive creation besides the grindadráp: wind-dried sheep known as Skerpikjøt.

•••••

From prehistory people have pooled sea water into salterns, evaporation pans for salt-making. The Faroese climate is too cool, and there isn't enough wood to fire evaporation, so the islands have come round to the Faroes-unique environmental necessity of wind curing skerpikjøt.

Skerpikjøt (approximately "shesh-per-jot") is dried leg of lamb with a pungent, curling, intense smell about which opinion is loudly divided - mostly, Faroese for and the rest of the world against. The Danes generally revile Faroese food as unspeakably foul. Skerpikjøt arouses passions like the southeast Asian durian.

About October the lamb's hind legs and parts in between are hung in the hjallur, an outbuilding with gaps in the walls like a picket fence to facilitate breezes for drying. The Faroes are a humid place because they sit right in the middle of the Gulf Stream, and so drying the meat takes at least months, but the salt-laden sea air is the perfect instrument for the job.

Hung up in the fall, the skerpikjøt won't be ready until spring (a fine fur of blue mold signals its ripeness), but there is an interim product. By December the meat is ræst, or fermented, and ready to boil or cook in the oven, ready just in time for Christmas.

(Gunnar, the diplomat, his wife Sigga and daughter Liv were more than gracious, welcoming us for an authentic Faroese family dinner. As it was March, drying of the sheep wasn't yet complete, and so the Holm-Jacobsens served ræst, or fermented kjøt.

It's one of those smells that the uninitiated instantly try not to breathe, try to just skip right on past, "keep moving, nothing to see here folks." But eventually, you gotta breathe. Thankfully you acclimate to smells. It's one the sense's strong suits.

But once past that barrier ræst kjøt is a treat. No, really.

As soon as we opened the taxi door for the ride home, the driver skipped the pleasantries and declared, "You have been eating Faroese meat." We weren't sure if it was an observation or an accusation and so ensued one of those hung-in-space moments while he seemed to consider us. Finally he said, "It's okay, I am used to it.")

When the meat is turt, or fully dry, you eat it as is, on open-faced bread. A Faroese lay person can tell whether a sheep is Faroese by taste, Kemm says, and can even tell the difference in skerpikjøt's taste from one island to the next, even whether the sheep have come up in a sunny place or not and whether they have been fed different grasses.

Kemm's personal favorite is sheep from a particular sunny spot on the island of Eysturoy. He, like Gunnar's wife Sigga, has his own supplier. He has been a customer of that particular farmer for many years. It is a bit like holding seasons tickets to a top tier UEFA team; there is a waiting list for the privilege. A yearly competition decides who makes the best Skerpikjøt in the land. Last year's champion was from the island of Sandoy.

Even with all this land and so few people, the Faroes import sheep from Iceland and even New Zealand, hundreds of tons a year. Most of the Faroese sheep, you see, end up hung up for wind drying, because Faroese sheep taste by far the best.

•••••

**TJØRNUVIK'S TALE: THE INVASION OF THE GIANTS**

Midday in Tjørnuvik. Sunlight dances across the water and the air is fair with a fine view across to Eysturoy island. Just off the coast two sea stacks called Risin and Kellingin take a battering from the sea. Once upon a time Risin (the giant) and Kellingin (the witch), traveled from Iceland on a mission.

Long ago, you see, Iceland was a land of giants, and the Faroes' beauty drove the giants to such distraction that they sent Risin and Kellingin to bring the islands back to Iceland. Kellingin, the witch, climbed onto the mountain Eiðiskollur to tie the islands together, meaning then to push them onto the giant's back. But when she pulled at the mountain the top broke off. The base of the mountain held firm through repeated attempts through the night.

Tjørnuvik

The witch and the giant worked so hard that they lost track of the time, and as everyone knows, if giants or witches are caught out in sunlight, they turn to stone. When the sun rose they were frozen in place and there they stand today.

The witch and the giant worked so hard that they lost track of the time, and as everyone knows, if giants or witches are caught out in sunlight, they turn to stone. When the sun rose they were frozen in place and there they stand today.

We are standing down by the rocks, way out at the tip of land somewhere, faces in the wind. Kemm offers a Cohiba he is proud to have summoned all the way from Havana and inhaling them furthers the conversation.

For a time when he was young Kemm was a fisherman in Iceland. He inhales, reflects, and in a voice borne away fast by the wind, allows that when a storm comes and you're far from shore and alone, you learn a lot about yourself.

•••••

## MURDER IN THE FAROES

Back in the car Kemm is fired with stories. Feel like a good murder yarn? Ah, well:

This morning? Just like every morning. Another baleful twilight, sun and gale, snow and hail. Jeezus, it's only autumn.

There's precious little glee in November. You're not going to see spontaneous dancing on the shore. Summer festivals are long forgotten and your daily prospects are nature-lashed today to April.

Danjal Petur "Pidde" Hansen fought off the morning as long as he could. He never liked it when he woke before he had to get out of bed because it was much more agreeable in there, inside his head in the bed.

It was early, it was late, he didn't know, it was night and it was dark and so there. He took those big looming red digits out of his bedroom and into the kitchen a long time ago and he was glad he did because who were they, lording over him, the only light he saw, engraving the dark minute by bloody unsparing taunting minute all night long.

Lots of mornings he woke with a start. Bed was better, so he turned and he tossed and he fought to get sleep back. When the sun found his window he covered his face with pillows. He strove to retrieve the warmth in his dreams because that was where he thrived. The wakeful world surely wasn't.

Pidde lived with his ex-wife. Yeah, that was bad right there. How could that be good? It was a non-marriage of convenience, but in the village of Runavik, population 3,794, you made the arrangements that you made.

Pidde's arrangements cost him his life. Some guy named Konovrat - for God's sake some guy from Croatia - and okay, wherever that is, was "dating" his wife. The last time anybody saw Pidde was 5 November, 2011, in the morning, outside his house.

When a recreational diver found Pidde's skeleton 150 meters offshore after church on a Sunday two and a half years later, his killer was already serving time for the crime in prison in Denmark.

At first they thought maybe Pidde had been thrown off a cliff. Because at first they treated Pidde's going missing as a "routine" missing persons case, as if there were such thing in the Faroe Islands, where the whole country needed only fourteen jail cells, but after all, even after their divers searched wave racked shoreline to no effect, they couldn't find him. Not a trace.

But they found a frying pan. And a pillow. With Pidde's blood. And they found them in Konovrat's house.

There hadn't been a murder since 1988 when somebody shot his girlfriend down on Suduroy. You could be 35 years old and not remember such a thing.

When Pidde went missing they held vigils around his house. They searched every hill, every shore, every basement and factory and container.

Everybody knew the cars that might be involved; everybody knew the whole story, in fact. All the details. If you didn't know Pidde personally you knew he ran a business selling fish. After ten days, two weeks the police called it a murder case. Something that happened in Denmark, not here. It was innocence lost, a scant few years ago.

•••••

## DOMESTIC SLAVES

Kemm is talking about how most Faroese men's DNA can be traced back to the northern Norwegian mainland, but that a surprising number of women's ancestors appear to have originated in Ireland. Faroes household words, for pets and cooking, for example, have Celtic roots while words for things like hunting come from Norse.

Back to Grim Cambán: The first name of the Sagas' settler of the Faroes is Norse, but his other name, Cambán, is Gaelic. Was Grim Cambán Norse, Gaelic, mongrel?

The answer is lost in the mists, but no matter; both were here. Even were Cambán a Gael, runestones declare that "eastmen," Norse, sailed to the Faroes.

It may be that not all Norsemen were bent on rapine and plunder, but that is certainly the legend. Kemm narrates tales of the Norsemen of old, swooping down on a terrified Ireland, stocking their northern islands with women. Wives, or sex slaves, depending on your attitude.

People captured other people everywhere back then. Germanic peoples, heathens from the forests, swooped down on Slavs, who gave their name to the word. Some say the largest slave market in western Europe in the eleventh century was at Dublin, and if that is true, northern explorers never lacked for a ready crew. Or wives.

•••••

## SAKSUN

To reach Saksun, in time we must turn left. Should we continue straight ahead we will cross the channel of Sundini to the smaller Eysturoy island, home of Kemm's favorite skerpikjøt and the Faroes' tallest peak. Spanning the channel is a bridge supported by eight columns known around here as the bridge across the ocean.

Five people live in Saksun now, way up at the end of Streymoy, 44 kilometers from Tórshavnon the far end of the island, at the end of the world. It's one of a kind, a real find, but around here there's one of a kind around every bend.

The air fills your chest so fresh it stings. The bay, the mists, the waterfalls that fill the hillsides, the pop-up rills after rain, everything in sight glittering, utterly pristine.

When Lars Gunnar Dehl Olsen was born in the 1990s, Saksun was home to 33. Tow-headed, lanky with a free range beard, Lars Gunnar stands in benevolent welcome at the end of the road. Which is also his farm.

For a time he rented a big white house from Johan Jogvonsson, a man in the "village." There are more than enough houses in the village for five or 33, because some are summer cottages. Now, out here on the point Lars Gunnar and his wife will endeavor to raise sheep and to do their part to keep Saksun alive, having just bought their own freehold in paradise.

Lars Gunnar calculates that 600 sheep is the minimum to make a farm viable and he has 700. Would more be better? If he had more he would need many more, enough to hire a farmhand. Seven hundred is about all he can handle by himself.

It's part of the old farm Dùvugarðar. Now a National Heritage Museum, its outbuildings - with turf roofs - recreate life in the old times. Today the museum stands tiny and deserted, locked tight, beside a hjallur, or curing house, those wooden, slatted buildings for air-curing skerpikjøt.

We can only peer through the museum windows at cooking pots and an iron tea kettle, a lambskin rug and a grandfather clock. There is bedding on bunks reminiscent of the tiny sleeping quarters at the Hanseatic League museum in Bergen, bunks much shorter than a grown man today.

Perhaps the Olsens' role is as much cordial host as lonely farmer. In the space of our visit, ours and two other cars call at their farm, for here at the end of the road is a fine panorama.

One thing for sure, the Olsens are safe from Viking raids. Sand has made the mouth of the bay so shallow that these days it is navigable only by small boats at high tide.

People may be a bit sparse out this way but the Olsens can rest content in their surroundings. Saksun is just utterly gorgeous.

Saksun

The ground never dries. The sheep squish-step about and drink from pools surrounded by moss. (How do they not get hoof rot?)

Forests of pine, birch and aspen covered Scotland, the Orkneys, Shetlands, Faroes and even Iceland up to around 5,000 years ago, when the northern climate grew cooler and wetter. Land waterlogged and trees died off, replaced by peat-forming mosses that sealed in rainwater, furthering the wetness. I have read that peat accumulates at the rate of perhaps a meter a millennium.

There are not many trees in the Faroes so settlers burned peat for heat and cooking. Like their ancestors, villagers make roofs of sod. Early inhabitants did it because sod was ubiquitous - and free. They still do it today because it works.

Here is how they do it: The earth is cut to manageable one-foot squares three or four inches thick and applied two-ply, with the first square grass/moss-down and the second upright so that they grow together into one impermeable unit.

While there are boards underneath (or birch bark where there are birch trees), the weight of the sod, about 500 pounds per square yard, helps to compress the logs in log homes and that helps to reduce the draft inside.

Life was hard for settlers and it still isn't easy, even here in gorgeous, glittering, scrubbed-clean Saksun. In his book *Harvest*, Jim Crace suggests the tenuousness of living on the edge of the world: "We do not press too closely to His bosom; rather we are at His fingertips. He touches us, but only just."

•••••

## TENSION WITH DENMARK

Dagfinnur, the man who took us to see the waterfall at Gásadalur, told us, "they say Putin eats Faroes lobster every single day. I don't know if this is true of course (chuckling to discount the notion), but if it is maybe that is what is wrong with him."

I appreciate Dagfinnur's defiance of the Russian leader. A couple of days ago Russia's ambassador to Denmark, Mikhail Vanin wrote in the Danish national newspaper *Jyllands-Posten*,

"I don't think the Danes fully understand the consequences of what will happen if Denmark joins the American-controlled missile defence. If it happens, Danish warships will become targets for Russian atomic missiles."

Maybe they don't but they used to. In 1972 a Danish politician named Mogens Glistrup founded the anti-tax, anti-immigrant Progress Party, a precursor to today's Danish People's Party, currently kingmaker in the Folketing, the Danish Parliament (175 representatives from Denmark, two from Greenland and two from the Faroes). Glistrup proposed that Denmark save money by replacing the Ministries of Defense and Foreign Affairs with an answering machine saying in Russian, "We surrender."

•••••

We are good friends now, disinhibited, and Kemm is loose. He drops into a sort of Faroese Rodney Dangerfield monologue. On the famous Putin lobsters: He read about that in a Norwegian magazine and everybody has heard it.

"You gotta lotta money when you can do that," he says.

"I saw a documentary the other day. Putin put in his election papers. Said he had a 70-square-meter apartment. Three-car garage, all Ladas. You think that's true?"

It all started going wrong, Kemm reckons, with Glasnost. The West started to sell the Russians all the stuff they needed to make mischief now.

On Obama: "I compare him with boiled spaghetti. His back is like boiled spaghetti."

The Faroes hope to rely on 100 percent renewable energy sources by 2030. Last summer they put up thirty windmills along the highway above town but none of us could figure why they weren't spinning in the blizzardy gale we drove through up there. They just stood still.

Faroese work hard at being green. While the EU might bless that, strains with the Europeans remain. The Faroese are in cahoots with other non-EU states Norway and Iceland - over fishing.

The Faroes are simply not a rich and diversified enough economy to suffer EU quotas on fishing, and so they go it alone. Back in Torshavn, this is Gunnar Holm-Jacobsen's principal preoccupation (shortly after our visit Gunnar was in Moscow for the opening of a Faroese "representation" there, unaffiliated with the EU).

Kemm raises his eyebrow in the rear view mirror. "A farmer never kills his last milk cow," he observes, "And we will never overfish." And you get it that he's right.

The Faroes' issues with the EU may be negotiable, but with Denmark, it's a wee bit more personal.

Kemm gets riled and sits up straight. He doesn't exactly throw out his chest but his invective comes with earned-by-living-here Faroese pride. So here is how it is:

Taxes are 50 percent and Kemm doesn't mind. Think about it, he says, turn it around.

We have 49,000 people, 23,000 taxpayers. Imagine, only 23,000 taxpayers provide these islands with fine roads, a port, public services. A place where everything works.

Sure, that's right, I'm saying, but after all, doesn't Denmark underwrite these islands?

Denmark topped the 2012 World Happiness Report, but that must be back on the mainland, only a Danish home truth. Because out here, I have sent Kemm into a splenetic fit.

All right, he declares, "They send 600 million Danish kroner a year." His voice rises, defiant.

"Thing is, we have to use a Danish agent for every last thing we bring over here," he says.

I imagine him slamming his mug on the bar. He spits and splutters, "they get their kroner back many times over!"

"We even have to use Danes to import stuff from China!" he declares.

When he was a kid and gonna get rich, he had a scheme to buy paint in bulk from a man in Norway, at a big discount from going through the Danes, but the Danish competition found out about it.

The Danish company threatened the Norwegians with their business if they traded with the Faroes and so the Norwegians backed away from Kemm. First they suggested a Maltese front, so the paperwork showed the paint came from Valetta, and Kemm wasn't against it in theory, but what if the Maltese connection went awry?

In the first place it wasn't reliable, and anyway why should Kemm have to engineer shenanigans in the first place? Could he not buy paint, PAINT for goodness sakes, from whomever he bloody well chose instead of through the Danes? And if not why not?

This is spirit kindred to the Boston Tea Party, a revolt against taxation but also against the British trade monopoly forcing the colonies to buy tea from the British East India Company. In the Faroes as in our own national mythology, you get enough of that vassal treatment, you want to up and rule yourselves.

•••••

**FALLOUT FROM FAR AWAY WAR**

Autumnal chill held mist to the shore like prison as the people of Copenhagen stood mute at the waterfront. Mouths agape, they watched as wind filled the sails of a convoy of ships, every one receding to the horizon.

Sixteen ships of the line, fifteen frigates, the entire Danish navy and ninety-two merchant ships besides sailed to England under the command of a British admiral in an audacious preventive heist. Some said the British even took the doorknobs from the Danish naval base.

Britain worried Napoleon would seize the Danish/Norwegian fleet. Word was that a multinational army was massing at Hamburg to advance on Jutland. So in August 1807 a British force sailed on Copenhagen to demand the entire Danish navy stand down and hand itself over.

J K Galbraith wrote that all foreign policy is a choice between the unpalatable and the disastrous. Denmark chose disaster. They refused and British troops bombed its capital into capitulation, the first time a European capital came under systematic bombardment. Some 3,200 Danes were killed or grievously hurt. The Brits destroyed the shipyards and sailed away with the Danish war fleet.

Things only got worse. Denmark allied with France and by November Britain had declared war. The besieged Danish kingdom endured bitter poverty. Deprived of grain, Norway, then in union with Denmark, starved. The country declared itself bankrupt. Denmark sued for peace.

The settlement, the Peace of Kiel, tore Norway from the Danish king and rewarded it to the Swedish kingdom as recompense for its loss of Finland. But the Faroes, Iceland and Greenland - overseas possessions of the Norwegian crown - remained with Denmark.

Way out here in the Faroes archipelago, not a lot changed. Except that from then Faroese nationalist ire was directed not toward Oslo (then Christiania, its Danish name) but toward Copenhagen. Arrogation of Faroese geography was neither new nor about to end.

Three months after the Nazis occupied Czechoslovakia in 1939, Denmark signed a non-aggression pact with the Germans, Copenhagen hoping to keep the country out of war. Germany had other plans. They began their assault the day the treaty was signed.

The Danish king surrendered straight away. Germany occupied Denmark on 9 April, 1940 and Winston Churchill went on the BBC to declare, "We are ... occupying the Faroe Islands, which belong to Denmark and which are a strategic point of high importance, and whose people showed every disposition to receive us with warm regard. We shall shield the Faroe Islands from all the severities of war and establish ourselves there conveniently by sea and air until the moment comes when they will be handed back to Denmark liberated from the foul thraldom into which they have been plunged by German aggression."

British destroyers sailed into Tórshavnharbor. Churchill stationed seven or eight thousand British troops on the islands alongside a population of some 30,000 Faroese. The British censored the mails, restricted vehicle movement and blacked out Tórshavnat night.

The German occupation of Denmark reverberated around the north Atlantic. The Icelandic Parliament, its suzerain occupied, declared home rule. Like in the Faroes, the British sailed into Reykjavik, ultimately stationing 25,000 troops on the island. By the end of the war responsibility for Iceland's defense rested with the United States, which built Meeks Field, the future Keflavik International Airport and NATO base.

Denmark's far-flung envoys ignored German edicts. A year to the day after the occupation of Copenhagen, Danish Ambassador to the U.S. Henrik Kauffmann authorized America to protect Danish interests in Greenland, acting "in the name of the king" and leading to the still extant U.S. airbase at Thule. Thus the U.S. acquired much of its far north Cold War military infrastructure directly from Berlin's invasion of Copenhagen.

Back on the Faroes, the governor generally backed the British occupation and in return for (mostly) local autonomy, the Faroes ferried deeply appreciated fish to the British Isles, which struggled under food rationing. The Faroes' economy boomed on the backs of sky-high prices in British ports. In the process though, 132 Faroese fishermen lost their lives "killed as a direct result of enemy activities."

Kemm speaks with near nostalgia and positive pride about the Faroes' role in the war, themselves occupied like their sovereign, their future uncertain. He tells tales of false flag supply missions that ran at peril to supply the U.K. with fish. Not all of them made it, not by a long shot, he says.

The British ended their occupation with the liberation of Denmark, but the Faroese wartime taste of autonomy rendered the return of the status quo ante no longer impossible. No one believed the Faroes would return to the old ways.

The emergent superpower United States wanted to locate its "Loran," or long-range navigation systems (since succeeded by the satellite-based Global Positioning System) and early warning devices on the Faroes, as they had in Greenland and Iceland.

Denmark saw an opportunity for income from the Americans and a chance to mitigate some of their own military spending. But the Faroese (who were never conscripted as had been the Danes) resisted militarization.

In a referendum the Faroese electorate just opted for sovereignty, the difference 166 votes. Copenhagen, distracted by its own occupation, was entirely unprepared for such an outcome. There hadn't even been an agreement whether the referendum would be binding. The Danish king did not accede, and instead dissolved the Faroese Løgting.

A new vote and further machination resulted in continued Danish responsibility for foreign policy, defense, police, justice and fiscal policy, while otherwise allowing home rule. No longer were the Faroes a Danish county, but now a "self-governing community within the Kingdom of Denmark."

Today's Faroese are citizens of Denmark, though no Faroese is obliged to serve in the Danish army. Still, in certain quarters, resentment at the Danes clings fast as peat to the roofs.

But times change. The NATO early warning radar installed in 1963 at Mjørkadalur (foggy valley) in Streymoy is now the islands' fourteen-cell jail. The one time Danish marine station is a nursing home.

The biggest British legacy besides that handrail at Gásadalur is the airport on Vagar, built in wartime. That and British chocolates, now more readily available in the Faroes than in Copenhagen.

•••••

**A DAY ON THE TOWN**

At the start of the day a smallish container ship approaches Torshavn's inner harbor. I can just about hear our friend Erich in Berlin, who observes these ships as a pastime. He would scoff, "ach, only 3000 tons."

Cloud cover hangs low and it feels like we may be beset all day, although yesterday immaculate sunshine, pelting sleet and gales jockeyed for position as fiercely as Viking raiders. And that was just in the morning.

A tender moves into place alongside the container ship, which reverses its screw and churns the water in place. A single crane, not heavy enough to exactly groan into action, swings up to grapple with the several dozen containers.

The inner harbor protects a small space calm and safe, enclosed by the shore and a reclaimed arm of land at the far side. They work the container ship into place with the bridge to the inside and containers pointing outward. This is Torshavn's industrial brawn, buildings reaching out to touch the waterfront, sturdy, three- and four-story merchants' buildings with many windows done up in red and yellow, small boats moored outside.

A wider, natural harbor extends beyond the built arm of land filled with longshoremen, crane operators and ships' hands, a space shielded from the open sea by a low-slung island called Nólsoy (from the tourist brochure: "During winter time you can enjoy the peacefulness and bleating sheep amongst the houses in the village"). Visible stem to stern, its entire breadth, from the hill above Tórshavn town, by my eye Nolsóy stretches a little more than seven kilometers across, with a tiny village at the shore in the center. On either side, either way into Torshavn, open water leads to the wide-open spaces of the north Atlantic.

The Tórshavn Cathedral stands back from the center of the inner harbor, around the corner from tiny glass-walled Etika, the islands' sole sushi restaurant, and houses crowd up the hills in a gentle jumble, not too close together, so that patches of grass grow in between.

Headlights make glossy the rain slicked road from up-island, which is also the road that connects to Vagar Island and the airport, and on to Eystroy and the north.

Salmon-farming sea-pens, circles with nets enclosing thousands of fish, run along the sound, accompanying the road north. Three or four big companies own most of that business and it is an important one. There are nine more rings just outside the harbor in Torshavn.

This is not a very big place and it is traditionally oriented, an outlier against the mainstream Danish post-religionism, with restrictions on alcohol sales and announcements of the confirmations of young people in *Dimmalaetting*, the local paper, a 56-page tabloid with an editorial in front and then features, most prominently in this issue, a look at Sigert Patursson's cattle farm.

In small places, little things mean more, and as the government puts it, "the old Faroese chain dance is our most important heritage." Dancing societies meet all around the islands, weekly in wintertime, except for right now, because the Faroese give up dancing for Lent and Easter is coming.

•••••

Forty percent of these islands' 50,000 people live in this city named for Thor. Their sovereign, Her Majesty The Queen of Denmark, Margrethe Alexandrine Þorhildur Ingrid, is also named for Thor.

On the limits of sophistication of our plucky little human race: It is useful to remember we still have cities, and leaders, and a day of the week named after a brawny, mythical god who never left home without his hammer. Then there is the day named after Thor's father Odin (Wednesday). Odin was a one-eyed, long-bearded spear carrier (whose present day Finnish admirers, the "soldiers of Odin," are racist xenophobes).

Anytime we get thinking that we humans are masters of the universe, it is healthy to remember that we still call the days of the week mystical things like "moon day" and "sun day" and "Saturn day."

They say that the Greek Zeus and Latin Deus are etymologically the same as the Old Norse Tyr, a once mighty god whose career took an unfortunate turn when he lost his hand to a wolf. No wonder he got a day as lackluster as Tuesday. And finally, in the grudging interest of sexual equality there is one day named for a woman, Freya, the Nordic fertility goddess.

•••••

The Føroyar Hotel sits low slung across ample rolling hills. Fine panoramic windows the length of it take in the whole town below. Above town is open hillside, separated from the first houses by what looks like an out-of-season, gnarly, wild-growing vineyard cut through with a footpath to town. They have built two layers of rooms into the hillside, each room with the same view, the whole expanse pasted with seasonally yellow turf roofs.

Tórshavn from the Føroyar Hotel

This morning the Faroes junior national football team buzzes around the breakfast buffet. They have already worked out before eating, a couple dozen boys dressed in the national team's blue, training for a qualifier against Azerbaijan.

The real Faroe Islands National Football Team (Føroyska fótbóltsmanslandsliðið) scored four goals in a match for the first time in its history in 2014. It was FIFA-ranked 102nd in 2015 and the highest it has ever ranked is 74th. When the Faroes beat Greece 2-1 in November 2014, Greece sacked its coach.

Later in the week they will play a Euro Qualifiers match against Romania. Everybody in town knows they will lose, they are sure about it, so when, as it turns out, they only lose one-nil it is a spectacular victory.

Tonight the hotel hosts a planeload of young people from Iceland. They suggest that if we need earplugs, just let them know down at reception.

## BOOM LAKKA LAKKA LAKKA

Nothing is quiet - or natural - at Café Natur. All the kids with coin are here after school, sneaking a pint before mom comes home. The drinking age must be fourteen. Myself, I try to enjoy a "Classic" Faroes beer whose smell and taste tend toward vinegar.

The Western world believes in the progress built into the Enlightenment. But the only enlightenment for the kids here this afternoon is blurred through the bottom of beer mugs.

Besides the kids and us, there are only sailors. Unlike any other harbor saloons in the world (besides Iceland), sailing to Greenland is a normal, workaday topic here.

When he was younger Kemm went to ply the fishing trade in Iceland. To work, but also to breathe the air on faraway shores. Sigurdur Oli, an Icelander, decided his ship both figuratively and literally came in in Tórshavn when his visit, after long weeks at sea, coincided with a volleyball tournament that brought all of the Faroes women's teams to the capital.

•••••

When the day of the Føroyska fótbóltsmanslandsliðið versus Romania match arrives we crowd in for the excitement down at the Irish pub, which is really two bars in one. Manners and acceptable dress are loose requirements on the top floor where Canadian girls pour Guinness and serve gravy smothered pork chops. Rather a different discernment prevails downstairs, not fifty steps from boats bobbing in the harbor, at Torshavn's closest thing to a true sailors' haunt.

In the movie version of what might be called *Tórshavn by the Sea*, wiry seadogs with prominent Popeye chins would cackle in a hopeless northern brogue, corn cob pipe smoke curling toward sunlight, its comforting fragrance filling a hardy oak-beamed room. But the real life Glitnir Tavern is not like the movies. Men congregate and rattle chairs in dark corners, erudite as unpaid whores, and take in, along with their beverages, the unscrubbable scent of year-old beer and baked-in deep-fried cod, presided over with the benign touch of the benevolent innkeeper and his wife.

Football chants and jeers at the bad-guy Romanians rise from here upstairs to the genteel Irish pub, where once in a while they shudder. Craig Robertson, in *The Last Refuge*, wrote that at Glitnir, aging patrons have "their backs securely to the walls, like one of those centrifugal-force rides that you get at a funfair. No matter how fast the room spun, they'd never fall off into the middle."

Perhaps these fishermen, whose jobs mean twice the time at sea as time on land, think thoughts made deep by the sea. More likely they simply contemplate their mugs until they are empty, then pony up for another round.

•••••

## THE LITTLE TRAVEL AGENT THAT COULD

Somebody at the Visit Faroe Islands office down on the harbor is the little travel agent that could. After fishing and related aquaculture, tourism is the islands' most important business, and up to recently, all of it has been jammed in around the national Ólavsøka festival in July, and more generally between March and September.

The push is on for more, and the tourist board does yeoman's work, snaring prominent feature placement in *National Geographic Traveler* magazine (one of its "best trips"), the New York Times and CBS. The islands have become an associate member of UNESCO, setting up a commission to promote a 700-year-old church as a world heritage site.

In 2011 they extended Vagar Airport's runway to 1,799 metres and upgraded navigation systems. The government doubled its funding to the tourism board in 2012 and cut taxes on airline tickets. They just finished a new terminal that forces arrivals through a duty-free gauntlet.

(Airport CEO Jakup Sverri Kass, 39 years old and a former marketing director at Atlantic Airways, apologizes for that, explaining that because the Faroes remain outside the EU, tax-free revenue is "a crucial part of the airport's revenue base.")

Hotel beds are a screaming need. The Føroyar Hotel up on the hill is the best in town, nominally international standard, hardly luxury. Otherwise, hotels Tórshavn and Hafnia in the center each have around forty rooms. The Streym Hotel, staffed by charming, disarming people, has fewer, and that's just about it.

They manage to run tourist numbers up over the stark limit of beds in summer by welcoming tourists who arrive as caravan campers aboard the Smyril Line ferry, which runs between Denmark and the Faroes, and Iceland.

•••••

**AND FINALLY**

The Mississippi River thrived in the days of Mark Twain, paddle wheel steamers and cotton. It was the lifeline of an earlier United States, but by the time I was growing up near the river, flood tides of trouble swept over our region's progress.

Synthetic fibers edged out cotton. The river trade shrank when the interstate highway system rose and long-haul trucks took hold. My town, Memphis, comprehensively failed at addressing the civil rights movement.

They shot Martin Luther King III on the landing of a Memphis hotel. They cancelled school that week. We could see downtown lit up at night from the riots and fires. Scared my parents through.

As the American south depended on cotton, the Faroese economy lived and died by fishing. In the 1980s all sorts of new high-tech gear led to overfishing. The resulting economic stress exposed the over-loose lending practices of the Sjóvinnurbankin, the Faroese national bank. When the Sjóvinnurbankin had to go hat in hand to Copenhagen for a bailout it started the Faroes' darkest ever depression, peaking with the collapse of the islands' two leading banks in 1992.

Unemployment approached 20 percent in Torshavn, more on the fells. More than five percent of the population fled, mostly for Denmark. Because they needed Denmark more than before, the Faroese dropped their independence claims (as they left Copenhagen with their unpaid bills).

But that was the 1980s. Unemployment has dropped and fishing stocks have risen and with them, again, the idea of independence. In 2005 the Faroes signed an agreement for a common market with Iceland. Besides that new trade mission in Moscow, the Faroes have bilateral trade agreements with the EU, Norway and Switzerland.

•••••

Is there something about wind-battered, sodden and remote spots like these trifling basalt assertions in the middle of the great big sea, places submissive to the larger forces of nature, that make a people stoic and stubborn?

"Fiercely independent" is a travel trade euphemism most commonly used to mean "asshole." Package tour brochures label the east African Masaai this way. What they really mean is "people unwilling to allow our minibus to stop where they live and shove our camera phones into their barns and houses."

They call the Faroese fiercely independent too, but they don't mean it the same way, maybe in part because there are no minibuses of tourists. I never met a Faroese person who wasn't charming. But just perhaps the island character runs a touch toward willful.

Fiercely independent may also mean "determined to protect their independence," and I think this is where the Faroese come down on the whaling and fishing questions and on further integration with the European Union.

The Faroese are a Scandinavian people whose history has opened fissures between them and their sovereign in their language, culture and economy. Fishing is politics here and distance from the EU is in the Faroese DNA.

Denmark itself is only a partial EU member, not having joined EU protocols on citizenship and legal affairs, and retaining its use of Kroner instead of Euros. The Faroes have winnowed their own connection still further.

When Denmark signed on with the European Community in 1973, the Faroes diplomatically declined. Maybe it was because of fishing rules; they've always rejected those. Or maybe it's just the way people get when they live way off on their own. Maybe solitude teaches you to make your own rules.

# PART THREE: ICELAND

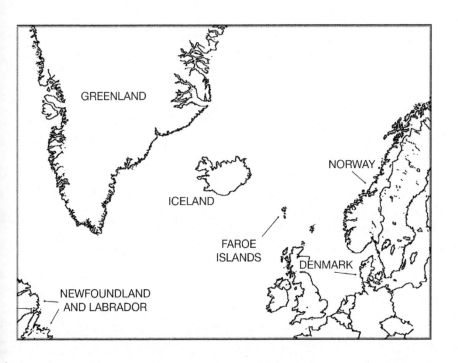

*Bill Murray*

## *NORRÖNA*

Time at sea is balm for the soul, respite from the workaday, a chance to contemplate the great wash of water upon the Earth. The sea is fluid. Change is the sailor's constant companion, and today we change countries aboard an obscure ferry across the north Atlantic to Iceland. A proper shipborne adventure.

Surely the passenger manifest holds no names of any ethnicity tied to terror. Here is a ship of Sigurds and Sigurdssons, Johanns and Johanssons. Still, when you change countries you offer your passport. In Torshavn's little harbor, though, the young woman in the window just smiles and flutters her hand. "Never mind."

Arriving at Iceland, no passport control. It's not that no one wants to stamp your passport. It's that no one is there to size you up at all.

Years ago I arrived at Stockholm on the party boat from Helsinki. That is what everybody called them (at least we young people), the Silja and Viking Line ferries that set out between capitals in each direction every night, their promenades overfull of food and drink and shopping, and a telephone in every room so you could call the United States if you wanted.

In my short-lived role as a businessman peddling my wares, I walked off the Viking Line onto a ramp into Sweden, where I expected someone to nod in recognition of my gravity. Nobody cared. Same thing. Nobody was even there.

A couple of days from now, flying from tiny east Iceland for the tiny capital, there will be no security. No x-rays, no walk-through machine, no questions. Just press a button on the counter to summon the clerk from the room behind a window where they can see you but you can't see them, to take your ticket.

•••••

The *Norröna*, the flag ship of the Faroese shipping line Smyril (the Faroese name for a type of falcon), runs this route between Denmark, Tórshavn and Iceland. Packed, it carries 1,500 people and 800 cars. In winter between Tórshavn and Iceland, it is never packed.

Up in the heated, enclosed outdoor view point a husband and wife knit together as we take our beers to the window and watch the spray spin off north Atlantic waves in a frosty, freezy way.

Spume slaps the window while the bartender allows that the Tórshavn to Seydisfjordur leg, she is the roughest. True enough; the red LED numbers read three a.m. sharp when buffeting rearranges the interior of the cabin in the dark. The *Norröna* sails with all the aerodynamics of a shoebox.

The *Norröna* tries to nestle into Seydisfjordur in the morning, but it is more of a wedge than a nestle. Seydisfjordur, where the sun sinks behind the mountains in November not to be seen again until the end of February, is a community of houses opportunistically assembled around the inside of a fjord steep and narrow, an entirely Arctic place with cliffs covered with snow, some buildings half-buried under drifts, with a wind across the Norröna's deck that will drive you straight back inside.

A man down at the docks, just the bundled form of a man really, claims Seydisfjordur should have been the main town in Iceland. No one but he makes that claim. When wild men ruled here, a long time ago before governments, Seydisfjordur started life around a herring fishery set up by Norwegians and they say it thrived. For a time the world's largest whaling station, also Norwegian run, stood on the shores of Mjoifjordur, today a village of 35 people just four or five miles over the ridge, the next fjord south.

Telegraph first connected Iceland to Europe from Seydisfjordur in 1906. Engineering feats like this buck up pride out at the far end, and this one helps Iceland insist it is part of Europe. Europe is like, whatever.

Seydisfjordur has scant relation to the Faroes. It is colder and meaner, harder core, smothered by snow, an outpost at the end of a water trail, cliffs along either side narrowing onto the dock.

It takes some time for the *Norröna* to find a fit. Husband and wife knit unconcerned on deck. Faroese and Icelandic men used to knit of necessity. Now it is sport, or perhaps chivalry. During endless winters people learn to entertain themselves. Fun is where you find it.

These *Norröna* passengers might not enjoy the Helsinki to Stockholm party boat. Not that kind of crowd. Neither do they exhibit any of the bovine wobble of Americans on a Caribbean fun ship.

Imagine history, long and dark. In living memory northern Icelanders read without electricity, learning their heritage, the Sagas, by the light of oil lamps. Because of Iceland's great isolation the original Norse language has held so fast that Icelanders can still read the original Sagas like they were last week's newspaper.

In this context the Sagas are not only the great historical epic of the northern peoples, but also social glue, nation-building tools, and in the living, breathing life of even a hundred years ago they were sources of wonder, fascination and high entertainment. Just those few years ago, you might never meet anyone you hadn't known from birth.

Consider that while settlements sprouted on the island more than eleven hundred years ago, only for about 170 years have people in this world had effective pain killing medicine. Prior to 1846 there was no anesthesia. Before the last century rudimentary medicine served to comfort the afflicted until they healed, or they didn't.

Before the invention of the telegraph in 1837, information could travel no faster than a sailing ship or a man on a horse. In Iceland's earliest days killing had not yet been outsourced to the gun, to a machine. It relied on hand tools and the brute application of pressure.

•••••

## WELCOME. NOW GO! HURRY!

See each place with child's eyes and embrace the moment you do. For the strange grows fast familiar, nevermore wondrous and new.

There is a lovely blue Lutheran church in the center of town, strikingly backlit by the sun's bounce off a snowy backdrop. Seydisfjordur touts itself as an artists' colony in summer. An arts camp in July, musicians at the church on Wednesdays. In summer there are 4x4 tours, bird watching, biking, sea fishing and kayaking and a nine-hole golf course over the hill in Egilsstaðir.

The blue church at Seydisfjordur

In winter it is tough. Home-bound knitters do their best to snare the passing tourist dollar. Buy a mitten, buy a bootie. A ski lift once ran up the hill, but it is closed tight this winter. The *Norröna* delivers its passengers, but only once a week in winter, and today despite cerulean skies, the buses hurry straight over the pass because the captain advised passengers by public address to leave the Seydisfjord straight away, forecasting a debilitating, road-closing storm.

Nodding to the wisdom of skating quickly over thin ice, we follow. Beyond the blue church and the ship from the Faroes is just the road out, over the hill to Egilsstaðir. Up toward the pass a Scania truck that was hauling fish lies on its side, a stark admission of failure.

Happened yesterday. Driver unhurt, fish still inside. They are frozen and unlikely to melt.

I scoff at the idea of a storm under these brilliant skies but by 14:30 the world is reduced to white and shades of gray, as snow sweeps the road. The horizon winks out. By then we have run up to the foot of Snæfell, "snow mountain," the ancient volcano that reigns over the highlands at 1,833 meters.

•••••

## EGILSSTAÐIR, EAST ICELAND

We are in the hearty care of a big man named Agnar. First time I see him I feel he isn't my kind of guy. Something about his slouch against the wall. Nobody slouches when the air is below zero.

Maybe Icelanders do.

Agnar is imposing, a ruddy man, ample and not naturally affable. He strikes me as a "from my cold dead fingers" sort and maybe he is, for he is an avid hunter, enumerating at length and in considerable detail the requirements for reindeer hunting - and his techniques.

Iceland's reindeer have no natural enemies. Their population is managed by government-controlled hunting between July and September. Reindeer meat is an Icelandic delicacy and there is demand enough for hunting permits to require a lottery.

Agnar wears a black turtleneck of thermally appropriate fiber, tight enough to display his girth. Flitty eyes in a big head suggest a distrust I don't think he means. Half me, half his lifetime among few strangers.

His on-and-then-off black wool cap and black fleece outer layer lay against his ruddiness to make him out as a confident outdoorsman. Might be just the guy you want around here, on second thought.

He has a Super Jeep. If super means how far off the ground you must step to climb in, it sure is super. It comes with its own Italian air compressor en suite. Essential equipment, for we haven't made it up to the glacier by the time we slide and our back end wobbles around in one place until Agnar hops out to let air out of the tires.

Lower air pressure flattens the tires. They relax a few inches, spread out and get a better grip. And it works. Eventually you'll need to re-inflate the tires, and that's where the air compressor comes in. Once we attain the main road back to Egilsstaðir toward the end of the day, Agnar stops at a junction with a billboard for us to regard in the whipping wind. It explains how geo-thermal power works around the region while Agnar sets about re-inflating the tires with the compressor.

The thing makes a lot of racket and he goes round to the tires one at a leisure time as if it weren't minus eight degrees, the wind howling like a penned sled dog.

•••••

Largarfljót, the longest lake in the country, flows down from our destination, so we run alongside it on the way up. We're headed to the great Vatnajokull, ("jokull" is "glacier") up onto the edge of Europe's largest glacier. The national park around it covers 14 percent of the country.

What is it about narrow northern lakes and worms? Lagarfljot has its own Loch Ness-style monster, 300 meters long with scaly humps and revolting spikes and a very, very long life. It has dwelt beneath these waters since 1345, spotted as recently as 2012. In legend its appearance augurs ill for the local folk.

It is just as well to contemplate a legend, for the landscape reveals little beyond the sweep of barren land and Iceland's largest organic vegetable farm. Four-foot trees, a reforestation experiment that I expect isn't destined to reach new heights, admit their discouragement in mangy patches on the road out of Egilsstaðir.

They hope the old saw about what to do if you get lost in an Icelandic forest (put the cork back in the bottle, stand up and look around) may one day get a challenge. The Forest Service claims 130 square kilometers of birch forest have taken hold in the past twenty-five years. That represents one and a half percent of the country, although you'd be challenged to find the first tree on the flight from east Iceland to Reykjavik. Still, they're hoping for 25 percent birch coverage one of these days.

They reckon birch forests in valleys and willow scrub along the coast covered about a third of the island at the time of settlement. Iceland's fate doesn't run as raw as Easter Island's, where the colonizers appear to have cut down every last tree, but the temptation to cut down trees in the Arctic for warmth and shelter must have been at least as mighty as on Rapa Nui.

Climbing toward Vatnajokull, sheep folds, circular pens for gathering and sorting sheep, line the Largarfljót flood plain. The herder might sort sheep into any of half a dozen pie-shaped low stone sections that comprise the circle, with a commonly accessible further circle in the middle.

Iceland has no passenger rail, and automobiles only found their way here in the 1920s, so horses were the main means of transport until very recently, especially for distance. Meghan O'Rourke, in *The New York Times*: "The Icelandic horse … is unique with its quick, short-steeped gait, so smooth a rider wouldn't spill a drink."

The horses in the valley of the Largarfljót graze at quiet farms on either side of the road, long manes and tails waving with the wind down the valley, white manes with dark bodies or the mirror of that, light bodies and dark manes. The river flows turbid and steady, scarcely a hundred meters wide, even less as it snakes through sand bars.

•••••

## NOT SO GREEN UNDER ALL THAT SNOW

The dominant politician of his generation, for good and considerable ill, was the son of an unmarried medical doctor and a secretary who as a boy aspired to be an actor, a man named David Oddsson.

In 1991 Oddsson's incoming national government inherited an economy built on three pillars: fish, geothermal power and the NATO base at Keflavik. With Oddsson's guidance the fishing business gentrified so that with time Icelanders tended more to buying fish futures contracts than actual fish.

Iceland's great bounty and enduring natural strength is renewable energy via glacial rivers and geothermal heat, generating nearly free electricity. Exporting these riches is difficult, so Iceland invites power-hungry industries to come and consume them onshore.

Oddsson cultivated Alcoa and by 2003, Iceland had become the largest producer per capita of primary aluminum in the world. Raw aluminum is now Iceland's main export, worth $1.97 billion in 2013. Fish fillets come second at a little under half that.

Aluminum derives from bauxite by the process of electrolytic smelting, using heat to get at valuable metals in rock. Smelting works by driving off other elements as gases or slag which tends to create nasty byproducts like acetylene, ammonia and methane. This requires vast electricity and hydropower is the most economical. Which means diversion of water. Which means dams.

The Alcoa smelter at Reyðarfjörður required the prior construction of the Kárahnjúkar dam project in a highland valley on the edge of the Vatnajokull glacier. Ultimately nine dams and dikes blocked two rivers. The dams and smelting by-products combined to spawn social upheaval and protest.

While the smelter provides jobs, opponents file lawsuits about high levels of fluoride in hay fields around the plant. Some say the smelter has killed Largarfljót, its aquatic plants and fish. But we know that is not entirely true, for how could the monster in the lake live without food?

Opponents believe that serving Alcoa has killed the lake. Agnar waves all that off and there is no changing his opinion, I am sure of it. A proponent of the plant and the jobs it has brought, he blames Largarfljót's turbidity on the glaciation process itself.

•••••

**THE EARTH ALIVE**

If Svalbard is nature austere, Iceland is a landscape afflicted, blemished and fidgety, a tempest uncomfortable in its skin as a teenager and every bit as inchoate. The whole island is a rage against the permanent, such a new spot of land that if all the Earth's history were a year, Iceland would have appeared the 30th of December. Lying across the mid-Atlantic ridge, Iceland is pulling itself apart at the speed fingernails grow.

Over 65 million years, a plume in the mantle below Iceland has poured out some 10 million cubic kilometers of magma, 50 times the volume of the island itself. It manifests on the surface as Bardarbunga, a volcano that most recently stopped erupting in February of 2015. Bardarbunga does its best to vex researchers, for it is buried beneath Vatnajokull. Scientists reckon that Bardarbunga collapsed after a cataclysmic ancient eruption, forming a ten-kilometer caldera 700 meters deep that today is filled with ice.

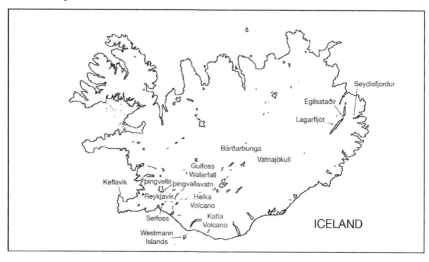

The Earth below Bardarbunga ground to life most recently on 14 August 2014. Earthquakes rumbled and migrated out beyond the glacier's edge until a fracture opened on the surface of the Earth to the north.

Two weeks later magma at a temperature of 2,150 degrees Fahrenheit broke through the earth at Holuhraun, a field of cooled lava from a 1797 eruption. Lava spewed forth for the next 182 days. Tour operators organized spectacular flyovers. By driving considerably longer than our route today, when the weather was right, Agnar could offer tours to a viewing site a safe distance away.

Volcanologists breathed sighs of relief when Bardarbunga's lava found a way to the surface. Had Bardarbunga cracked the icy dome of the Vatna glacier it would have unleashed catastrophic floods.

Just such a thing occurred at another subglacial volcano called Katla. Legend tells us Katla is named for a cook at a monastery who owned a pair of trousers in which the wearer could run forever. When a shepherd stole them to help him bring in his sheep, Katla drowned him in a barrel of whey. In despair when she realized she would be caught for murder she ran up the volcano and threw herself inside. An eruption sent a jökulhlaup, a glacial flood, down on the monastery.

(Volcanism can hold in reserve all kinds of nasty surprises. Lake Nyos fills a crater along the "Cameroon Line," a fault along which the African continent is separating. One night in 1986 heavy rain pounded the land and so a local health care worker named Emmanuel Ngu Mbi took shelter in the village of Wum, and slept.

The next morning he hopped onto his bicycle and began pedaling. He saw an antelope lying dead along the path, and then rats, dogs, other animals. At the next village he was astounded to see dead bodies everywhere. Overnight a cloud of volcanic carbon dioxide rent the lake and displaced all the air. It crept along the ground and some 1746 people and all their livestock died.)

•••••

Compared to the evil, sloshing, 600-meter active Holuhraun fissure that Bardarbunga served up for six photogenic months, it is hard to understand how little Eyjafjallajökull volcano caused enough pain in 2010 to shut down trans-Atlantic air routes for almost a week, costing airlines alone something like $1.7 billion and affecting 10 million passengers.

Europe's three largest airports — London Heathrow, Frankfurt Main and Paris-Charles de Gaulle — were all shut by drifting ash or the threat of it. U.S. military supplies for Afghanistan were disrupted. At least a dozen delegations canceled plans to attend the funeral of President Lech Kazinski of Poland. All because when Eyjafjallajökull blew, winds were at just the angle to move the ash toward Europe.

Eyjafjallajökull started out as what Icelanders call a "tourist eruption," scenic but not very dangerous. Except that ash can melt in jet engines, forming a glassy coating that clogs their turbines.

In 1982 a British Airways flight flew through an Indonesian volcanic cloud and lost power to all four of its engines, and likewise a 1989 KLM flight over Alaska. Both pilots restarted their engines and landed safely, but new rules forbade aircraft in airspace that might include any ash at all. After Eyjafjallajökull cost global commerce some five billion dollars, new rules raised the limits on the amount of ash airplanes can fly through.

The 1783 eruption of Iceland's Laki volcanic fissure south of Vatnajokull produced the largest recorded lava flow in history, and sent a gaseous haze of ash, sulfuric aerosols, flourine poisons and other gases across all of Iceland killing some three quarters of the island's livestock, in turn starving nearly a quarter of the humans.

Lava shot 1.4 kilometers into the sky. The English Channel was blocked by a gritty fog of ash. The next winter the southern Mississippi River froze over. Failure of the Nile's annual flood brought drought that reduced the population of the Nile valley by a sixth. The European Science Foundation called it "one of the most important climatic and socially repercussive events of the last millennium."

Through the years travelers returning to Europe claimed that physics obeyed its own rules in Iceland. Iceland's most famous volcano, Hekla, was the Gateway to Hell. In *A Journey to the Centre of the Earth*, Jules Verne made Iceland the route to get there.

In Verne's telling, Professor Otto Lidenbrock and his party descend into the crater of Snaeffels volcano, northwest of Reykjavik, encountering gases electrically charged and combustible, geysers and a sea, giant insects, mastodons and a twelve-foot-tall prehistoric man. A poem from around 1120 calls Hekla Judas's prison, and witches, they say, still gather there on Easter.

In November 1703 a windstorm destroyed some 400 windmills in the New Forest in Hampshire, England, opposite the Isle of Wight. They burned to the ground from the friction of their blades set spinning against wooden gears. The July, 1783, eruption of Laki summons images just like that. Alexandra Witze and Jeff Kanipe's frightening book *Island on Fire* tells the horrifying tale:

"Inside the church the only light came from lightning flashes, followed by claps of thunder so loud the steeple bells chimed in response."

• • • • •

## NAKED AND FREEZING ON VATNAJOKULL

Reindeer break at once across the hill above the road - a herd of forty - and kicked-up snow gathers speed rolling our way. No apparent reason for their stampede. These beasts, magnitudes more hearty than the dispirited troika that pleaded for handouts in Russian Barentsberg, appear to run for pure joy.

In the world of Icelandic reindeer, the ladies are both the fairer sex and the tougher. Females and males alike shed their antlers annually, but bulls shed right after the rut, in autumn (and it must be a relief, because reindeer antlers represent the fastest tissue growth known in mammals, up to two and a half centimeters every day. They can weigh ten kilograms).

Cows fight, physically, for the best feeding spots in the winter when they are pregnant, so they keep their antlers through winter. Collectors fan out across these hills as soon as the snow melts searching for shed antlers that soon after appear shortly after, carved into every kind of bauble in the boutiques of Reykjavik.

The day of the eclipse Agnar was guiding a group. "We were standing on that hill there," he says, pointing, and for a few minutes at maximum eclipse "the reindeer all got into a group," as they do at night. "For the reindeer it was a very short night."

The Arctic fox (that they reckon has been around for 10,000 years, turning brown in summer and white in winter) is Iceland's only native terrestrial mammal. Reindeer, Iceland's entire cadre, were introduced from Norway. Unlike the Lapps of northern Scandinavia, Icelanders never took to domesticating reindeer, so they live up here in the eastern highlands in winter and come down toward the shore for better grazing in summer.

Agnar parks the Super Jeep in front of a completely improbable guest house built for twenty or thirty, perched at glacier's edge and across a road marked only by reflective yellow poles along one side. Truth is, the glacier looks the same as the mountains it lies between this time of year, undifferentiated, everything bathed in white.

Agnar sets about digging places to make footfall in the snow, a spadeful per step, from the vehicle to the door. Just several meters away, but over the snow horizon, he claims heat glows beneath the snow and that we should shed our clothes and jump into a hot pool.

At minus eight degrees it sounds like an act of dubious wisdom, especially since we can't even see that such a thing exists.

"Most people," he smiles, "take their clothes off and run with their coat and boots on, maybe a towel."

He points to the changing rooms, leaves us towels and sets off with his spade digging a path.

No one within twenty miles. We do as he says.

We imagine that once we commit we will see the tail lights of the Super Jeep driving away down the hill, Agnar cackling with evil, the two of us locked outside and naked.

Shedding my clothes, I read a sign on the wall that explains the water in the pool stays at a constant 48 - 53 degrees celsius. Stand at the edge and the snowy rim reaches above your private parts, not that there's anybody around. You jump in - quickly - and find a place not too near the hot vents, and your feet float up like in the Dead Sea except it's not salty.

Whoever made the pool rimmed the water with stones and today nature has laid fresh snow around the pool so that when you get down low in it to expose only your head to the cold, you can't see above the snow rim. It's quiet as a scared kitten, so quiet I imagine hearing individual snowflakes land on the glacier. This tiny mote of space is all that exists in the world. It's snug in the water and morsels of ice tickle your face.

Refreshing, renewing. And like so many other things around here, utterly incongruent. Elsewhere on this island, with heat so near the surface, Icelanders bake Rúgbrauð, or Geysir Bread, buried in a pot two feet underground to cook overnight.

•••••

Guides the world over fix on their favorite landmarks. For our Burmese guide it was factories. "That is milk factory," "That is rice factory," "Do you want to see brick factory? Take photo?" Kemm on Streymoy Island liked churches.

For Agnar it is power stations. He shows us all of them (and there are many) big and small, and tells the tale of a farmer and his own personal power station. Power shed, really. It seems that one summer, when there was no snow, the electricity went out and the farmer went to investigate.

He found the door blown off and snow tumbling out of his shed. Failed electricity led to a burst pipe, turning the shed into the farmer's own personal snow machine. His neighbors snickered that he could hire himself out to ski slopes.

•••••

Agnar's tires are straight-from-America and too big for him to carry a spare. Only America, where bigger is always better, he says, would make these tires. He scoffs at an Icelandic company that has 38-inch tires made in China and imported. They won't do in EAST Iceland.

And since they are too big to carry a spare, what do you do if you have a flat?

"You have to fix it."

He glued his tires right to the rims and the mechanic who helped him told him he was crazy. But he didn't mean for them to come off. Ever.

I was wrong about Agnar at first. All this derring-do makes Agnar's fine company on the side of a glacier beat that of any neurotic city boy, or gentrified psuedo-farmer like me.

• • • • •

Back to Egilsstaðir, one of Iceland's few inland towns and the transport hub for the east. It is the first proper town if you arrive on the Norröna ferry and home to an airport with multiple daily flights to Reykjavik. Population, about 2,750.

There is a cafe in the red house (they just call it the red house) in the middle of town. Tonight maybe thirty people socialize in a light, Egilsstaðir way, gathered in groups around laminated diner-style tables like the Hvonn brasserie in Torshavn.

(Most people on the island are related at least at the eighth or ninth remove. To avoid striking up a relationship with your cousin when out at the pub, there is an "incest prevention" app based on genealogical data that allows people to bump phones and determine how closely they may be related. Just in case.)

An Indian fellow in the kitchen serves up tandoori chicken dishes, Gull Icelandic beer in big mugs and "wood-fired" pizza, surely exotic in a place with no wood. People come for the food and the free wi-fi, or to play chess.

Icelanders play a lot of chess. It is one of the ways to pass the long winter. In the off season fishermen carve chess pieces from whale bones (wood being more scarce) and people knit. There is a fine selection of yarn in the store. Families, friends, the community, everybody nods closer in the winter.

And Icelanders read. In the 1960s there were a dozen daily newspapers and forty bookshops in Reykjavik. There are more books published and more books read per head here than anywhere else. Every tenth Icelander is an author.

Meanwhile, in the Icelandair Hotel Herad across the way, mod furniture that may have found exile here from the rest of Europe after the '80s swivels in place beside the overbearing silence of its restaurant. The Hotel Herad's most notable feature may be ahead of its time. Its default TV news channel is not the advertising wasteland of CNN, but France 24 TV news.

•••••

**UP IN THE AIR**

I throw open the blinds the day of our flight from Egilsstaðir and flop back down on the bed, self-satisfied because I've built an extra day into our itinerary and this will be it, the day we are socked in with a full blizzard. The street is scarcely visible and the flags outside stand straight, towel-snapping in the wind. No plane will fly here today.

Snow-whipping wind bends the trees sideways while I imagine a day of amniotic calm in which I needn't be kempt nor ept nor sheveled. I imagine ordering modest room service fare in the modest Icelandair hotel, never progressing beyond my underwear and soaking in the state of the world as France Vingt Quatre sees it, nibbling the admittedly graying grapes on the Herad's fruit platter. Until the next time I look and blue sky and calm reign, and the occasional car makes wary time down the highway.

All flights lead to Reykjavik, four of them, at 8:55, 12:15, 12:55 and 16:10. They ask that you arrive thirty minutes before your flight, but still you have to ring the bell on the counter for service. It's a little whacky. There's a video monitor on which Saevar the Reindeer Whisperer offers tours of East Iceland.

Americans have tried to convince ourselves since 9/11 that a more prominent display of intolerance, flags and belligerence by Homeland

*Bill Murray*

Security will take care of the security threat. Back home we have made the dour airport experience the new normal.

In Egilsstaðir, the old normal never left. There is no security and there are no security personnel. You are hard pressed to find any personnel at all except the lady behind the counter at the coffee shop. And there are no bag scanners or x-ray machines. Just jump on and ride.

By this time we have had any number of alternating gales and lulls since that first look out the window. Three Caterpillar tractors with big blades race up and down the airstrip. In winter, I guess clearing that bit of land is a full time job. The 8:30 arrival, a Fokker 50, roars in ten minutes late and we are southbound within a half hour.

A pilot on the Savusavu airstrip in Fiji once lauded the entire Fokker line to me, saying these little worker bees *demand* the air and you have to hold them on the ground. So it was with today's flight in a Fokker 50, as we roared down the airstrip and out of east Iceland like lightnin'.

When I was a teenager my friend Jim and I found some of his dad's money, paper bills that said "Landsbanki Islands," and we scoured maps to find these islands. We couldn't and came to realize the translation would be something like the "National Bank of Iceland." In fact, the failure of Landsbanki, alongside Iceland's other two big banks Kaupthing ("marketplace") and Glitnir (as we learned in the Faroes, Norse heaven), precipitated Iceland's bankruptcy in 2008.

The word "Islands" works the same way here. The airline is Air Iceland when you book your tickets in English on the web; here it's Flugfelag Islands in its livery, and in-flight magazine.

They keep Reykjavik city airfield busy with domestic flights to Isafjordur, Akureyri and then on to Grimsey in the Arctic, Þhorshofn, Vopnafjordur and Egilsstaðir, to Tórshavnin the Faroe Islands and to Illulisat, Nuuk, Narsarsuaq, Kulusuk (where we are bound soon) and Ittoqqortoormiit in Greenland.

124

From my seat 2A I lean forward and guess that if that propeller comes loose so will my head, because before they start it up and it spins too fast to see, I reckon it is maybe just a touch more than a meter from my head. Which might be just as well if the prop flies off, anyway.

• • • • •

## THE FEARSOME NORTHMEN

> "Blond was his hair, and bright his cheeks.
> Grim as a snake were his glowing eyes."
> - Tenth-century poet

Many a more southerly European prayed for protection from the fury of the Northmen, for their legend cast a dark and fearsome Arctic shadow. The word "berserk" originates with the Vikings: Berserks, literally "bear-shirts" in Old Norse, fought "like wolves or dogs," strong as "bears or bulls."

One, suddenly possessed, "furiously bit and devoured the rim of his shield; he gulped down fiery coals without a qualm and let them pass down into his belly; he ran the gauntlet of crackling flames...." Ransack came into English from the Old Norse Rannsaka, to search a house.

The first known Viking raid befell the island of Lindisfarne on England's east coast, home to a Celtic priory, in 793. The Vikings destroyed the church by "rapine and slaughter" in one of the early quick-in, quick-out raids they perfected in estuaries and along coasts.

Gwyn Jones, in *A History of the Vikings*: "The unexpectedness, the swiftness, and the savagery of the viking raid ... came as a bolt from the blue not only to the monks surprised and slaughtered there but to ... Charlemagne's court."

Neither civilization was modern, though. Charlemagne, the first Holy Roman emperor and the greatest of all medieval rulers, was illiterate. Over the next two hundred years the Vikings, unconcerned by any

"Holy Romans," occupied Galway and Cork and the Isle of Man, and built the town of Dublin in the 840s.

Overcrowding may have set off Viking exploration. As we saw with the Danes in Jutland, in the first settlers' time there was room to pick the best place for your farmstead, but Norway grew from 17,000 people in 30 CE to almost 250,000 by 1000. By the beginning of the ninth century the bulging population burdened the just 3 percent of the country suitable for agriculture. Farmland became precious.

People who lost their farmsteads formed towns that afforded new ways to earn your keep but also contained mouths to feed, prompting a need for commercial goods. In *Visitors to Ancient America*, William F. McNeil makes the case that this combination of needs could have been the genesis of the Viking age.

Viking longships were well suited to coastal waters - sleek, of shallow draft, able to go either direction changing quickly, fast, maneuverable, moving with or against the wind. They had shields along the sides, and frightening dragonlike figures rose up forward and aft. They were made for medieval marauding.

With the Swedes controlling the east and the Danes much of the more southerly parts of the North and Baltic seas, the Norwegians operated in the northwest, and over time explored further and further offshore. This required developing new science - the ability to navigate in the open sea, out of sight of land. Vikings learned to use the sun and stars.

McNeil suggests they used the sky for navigation in the same way as the Polynesians. "They knew the position of the sun at different latitudes for every day of the year," and the locations of the constellations throughout the year, giving them the ability to determine how far north or south they were from any given location.

The longship was suited to sailing into estuaries, along riverbanks and coastlines, but not a good fit for longer ocean voyages. For this came the Knorr, or cargo ship. The stubbier knorr, perhaps 16 by 70 feet, kept crew to a minimum (perhaps a dozen people tops versus 25, 60, even a hundred to row and fight from the longboat) and had a hold in the center for cargo. With less rowing manpower, the knorr was almost entirely dependent on wind for sailing, and hoisted a massive square sail.

If overcrowding initiated the Viking Age in the late eighth century, organized westward migration probably began with the wars that swirled around the consolidation of Norway by one Harald Fairhair.

•••••

## A ONE-MINUTE HISTORY OF KING HARALD FAIRHAIR

King Harald in his ill-mannered way did as much as any man to populate the north Atlantic, though that was not his intent. The unifier of Norway in Norse legend, he was reviled beyond Norwegian shores, for his rise caused wholesale flight from established homesteads in Norwegian fjords to frigid and miserable outposts in the Faroes, Iceland, Greenland and beyond. Refugees resettled in the Shetlands and British and Irish isles. Normandy, in northern France, translates from Germanic as land of the north man.

The Saga of Hord tells us that "Most of Iceland was settled in the days of Harald Fairhair, for men would not tolerate his oppression and tyranny." Freedom-seeking tax dodgers fled Harald as he consolidated petty kingdoms all across Norway and demanded tribute.

Yet improbably, the legend of Harald is also a love story. Consider these excerpts from a 1923 children's tale by Mary Macgregor:

> *In eight hundred and sixty-one, when he began to reign, Norway was divided into thirty-one little kingdoms, over each of which ruled a little king. Harald Fairhair began his reign by being one of these little kings.*

> *Harald was only a boy, ten years of age, when he succeeded his father; but as he grew up he became a very strong and handsome man ....*

*Harald sent ... some of his men to a princess named Gyda, bidding them tell her that he wished to make her his queen. But Gyda wished to marry a king who ruled over a whole country, rather than one who owned but a small part of Norway, and this was the message she sent back to Harald.*

*... King Harald ... said, "... now I make a solemn vow and take God to witness, who made me and rules over all things, that never shall I clip or comb my hair until I have subdued the whole of Norway with scat (land taxes), and duties, and domains, or if not, have died in the attempt."*

*Then, without delay, Harald assembled a great force and prepared to conquer all the other little kings who were ruling over the different parts of Norway....*
*It took King Harald ten long years to do as he had vowed, and make all Norway his own. During these years a great many new bands of Vikings were formed, and led by their chief or king they left the country, not choosing to become King Harald's men....*

*Meanwhile Harald, having fulfilled his vow, had his hair combed and cut.... After his long, yellow hair was combed and clipped, he was named Harald Fairhair, and by this name he was ever after known. Nor did the king forget Gyda, for whose sake he had made his vow. He sent for her, and she, as she had promised, came to marry the King of all Norway.*

•••••

Fleeing Harald, a man named Floki Vilgerdarson sailed first to the Shetlands, then the Faroes and from there set out on the first specific attempt at building a settlement in Iceland, guided by three ravens able to smell land. In the legend Floki became "Raven-Floki," and Hrafn is a common Icelandic name today.

Behind Floki a cascade of emigration swept to sea. This refusal to knuckle under Harald's rule feeds the foundation myth of Icelanders as free and independent souls, wild adventurers, long-haired, wild-eyed, skin-wearing men willing to toss their whole world and their families' fate into a tiny ship and chance a storm-wracked four day slog from the motherland.

These men sought to live free, to escape the scat Harald imposed on the conquered. So for all the beseeching about freedom and independence, Iceland was born as a redoubt, a lair for scheming scofflaws.

At the end of the settlement period, around 930, Iceland was home to about 20,000. By 1100, 50,000.

•••••

## A CESSNA'S EYE VIEW

I first came to Reykjavik at the darkest time of year, in January 1991. I stayed at Icelandair's Loftleidir Hotel out at the city airfield. My friend Jim and I walked over to the airport building, behind a tarmac fence and a row of bare and determined five foot trees. We hired a charter Cessna piloted by a very young man who had trained in Florida.

Aloft from runway 140 eastbound we turned north, and the green and red rooftops of Reykjavik disappeared. Everything man-made disappeared. Snow masked things visible in summer, like all the roads.

I had been on the equator six months before and saw how satellite dishes pointed straight up to the sky. Here giant dishes, bigger than buildings, pointed straight south, searching the horizon. Narrow bands of ice spread like waves frozen in the act across the surface of Þingvallavatn, Iceland's largest lake, a rigid, dull ice sheet.

Snow covered everything but the shadows. The pallid yellow of the sun defined the only color, the disc bright, Earth below black and white. Summer cottages dark and empty populated the lakeshore. Geysers spattered and scalded rocks and sent up steam that sank and sulked away beyond the hill.

Hallgrim's fearsome church

A few clouds stood out higher than the others. They nodded and drifted and they grew and gathered until we had arrived over Mount Hekla. On a Thursday afternoon a month before, long past dusk, Hekla woke from eleven years of malevolent dreams, gushing coal and cinders still not covered by snow.

Tour guides scrambled to organize excursions, a half hour by small plane or four hours with "specially trained drivers." But as we banked to pull away I couldn't find anybody down there. Still no roads.

We rolled right and bore down across the southern shore over whitecaps roiling and evil, to Heimaey, on one of the Westman Islands, an outpost of fishermen, virtually all of the homes concentrated in a bowl where eighteen years before a 2,000-meter-long crevice rent the Earth and rained lava and ash over 5,300 hapless villagers. They evacuated the town in an hour, a heroic feat, but every resident's last possession was lost.

Returning, the coast led us back over Mount Geitafell, just a mount-let really at 509 meters, and into Reykjavik, dominated by Hallgrim's church. Hallgrímur Pétursson, a wayward lad who ran away to Copenhagen in the 1600s, later returned to become a hallowed figure, a religious poet for whom the dominant building in Iceland is named. Hallgrim's church imposes itself on Reykjavik, arms leaden and Communist-crossed, with a glower heavy and mean.

**SHAKE HANDS WITH THE PRESIDENT**

Reykjavik occupies a hill on the southwest corner of Iceland, surrounded on three sides by water, like downtown San Francisco. You can see downhill to the water in most directions, and in mid-January a furious wet wind from the Atlantic whips right through you.

In those days the *Morganbladid* newspaper building anchored one end of the main pedestrian mall Austurstraeti, just a block from the Althing, the Parliament. Now better known as mbl.is and *Iceland Monitor*, the newspaper has made the move to the suburbs. Way back in 1991 a loud, wild-haired man in a red headband hawked newspapers. At first we thought he was a madman, maybe dangerous.

A big square clock with four faces showed four different times. An ice cream shop between the apotek and a neon "Drekkid Coca-Cola" sign did brisk business. Cones in the cold. We headed along Laugavegur Road until we found a place that called itself "avant-garde," Club 22. That's where we met Raven.

Raven was his suggested pronunciation for Hrafn, son of a now-deceased well respected writer, who fit into the local literary scene in his own right. At 26, he had already written several books. He gave me one as a parting gift - "*Nazistar,*" a 412-page history of the Icelandic

Nazi party. He had worked at the state radio network, now worked at a newspaper, and he took us to meet the President.

•••••

We didn't know where we were and followed Raven up the stairs winding around the lift to the second floor of a multi-story, bureaucratic building like the others in the neighborhood, and found that it was the Ministry of Education and Culture.

Speakers' remarks were piped into the lobby from a conference room. There was coffee from a great silver urn and a table with copies of the day's agenda and the speakers' prepared remarks, nothing to us, in Icelandic.

We arrived both sweaty and freezing, unwrapped and warmed up with coffee, waiting for a post-conference reception. Raven explained we would soon meet various national literary luminaries. He slipped into the conference room and returned, motioning for me to quietly follow. He thought I had enough camera gear to look like a journalist, and that I could get some good pictures.

No one else on Earth could read the first thing the accomplished men and women in this room have written, but here sat one author for every 1,250 (then) citizens of the country, 200 of Iceland's most promising and revered authors.

One other person sat taking pictures so I joined him on bleachers beside the podium, scowled with my best journalist's concentration, and surveyed the room, determinedly changing lenses and generally camera-fiddling.

Today's conference took place in a room of light Scandinavian wood, nautical theme, port holes for windows, a view out over the harbor. Tables for eight radiated in a semi-circle from the center. The Minister of Education and Culture, intense in a goatee, held forth across a green felt cloth, leaning forward and using his hands as he spoke.

Raven whispered and pointed this way and that and I clicked away at "our finest novelist," "our most respected poet" and so on until Raven whispered, "and there is our President."

•••••

During the Reagan/Gorbachev Reyjkavik summit, the Soviet leader used an old Russian quip that the woman is always at fault, joking "You're asking me the eternal question of who is responsible: the wife or the mother in law."

Vigdis Finbogadottir wasn't in the room, but if she had been, chances are Europe's first female president, the summit's host, wouldn't have taken kindly to the General Secretary's attitude. Serving as artistic director at the Reykjavik Theatre Company in 1975, she cancelled dress rehearsals so she, her mother and three-year old daughter could join an astounding 90 percent of women in Iceland in a "Women's Strike."

A bit of a cultural and linguistic purist, the President was among friends at the Ministry of Culture. She sat about twenty feet away: gold earrings, navy blazer, blue silk scarf. I snapped away and tried to look photojournalistic.

When the conference broke up she and the Minister of Education and Culture stood for pictures with us, one of which she signed for me. You don't get access like that everywhere.

The conference was all the buzz in Reykjavik that winter's afternoon. We met writers, poets and Stefan Jon Hafstein, manager of the state radio networks who arranged a tour, and Hughes Beaudouin, the press attaché at the French embassy, with whom we dined.

Hughes was on his first diplomatic assignment, having picked Iceland over Czechoslovakia because he had gone to school here. Over the next couple of days he became a sort of French/Icelandic goodwill ambassador. He told us that the conference was a fire and brimstone appeal for preservation of Icelandic culture. Some participants suggested banning CNN.

L-R: The author, the President and the Minister of Culture

•••••

Raven arranged a Chevrolet taxi with big tires and deigned with a flourish to personally guide us on a three-hour city tour. He kept up a running narrative and kept available a bottle of Ballantine just inside his coat.

We began to suspect a couple of things. One, that everybody knew everybody else, and another, that Ballantine may lurk behind more than a few lapels. It's cold in Iceland in January.

First stop was the highest vantage point in town, the bell tower of the fearsome Hallgrim's Church, with its statue of Leif Eriksson, discoverer of North America, on the sleety square outside.

It cost a few kroner to climb to the top where you could survey Reykjavik and beyond. The bells rang just above our heads and jangled our nerves.

Somehow, Raven procured from an ice cream shop a round of Beck's beers for which we did not pay, and we took them to a hill outside town where we stood underneath a fantastic array of imposing, vaguely sinister unlabeled antennae. In one direction Reykjavik, in the other a visual demonstration why Armstrong and Aldrin came here to practice their lunar excursions.

•••••

**THEORIES**

Hrafn bundled us into a crowd of flask-pulling partisans in their coats, scarfs and hats, close-pressed into a stuffy space, rowdy, holding cocktails close to the chest. Parliamentary campaigns were running full throttle toward election day three months away. Tonight's rally, for the conservative Independence Party.

The candidate, entirely unknown to the Americans, bounded to the stage and exhorted the crowd. In Icelandic. The idea that we were attending a political rally that was unintelligible struck Jim as funny, so he decided to become the world's biggest supporter of … whoever the candidate was.

Jim cheered. Jim applauded. Jim stomped approval and shouted and eventually, Jim got thrown out. Hustled with burly hands under both arms straight out the door. We gathered him up after the rally.

Jim was booted from a rally for Iceland's next prime minister, the young politician David Oddsson. Oddsson, then Reykjavik's mayor, became prime minister and later, Iceland's Central Bank Governor. More important, Oddsson would set in motion the most ignominious episode in his country's history.

•••••

*Bill Murray*

I think it is safe to say that in practice capitalism happens at some distance from theory, from Adam Smith's rational self-interest to Ayn Rand's objectivism to the dictatorship of the proletariat. We live and transact amid haphazard accretions of laws and customs in systems of diverse competence, from the self-satisfied prosperity of the City of London to the utter helplessness of the former Communist side of Europe, where half the population of Moldova lives on less than $5 a day. Like Moldova this island on the far boundary of Europe has had its recent trials, and our story begins with David Oddsson's outsized ambitions for his tiny land.

Oddsson was a fabulous mayor. As a very young man he sold off the city's holdings in the fishing fleet, built a new city hall and midwifed the Pearl up on Öskjuhlíð hill, an attempt to make something novel of hot water tanks that loom over town by putting a restaurant on top. After nearly a decade running the capital, at just 43 he set out to run the country with one big idea in mind. He was going to bring Iceland global.

He lowered corporate taxes from 45 to 18 percent and business loved it. Inflation plunged from double digits to three percent in 1992-1993. Under the young prime minister, Iceland became the most free market Nordic economy. Long before the British cliché of the Polish plumber, Poles came here to do Iceland's dirty work, the toughest fishing jobs, construction, "to push old people in their wheelchairs."

Icelanders with foreign nannies. Haldor Laxness, who indelibly portrayed the hopelessness of the feudal Icelandic crofter in his Nobel prize winning *Independent People*, would have scarcely believed it. But there it was.

The prime minister thought Ronald Reagan and Margaret Thatcher hung the north Atlantic moon. When supply-side economist Milton Friedman came to Reykjavik then-Mayor Oddsson brought all his friends and made like my friend Jim, bouncing and applauding and elbowing his friends to join in.

Oddsson meant to make Iceland's financial sector big enough to play in international markets. Privatizing the banks would be his crowning achievement. He made the banks bigger, no doubt about that. They ultimately swelled to something like ten times the size of the entire domestic economy.

Privatization is a fundamentally political act. Roger Boyes writes in *Meltdown Iceland* that, besides the allure of Reaganism and the glow of Milton Friedman's theories, if Oddsson's government privatized the banks it needed to retain at least some level of influence over vital institutions, if only to steer broad policy.

Early on, Oddsson had reason to feel insecure. The first privatized bank, Glitnir, emerged under the control of a relatively new business group. Turned out privatizations might let in rather more new players than old money would prefer.

Since people could remember, clans collectively called "the Octopus" ran Icelandic business, an insider clique of twelve or fourteen families with deep interests in everything. Timber and transport, for example, in a land with no trees, where timber must be brought in - by transport.

As long as money was earned, kept and spent in Iceland the Octopus stayed in the background, comfortable in their wood-paneled clubs. But new actors had an irritating itch to play in new markets. The cephalopods were determined that new blood in banking be bound to the old boy network. Oddsson closed bidding on bank privatization to foreigners. That way the Octopus stood to come home with an outsized share of future privatizations. Everything got far too cozy.

The Icelandic journalist Iris Erlingsdottir wrote, "Politicians were never asked to report family ties to the banks, and were never required to recuse themselves from voting on measures that benefitted them personally." Majority ownership of one of the two big banks went to families associated with Oddsson's party (Independence) and control of the other to families with ties to his coalition partner (Progressives).

Roger Boyes calls it Oddsson's "Original Sin, the beginning of Iceland's fall from grace." There was more sinning to come.

After the crash Erlingsdottir wrote: "The Icelanders saw themselves as innately superior businessmen destined to lord over Europe, just as Europe had lorded over Iceland for so long. They weren't tied down by archaic concepts, such as generally accepted accounting principles ... independent boards, or lending standards...." You can hear her clenched teeth clattering through her keyboard.

With banks in his allies' hands and unbound by government regulations, Oddsson expected his dreams of Iceland at the grown-ups' financial services table were set to be realized. He left the prime minister's job in 2004 and became Central Bank governor in Oct 2005; he must have considered it a promotion. In fact, the stage was set for mayhem.

Iceland's bankers borrowed more than ten times the country's Gross Domestic Product on international markets. The big three newly private banks went on international buying sprees, concentrating on the British high street and buying a Premiere League football club.

For Icelandic bankers, more was more. At home they marketed foreign currency loans. Boyes quotes a "now-unemployed architect:"

> "We would get cold calls from the bank ... and a young voice would offer us the possibility of buying a new car in a parcel of currencies from countries we had never visited."

The suburbs of Reykjavik grew by a third in the decade to the crash, fed by 100 percent mortgages loaned to first-time buyers, many of whom had two cars in brand-new garages, bought with 100 percent loans in Japanese yen or Swiss francs.

Between 2003 and 2004, while the value of the U.S. stock market doubled, Icelandic stocks grew by a factor of nine. Yet the economy was *achingly* small: In 2007 Iceland's GDP was a third of Luxembourg's, 1/20 of Denmark's and little more than 1/1000th of that of the U.S. The few at the top of Iceland's pyramids began to be called "oligarchs," after the louche displays of the richest Russians in the 1990s.

The nadir surely came at nine o'clock on Saturday night, 20 January, 2007, when Elton John walked onto a Reykjavik stage and sang "Candle in the Wind" for the owner of a container ship company who had bought into Kaupthing Bank. Ólafur Ólafsson hired him for his 50th birthday party.

As events came to pass, all the sins and intrigue of the Sagas would play out once again in 2008.

•••••

**CRASH**

In 2008 the state channel broadcast no daytime TV, just a test pattern. So David Oddsson's successor as prime minister, Geir Haarde, who had been Oddsson's Finance Minister, was quite literally correct when he appeared on the screen in the middle of the afternoon of 6 October, 2008 and said:

"Fellow countrymen:

I am well aware that this situation is a great shock for many, which raises both fear and anxiety.... If there was ever a time when the Icelandic nation needed to stand together and show fortitude in the face of adversity, then this is the moment. I urge you all to guard that which is most important in the life of everyone of us, protect those values which will survive the storm now beginning.... It is very important that we display both calm and consideration during the difficult days ahead, that we do not lose courage and support each other as well as we can. Thus with Icelandic optimism, fortitude and solidarity as weapons, we will ride out the storm.

God bless Iceland."

*Bill Murray*

Geir Haarde had just admitted his country had gone bust.

Icelanders traveling abroad found that hotels declined their credit cards. Currency exchange outlets would no longer sell real money for Icelandic kroner, which was no longer real money.

The proximate cause was the seizing up of the interbank markets when Lehman Brothers collapsed. The Icelandic Central Bank had the money to bail out Glitnir, the smallest of Iceland's big three banks, but the combined balance sheet of the big three was €110 billion and the whole country's GDP in 2007 was €14.7 billion. The Central Bank didn't have the money, so Iceland let its banks fail.

Having largely depleted its reserves on Glitnir, Oddsson's Central Bank needed a loan just to keep the government on life support. The IMF loaned $2.1 billion and neighboring countries another $2.5 billion (including the tiny Faroes, which offered a no-strings attached loan).

Now the government could afford to protect domestic deposits, but not foreign ones. The Brits were left holding a raft of unfunded commitments, bunches of British institutions having been lured by high Icelandic interest rates (Oxford University £30 million, London Transit £40 million), leading to "the common British view of the Icelanders as amoral plunderers."

The furious Brits, facing potential losses of millions of pounds for a half million British savers, used anti-terror legislation to freeze one of the bank's (Landsbanki) assets. For a while the U.K. Treasury's home page listed Iceland's Central Bank and Ministry of Finance alongside sanctioned terrorist groups and regimes, including Al-Qaeda, the Taliban, Burma, Zimbabwe and North Korea.

Icelanders returned the love. The In Defense movement, which launched the career of Iceland's most recent disgraced politician, Prime Minister Sigmundur David Gunnlaugsson, showed on its website the forlorn image of a girl waving a sign, "I am not a terrorist, Mr. (Gordon) Brown."

Net worths plunged and the cost of living soared. The savings of more than 50,000 people disappeared. The stock market fell 95 percent and interest rates on loans ranged toward 300 percent. Ads offered thousands of dollars to anyone who would take ownership of cars and their payments. Repossessed Range Rovers became known as "Game Overs."

Inflation eliminated savings while unemployment took second incomes out of the workforce. Families lost their houses, retirees their pensions. The atmosphere turned raw as the Icelandic new year. Anger welled up that the government should even presume to remain in office.

Iceland is tiny. When the crisis blew up some of those demonstrating outside Parliament were related to those debating inside. Riot police were cousins to the rioters. It was a family affair and as family affairs do, it got hot-blooded.

The protests became known as the kitchen revolution because protestors banged pots and pans. They held signs that read "!" and "?" They raised the flag of the supermarket Bonus - a cartoon pig - over the Parliament. Someone printed T-shirts: Helvitis fokking fokk.

•••••

A land that survives miserable winters, deforestation, failed fish harvests, famine and volcanoes as necessary had been outdone by thirty men who had gone out into the world and come back, humiliating the nation. It only took seven years from the beginning of Oddsson's privatization.

A thousand-year heritage will produce a strong resistance to nouveau anything, including riches, so a strong undertow tugged back against the ostentation. The country's pride was hurt but the political class showed no remorse. Oddsson blamed the oligarchs. The oligarchs blamed Oddsson. They all had a go at blaming the Brits.

*Bill Murray*

The entire country has the population of a modest American town, Lexington, Kentucky, say, or Corpus Christi, Texas. As in Greenland, most of Iceland's population lives in sparse settlements on the coast, poorly connected by land transportation except around the perimeter, on roads that run up and down fjords (the road from Seydisfjordur to Reykjavik via the ring road, some 655 kilometers, may take eight and a half hours in good weather).

This separateness furthers Icelanders' pride in their independence. It also tamps down attention to the greater national good. Asgeir Jónsson writes in *Why Iceland?*, that Iceland "has never needed a strong central command to organize for war or national defense, and because of its diminutiveness, it has never required the construction of a sophisticated bureaucracy." Which helped set the table for financial collapse.

In the way of a small society - or a totalitarian one - the party had produced the prime minister and the Central Banker. It had allowed ownership of the former state bank to fall to party loyalists - who loaned money to the party.

David Oddsson became the most hated man in Iceland. Thing is, his career-long wariness of too close a union with the Europeans - just like in the Faroes - and his longtime resistance to the Eurozone, helped Iceland bounce back.

The country devalued the krona by about 60 percent so that while domestic salaries felt the same, Iceland's exports became more attractive abroad. Iceland's output today is greater than the year before the crisis. In 2007 Iceland's GDP was $14.5 billion, and in 2015, $17.07.

The retrospective press hasn't been kind to Oddsson, whom most portray as an ambitious fish with outsized aspirations for his tiny pond. Oddsson once fancied himself a Central Banker. For a time after the crash he fashioned himself a poet. Then he settled in to write plays and short stories, and edited the daily *Morgunbladið*.

Which brings us to the present.

In the election of June 2016, Oddsson quit his job at the newspaper and summoned the audacity to run for President (Iceland's system has a prime minister and a ceremonial Presidency). Oddsson finished fourth, with 13.54 percent of the vote.

The winner and new President of Iceland is the independent Guðni Thorlacius Jóhannesson, a historian and lecturer at the University of Iceland, who had no previous political experience. The field of nine candidates included my friend Hrafn's sister Elísabet, who is a poet. There was a financier, the founder of a children's charity, a truck driver, an ethnologist, an "entrepreneur and peace activist," another author and Oddsson.

The year 1991, when I first visited Reykjavik, feels like half a lifetime ago. But since the Presidency of Vigdis Finnbogadottir, to whom I introduced you, her successor, Ólafur Ragnar Grímsson had been President until this very election.

Eleven weeks before the Presidential election Sigmundur Davíð Gunnlaugsson, Iceland's youngest-ever prime minister, resigned, caught with his wife in the undertow of the Panama Papers scandal, the release of some 11.5 million documents detailing secret financial dealings among many of the world's rich and powerful.

Gunnlaugsson had failed to disclose his ownership (with his wife) of an offshore company that was a creditor of the failed Icelandic banks. The existence of the company came to light in a scorching, hard to watch television interview with a cold-blooded Swedish journalist in April 2016.

When Sven Snorri Sighvatsson, whom we are soon to meet, says "We are sick and tired of dishonest people," you can see his point.

•••••

*Bill Murray*

**FAIRIES**

Back on Streymoy in the Faroes, Kemm pointed out the rock they built a highway around because fairies lived there. In Iceland Borgarfjörður Eystri, a fjord northeast of Egilsstaðir around which a hundred people have settled, is capital of the elves. You may visit the Kirkjusteinn, the church of the elves. The elf queen, they say, is from here.

The huldufólk ("hidden folk") held up a road project in 2014 when a judge ruled that there was a chance elves could be living on the barren landscape.

Builders narrowed a highway just south of Reykjavik instead of moving a stone where elves are said to live. The Hotel Klettur ("boulder") in Reykjavik incorporates a rock on its ground floor about which its marketing material is coy. If it is connected to elves, the hotel suggests, "The boulder on the side of the hotel would then possibly be the entrance to their home."

Public officials humor the huldufólk where possible. The head of Iceland's Public Roads Administration explained to the radio series *This American Life*, "You really have to listen to everyone because you are probably going to meet them at a party after awhile. You know, when you scream at someone in traffic in New York, you know you're probably not going to meet them again, so you do it. But not so much here."

An oft-quoted expert on matters elfin is a professor at the University of Iceland named Terry Gunnell. Here in the *Guardian*:

> "This is a land where your house can be destroyed by something you can't see (earthquakes), where the wind can knock you off your feet, where the smell of sulphur from your taps tells you there is invisible fire not far below your feet, where the northern lights make the sky the biggest television screen in the world, and where hot springs and glaciers 'talk'.

"In short, everyone is aware that the land is alive, and one can say that the stories of hidden people and the need to work carefully with them reflects an understanding that the land demands respect."

Elves and fairies, demons and angels survive from the time of a different human, a more insular one, who granted sentience, awareness and feelings to objects - trees, streams and living things - and made room for loosely interpreted spirits like elves. A previous president, Ólafur Ragnar Grímsson, says that rural folk invented the huldufólk to keep them company.

While nominally Lutheran, Iceland generally ranks among the top ten countries in "convinced athiests," and a 2013 survey declared Iceland has the largest percentage of heathens in the world.

•••••

Up on the south side of Öskjuhlíð hill opposite Reykjavik, a real-life, modern-day pagan temple rises, the first built anywhere in perhaps a millennium (and the first building in Iceland in modern times constructed entirely from native trees - larches from a century-old reforestation project).

This shrine to the Norse gods Thor, Odin and Frigg is the brainchild of the Ásatrú Association, formed in 1972 and led by Hilmar Örn Hilmarsson, who has been its allsherjargoði (roughly "high priest") since 2003.

When Iceland converted to Christianity under pressure from the Norse king, politicians tacitly agreed that if worshiping of the Norse gods had to continue it should do so in secret. Hilmarsson doesn't think it ever went completely away.

Commingling of more than one tradition - like Muslim and traditional beliefs in Indonesia, Buddhist and Bon traditions in the Himalayas and Christianity, Santa Claus and the Tooth Fairy in the U.S. - feels completely natural to Icelanders. There is a sense that God is far away, but the hidden folk are all around.

Hilmarsson: "Monotheism is one truth for the masses, but polytheism is many truths for the individual ... You may have a need for Freya on Monday morning, and Thor may be absolutely essential for you on Tuesday afternoon."

If you ask me, the evolutionary pinnacle of Icelandic witchcraft was the "scorn pole," a fetish that set out to cast public shame. "It was commonly a pole placed in front of someone's home with curses carved on it and a horse skull or in more extreme cases a severed horse head on top of it" to scare away the good spirits protecting your land and, witchy cauldron-stirrers willing, ruin your harvest.

Hilmarsson made a scorn pole in 2003 to oppose that Alcoa hydropower project up east at Kárahnjúkar.

•••••

**THE ÞINGVELLIR**

The flight from Halifax is short as Canadian summer. No night on this overnight flight, just a twilight lull, and all at once before anybody really wants to do this, our new man Sven stands outside the Keflavik arrivals hall and to his considerable credit, he looks game. By 4:45 we are thundering across lava fields.

Southbound on rough tarmac on the 425, we drive along an emergency road they built ten years ago that skirts the coast. No one out here this time of morning and I'm not sure anyone ever is. We stop in the middle of the road and climb a hill, scrambling over pumice, skittering it down.

We have known Sven for less than an hour, but already it is clear that he is a fabulist. Alighting from the Super Jeep he notes offhand that he cracked two ribs and punctured a lung rescuing an old lady in his tour group who was about to take a fall. Just a couple days ago. When movie stars come to Iceland they always ask for Sven because if they treat him like shit he treats them the same right back. They respect that.

On the reality side of the ledger, he presents as an agreeable fellow, ranging between engaging and bubbly. And he was game enough to drive out and pick us up at such a small hour of the morning that his friends in Reykjavik (for he must travel with only the trendiest crowd) must have just been turning in.

I can not tell if this is a tic of the Icelandic language or of Sven: He personifies inanimate objects: On the Strokkur geyser, "I guess living here all my life, I've got used to it. They tell me he smells but I don't notice." On the Faxi falls, "He outdoes himself."

Sven has a peculiar wide stance, skinny legs planted across loose pumice, swaying forward and back between the balls of his feet and his heels while he explains that certain mosses grow as little as a millimeter a year and are so delicate that if you press on them, they die. There is no danger of that where we stand, for nothing here grows, right to the horizon, right down to the sea.

It is light and porous, this pumice, bouncing in your hand like astronauts on the moon, what you get when a volcano throws glassy lava up from beneath the earth and it cools in an instant. We turn it over in our hands. It is the color of the terra cotta rooftop tiles of Tuscany.

The air in pyroclastic rock makes it natural for insulation. The Icelandic firm JEI processes pumice from Mt. Hekla for use in green roofing and to aerate soil in horticulture. It exports to the Nordic countries, Belgium, Germany and the United States. Another use for this rock field: LAVA®, THE HAND SOAP (with pumice!).

Out of the lava down at the shore rises the very small fishing settlement of Grindavik. The "vik" in Grindavik, Keflavik and Reykjavik means "bay," but the "Grind" apparently isn't kin to the Faroese word Grindadráp, meaning whale hunt. Sven says the Icelandic "Grind" doesn't have anything to do with "whale." Or "hunt."

It is very early in the morning, still not six o'clock, but it's happy hour for tiny black flies, some kind of midge, and we are free hors d'oeuvres. Sven says the local name is "Mýs." There is a Mý Lake up in the north, not far from the main town up there, Akureyeri. Irritating little bastards, these Mýs.

We run through a mental checklist of less torturous Icelandic fauna: The reindeer we saw on Vatnajokull in winter, there is mink, there are foxes, a formerly domestic rabbit that has turned to a life of crime on the lam, and, Sven winces, "We are living in harmony with the rats in Reykjavik."

Seals share tidal flats with salmon fishermen on the run-up to Eyrarbakki, home of the Litla Hraun prison, a nine building complex inside a security fence where they actually do make license plates. While it has more cells than the Faroes' tiny prison it is not a big place, with room for 87.

The prison is the only real employer in Eyrarbakki for those who are not fishermen, presenting a wee civic challenge, for a new prison is nearly ready up on Hólmsheidi Road near Reykjavik, set to open in August 2016.

And no, none of Iceland's most notorious prisoners serves here. They have their own private facility, behind whose walls Sven is certain they play tennis, enjoy special meals and keep the nails on their grasping bankers' fingers well tended.

•••••

We join Route 1, the ring road, northbound. It smooths out the island's more than 5,000 kilometers of coastline to a more drivable 1,332 kilometers, but still takes around eighteen hours to circumnavigate, weather permitting.

A handsome town of 6,500 called Selfoss, dominated by the chalky sky-blue Ölfisá River, looks positively Finnish architecturally. Selfoss is just 60 kilometers southeast of the capital. A few dozen city folks' summer houses reach up the hills.

David Oddsson was brought up here. One tough bastard, Sven shakes his head, always three, four or five steps ahead of everybody, but he says "If you shake the Blue Hand, be careful." He means the hand, tentacle, with which The Octopus once gripped the island.

Here in Selfoss lies the body of Bobby Fischer, former World Chess Champion and determined eccentric. Fischer violated U.N. sanctions on Yugoslavia by playing a chess match in Belgrade during the Bosnian War, leading U.S. authorities to issue an arrest warrant. This country granted Fischer asylum for putting "Iceland on the map" in his World Championship match in Reykjavik against Boris Spassky.

In winter, weekenders in Selfoss might pop over to Friðheimar, a restaurant inside a greenhouse, to enjoy premises-grown tomatoes on fresh salad while watching snow drifts pile up outside.

Today, in summer, we stop to admire the Kerið volcano's well-preserved, 3,000-year-old caldera, the severity of its red volcanic soil softened by new grasses and an explosion of wildflowers. Atlantic lupin, introduced in the 1980s, reaches for the sky, but Sven calls the lot "little cockroaches," for it crowds out the grasses, sedges and clubmoss. Whoops. I thought it was pretty.

•••••

All these Super Jeep cowboys love their hardware. Sven's company fleet uses tires that range from 38 to 46 inches and all the vehicles are air compressor equipped. He hauls me around back and underneath to show how they install air bladders above each tire so they can pump up the back or the front of the vehicle for climbing or descending.

Retrofitting Jeep frames is big business in Iceland nowadays, with lead times stretching out six or seven months. A total retrofit can run 25 million kroner, around $200,000.

149

*Bill Murray*

Sven points to a farmhouse with an industrial boiler-looking contraption alongside. This is a farmer, he says, who, having found a spot of hot water bubbling up on his land, inadvertently became a utility company. He rigged up a generator and sells power to his neighbors.

Sven explains just how cheap electricity is. Even in dark and cold - really cold - winters it costs him the kroner equivalent of about $48 a month to heat his 120-square-meter (+/-1300-square-feet) flat.

Ample energy lured the aluminum business here, but at last, says Sven, there are plans to sell electricity offshore, by undersea cable to the United Kingdom.

These plans are hardly a sure thing because of strident local opposition, because it seems local electricity bills will go up. Iceland, by agreeing to sell the power, will be newly bound to pertinent EU agreements, which somehow gum up the works. Having to play by the EU's rules is an enduring bone in the throat out here on the edge.

"That debate is still to come, and I will oppose it. Why should the government get money from England at our expense?" asks Sven.

Which segues right into the corruption thing, kept more or less regularly raw since 2008 and chapping the citizenry just now because it has been scarcely seven weeks since Prime Minister Sigmundur Davíð Gunnlaugsson resigned in humiliation amid the Panama Papers scandal.

When pressed on how to demand better governance, Sven grows quiet and says simply, "We are just a small nation up in the north. It's...." And he trails off.

•••••

The tour buses don't call at the Reykjavik hotels until 9:00 so at this hour we have the island to ourselves, even in the tourism-vital month of June. Because of our evil-early start, we have seen the sights, the

150

waterfalls Faxi and Gullfoss and the Strokkur geyser, been out to the shore and over to Selfoss and climbed a volcanic mountain all unimpeded by tourists. We have been out half a day and still it is just time for breakfast. I believe Sven is anxious we might feel short-changed.

Gullfoss

He wants to take us to one of his favorite spots and so we climb, achieving altitude quickly, and soon we are navigating among patches of snow, tearing across a graveled tarmac far from the nearest human, destination Langjökull glacier, Iceland's second largest after Vatna.

We stand taking in the expanse of Langjökull, and Sven observes, "You can see as long as the eye takes." After years of global warming-induced melting, Langjökull is still up to 580 meters thick.

With no one else in sight, I duck behind the Super Jeep to pee. "Don't let the elf bite it," Sven says. Local humor.

Dark and imposing above us, the glacier turns Sven to talk of the rescue work in which he is trained. While his stories of personal heroism strain credulity, he says that 44 people have gone missing without a trace across the island and are missing still since he got involved, and on that at least I have no reason to doubt him. It is a rugged land.

On the other hand, over the course of the day Sven claims not only to have cracked two ribs and punctured a lung the week before, but also to have:

- been trapped for four days under snow in an avalanche, surviving by sharing dog food with his rescue dog,
- swum across Kerið's caldera naked before his own tour group on a dare,
- dropped a 50-million-kroner video camera out a helicopter during the 1986 Vatna flood (I'm not sure what 50 million kroner was worth in 1986, but currently that would be about $400,000), in his previous career as a journalist,
- been on hand by chance for both avalanches up near Langjökull last year, and
- saved a little boy from drowning in zero-degree-Celsius water after the boy fell in when Sven happened to be walking by.

Sven is more packaging than product. For all that, he had me with his elf tale.

•••••

**SVEN'S ELF TALE**

"In 1986 I was in a boarding school on the south coast. I was sitting on a stone near a very big waterfall called Skógafoss ("Forest Falls"). I went up into these hills, up and forward, and often I went out at night to this waterfall to take a look. And there was this beautiful, beautiful woman one day that tapped onto my shoulder. And she sat down to me on the stone. She was a very small lady, had this wide, silky dress on, blonde hair, small woman, very beautiful, and we talked about her world, and my world and how we were doing and about our lives and so on.

And she told me a secret. It was the biggest elf church that we have. And she pointed to me how I could see the entrance, the door of the church. And she said, there is a trick about it. You have to believe. And if you look into the waterfall for a couple of minutes and then you turn to a special rock, then you can see it move and there is the entrance.

So I did that and she helped me to do it. And when I had looked into the waterfall for a couple of minutes and I turned my head around, I saw the entrance of the church.

So many of us have the experience of seeing those hidden people.

I've never seen a troll, but I know a few rocks that have turned into a troll.

So if you ask me Sven what is your religion, well basically we the Icelanders, we are Lutheran, but we have Catholics, I guess Muslims and Hindus but I believe in the elves, I believe in the trolls, and I believe in the Santa Claus and I believe in myself, and all the good things that we have in our spirit. And that's it!"

•••••

## THOUSAND-YEAR-OLD PARLIAMENT

An hour's drive east of Reykjavik family sedans fill a parking lot. Sven seems to think *our* Super Jeep needs more room, for he scoffs at that lot and aims for an empty one that looms ahead. We spin to a stop and scatter some rock and the monster asserts our arrival.

We set out along a footpath over one of the more remarkable bits of land on earth, the boundary between two tectonic plates. The bulk of the mid-Atlantic ridge lies beneath the ocean, so along almost all of its reach, standing in witness to its downright remarkableness is impossible.

It is the longest mountain range in the world, here separating the diverging Eurasian and North American tectonic plates. As manifest in Iceland, to the east rides a raised lava ridge, the Eurasian plate, from which the North American plate, to the west, pulls up from the Earth and apart.

Its width varies. Just here it presents as a three foot deep grass covered crevasse just wider than your arms can reach. You can jump inside and stand on the spot where the Earth is coming apart.

Elsewhere the crevasse deepens to twice the height of a man and fills with icy, transparent-as-the-ether water.

We stop along the path.

"Now we are on the Eurasian plate."

With a hop, "Now the North American."

Hop. Europe. Hop. North America. You can change continents in Istanbul too, but you have to drive across a bridge.

• • • • •

Most places, a morning walk along a fault line would make your day right there at breakfast. Here in Iceland, two for the price of one, you get epic geography and epic history too, for on this spot lies the heart and soul of the Icelandic nation.

Sven stops farther along the path. Just … HERE, he thinks, this may be the spot where was held the world's original Parliamentary meeting in 930.

• • • • •

# A WORD ABOUT WORDS, AND TALKING ABOUT TALKING

"Parliament" derives from the eleventh century Old French "parlement," and every schoolchild knows "parlez-vous Français" means "do you speak French?" so quite literally, a Parliament is a talking shop.

Turns out, even before they worked out a word for it in French, way up here the real thing existed. "Thing" in Old Norse and Icelandic translates as "assembly," and it is spelled "Þing" in Faroese and Icelandic. Resist the natural inclination to pronounce the letter (called "thorn"), written "Þ," as "p." Rather it is pronounced as an unvoiced "th."

In modern Scandinavian tongues "thing" has become "ting." The Faroes' assembly began life as the Althing, a "general assembly of all free men," and was later renamed the Løgting, "law assembly". It began on the Tinganes peninsula in Torshavn, still the seat of Parliament and the city's pride.

The Faroese Løgting and Iceland's Althing carry on a rivalry to the claim of "world's oldest Parliament." The Faroese might logically claim the crown since expansion from the Norse mainland reached the Faroes before Iceland, but memory gets hazy when you gaze so far into the past.

Iceland claims its Althing was the world's first, established here where we stand on the Þhingvellur plain in the specific year of 930. There are other "oldest" claims. The Tynwald on the Isle of Man claims to be the oldest "continuous" Parliament at over age one thousand, but without a great deal of evidence. And the Jamtamót, the Parliamentary assembly of a Swedish province claims, like the Althing, to have been created in the first half of the tenth century.

Whoever convened first, we know that each year at the summer solstice, leaders, village chiefs from around Iceland, convened on this spot to discuss common interests, and make policy. Though this plain was a more or less central spot, those from farthest east Iceland traveled as long as seventeen days around mountain and glacier.

The base of a cliff served as a natural amplifier for a speaker's voice, allowing him to address the assembled. Each year, for two weeks in high summer laws were made, disputes settled, foreign VIPs petitioned.

History played out for centuries at this place they called Þingvellir, the "Parliament Plain." After that first meeting in 930 the Goði, or chieftains, convened on the same spot each year until 1798.

At one particularly fateful meeting in 1000, 39 Goði met under pressure, for Olaf, the king of Norway, had issued a threat. The wrath of his kingdom, and the most fearsome fleet of war-fighting longboats in the Atlantic hung poised to hammer the island if the Goði failed to accept Christianity. This was the king's demand.

Iceland's founding some seven decades before came about in flight from the tyranny - and taxes - of Harald Fairhair of Norway. The Goði meant for their new country to be a land of laws and not kings. That was why they were here, assembled at Þingvellir to make their own laws in the absence of a king.

Now, these elders were reasonably confident the king wouldn't risk his fleet in a peril-fraught adventure to Iceland. As Frans G. Bengtsson wrote in *The Long Ships*, "... in the border country, few men's authority extended beyond the limit of their right arm."

Their grandfathers hadn't been wrong fleeing Harald for the island (in fact, Icelanders specifically and knowingly benefitted from the lack of taxation needed for defense). Still, the Norwegian fleet could block Iceland's tenuous European lifeline. King Olaf held the sons of some Goði hostage even as they met.

Legend tells us that as the men debated, a messenger arrived with word that an eruption had sent lava toward the farm of one of the attendees. That put a little bit of the fear of (Norse) gods into the assembly. Message: The gods won't stand for this changing religion nonsense.

Christianity had come to Norway after most of these pagan Icelanders left. Some learned of Jesus while passing through the British Isles, many absconding with wives. Synecretism led some to worship both the Christian and pagan gods, but in hard times Thor was still the go-to god.

What to do?

Heads turned to a wise man called Snorri Þhorgrímsson, a chieftain from the west of the island. The Sagas reckoned him "... a very shrewd man with unusual foresight," and "... the wisest man in Iceland not counting those who were prescient."

Snorri asked, "What angered the gods when the lava burnt which we are standing on now?" He meant that eruptions were just part of life on their blasted isle, gods or no gods. The attendees saw his point. A vote was held and the Þing adopted Christianity as Iceland's religion.

Besides, in accepting Christianity the most powerful men in Iceland surmised - correctly - that an appreciative hierarchy of Christian bishops and officials from Norway would look favorably on the Goðis' power and rule.

In the event, the Þing had opted for the best of both worlds. Hoping to hold Harald at bay, the Goði proclaimed "one faith and one law" - the faith would be Christianity, but anyone wishing to worship the pagan gods were free to do so in private. Snorri had a church built at Helgafell, his farmstead on the western Snæfellsnes peninsula.

•••••

Everyone with power and influence attended the Þing. Crimes would be adjudicated, laws recorded, marriage alliances arranged. But besides the chance to forge and strengthen ties among the Goði, beyond their heavy responsibilities, most marvelous of all, the Þing was a flourishing Nordic medieval bazaar.

I try to conjure the spectacle of a Þing in progress a millennium ago; a governing experiment, societal pageant, a kind of grand plenum and Icelandic Burning Man, all tossed together and served on the volcanic plain:

Having come from far and wide, the villages chiefs have brought an entourage of family, competitive athletes and horsemen, traders and cattle. Over the years they have built structures of boulders and turf (ruins exist today) and each year they cover them with temporary roofs of wood and turf.

The Þingvellir is utterly unlike the attendees' home villages. Just a few months ago back on the croft, the silence was unrelenting (save for the howl when the wind got going, and the raking sleet across the roof); the nights went on and on, with stimulation scarcely more potent than the strength of a candle.

Now, in high summer, headmen are free from home affairs, laborers from the dismal croft, to a man exhilarated in the runaway intoxication of it all. News of the welfare of kin. Gossip from the farthest ends of the island. Intrigue at time-worn lies told over mead. Barely mediated chaos.

Every kind of merchant, sword-sharpeners and brewers, coopers and tanners and peat-cutters, clowns and tale-tellers, holding forth while itinerant farmhands seek seasonal work and traders probe for deals, some coming from abroad in search of exotic exports.

Villagers delight at the smell of grilling meat until they encounter the pungent atrocity of the tannery. Everywhere, in every direction, for days, Icelanders august and modest share in the spectacle.

Athletes astound. Ropes are tugged, cabers heaved, sheaves hurled, dice tossed and fortunes lost, challenges taken and gauntlets thrown, blood feuds resolved and new ones begun, all in a mad fervor to drink in life and all of it, here in high summer, on this lovely spot, softened by greenery and painted by wildflowers with waterfalls and cascading rapids in the river Öxará swaying across the plain.

Stories are humans' most enduring possessions. Since the campfire and the cave we are a narrative species, and the tales we tell shape the people we become. The tales of this country's founding were told and retold year after year at the Parliament Plain, the hardships of the earliest settlers, the privation, the fights for survival.

Stories told at the Þing traveled home to every corner of the land, and over the years and through the retelling, a common heritage was born and the people's allegiance was bound to the nation, which duly bound itself back to Þingvellir. By a 1928 law Þingvellir, by the river Öxará, shall remain the protected property of the Icelandic nation.

•••••

**GETTING FROM THERE TO HERE**

Norway and Denmark united in 1380. From then the Danes monopolized Iceland's trade and controlled entry to its ports. Kemm complained about this in contemporary Faroes.

British ships called to trade for sulphur for gunpowder. The Danes forbade it; islanders ignored them where they could until the 1550s when Denmark resolved to occupy the island, seize the sulfur mines, harbors and a quarter of Icelandic farms.

Denmark conspired in a trade monopoly with the Hanseatic Germans against British trading interests. Their monopoly and low state-imposed fish prices kept Iceland in poverty for more than two centuries.

Allowing Iceland to stagnate while raiding its resources befit a Danish nation that itself was primarily agricultural, a laggard between its British and Germanic neighbors. Denmark's main business was exporting food, primarily bacon, to Britain. It is still the U.K.'s largest supplier.

History won't be hurried in remote places. Icelanders debated home rule into the twentieth century. At the end of World War 1 Iceland achieved sovereignty in a referendum approved by 92.6 percent of voters, but remained ultimately under the Danish crown.

Finally, as in the Faroes, the German invasion of Copenhagen in April 1940 inspired Reykjavik to sever its connection to the Danish crown. A month and a day later Reykjavik woke to confront a rude reality, an uninvited British occupation force.

Churchill knew Britain could scarcely survive without supplies via the sea bridge to the United States and Canada, and reasoned Iceland's fjords could provide perfect refuge for German U-Boats (the Reich had already petitioned for landing rights for Lufthansa). The Brits meant to deny German submarines the safety of the fjords.

No sooner had Icelanders resolved to take the final fateful leap to independence than Reykjavik, like Torshavn, had been shown the limits of its aspirations to sovereignty.

Some called it a British invasion. The Brits, it seems, weren't storybook occupiers; "careful with their money, complaining about the weather," and their rations weren't enough to feed a black market.

When the Americans offered to relieve the Brits and take over protection of Iceland they "swept the Icelanders off their feet with their brashness, wealth, generosity, naïveté, loudness, friendliness." To formalize the arrangement Reykjavik sent a provisional invitation demanding full recognition of Iceland's independence and a promise to withdraw at the end of the war. The Yanks promised and then stayed for the next 65 years.

Icelanders resented the intrusion of another invasive culture. Keflavik resented becoming a garrison town. Icelandic girls got pregnant. The government asked the U.S. not to send black soldiers and the U.S.

complied. U.S. TV shows were banned from Icelandic sets (causing the birth of "an independent Icelandic television service, family friendly and purged of American influence").

But there was more than resentment; there was also fear. Just as the Faroes ultimately required a protector, Icelanders found that they, too, were unable to define their future entirely on their own.

The Americans and then NATO promised prosperity and protection. Fishermen trawled for five years without worry of predators. They sold into the limitless U.S. market. Farmers sold milk, sheep and chickens to the U.S. base.

At war's end construction equipment was donated, roads were built and fishermen had construction work outside fishing season. A cement plant and a fertilizer plant rose from the volcanic soil. A program for hydroelectricity began with Marshall Plan money.

When the war started Iceland was in debt. By the end of the war it was a creditor nation with currency reserves and a positive balance of trade. It became a founding member of NATO in 1949.

The government fretted about a depression if the Americans withdrew. Now, politicians thought, Keflavik should stay a military base. By 1955 the base generated 18 percent of Iceland's foreign exchange. But not without protest. Demonstrators lamented the loss of neutrality and "the branding of a proud community as a mere garrison."

Icelanders may have come to accept the NATO base, but that's not to say that a pack of pink-cheeked American enlisted men was welcome in Reykjavik for a loud, American-sized weekend on the town, competing with the local boys for the local women. It was probably for the best that with its $10 beers, Iceland priced a wild weekend beyond most soldiers' means.

On my first visit in 1991, Hughes Beaudoin, the French diplomat, heard on the radio about some trouble with soldier/Texans playing rowdy cowboy on a Friday night in town and being tossed from a nightclub. Perhaps that's illustrative of Icelandic resentment. For sure it's an example of the paucity of Reykjavik's local news.

•••••

Even as the debate continued, the base recruited a certain set of new supporters in its own unique way; it was a magnet for kids. A man I met in Reykjavik named Sigurdur told me that when he was a kid in the mid-eighties their field trips to the base exceeded cool. The people there had guns, and he could eat at the Burger King on the American base, long before fast food came to Reykjavik.

•••••

## COLD WAR, COLD SUMMIT

When Mikhail Gorbachev arrived for his summit with Ronald Reagan in 1986 he became the first Soviet leader to step onto a NATO base, at Keflavik. He was hardly the first Russian to visit, though. During the Cold War Reykjavik hosted one of the Soviet Union's biggest embassies at Garðastræti 33, just two long blocks from the Althing, providing diplomatic cover for robust spying.

The Reykjavik summit was like nothing Iceland had seen before, the block-booked hotels Holt and Saga, the heavy black Zil limos and dark-windowed KGB vans, Gorbachev's ship the Georg Ots in Reykjavik's harbor alongside the Baltika, the ocean liner that had carried Nikita Khrushchev to the United States for his kitchen debate with Richard Nixon in 1959.

Alongside the high affairs of state, low comedy. Ken Adelman, in his book *Reagan at Reykjavik:*

> "A massive copy machine had been hauled into Höfði House ... but no one knew how the behemoth worked. ... We were all flailing around ... when a Soviet colonel pulled out a pack of carbon paper

from his briefcase, waved it about, and ... said: "Here - Soviet high tech!"

•••••

The summit inspired events beyond Iceland's borders. A young German named Mathias Rust caused a sensation the next year when he evaded Moscow's air defenses and flew a tiny rented Cessna into the shadow of St. Basil's Cathedral, landing right in Red Square. The summit had induced Rust to travel to Iceland as a sort of training run for his planned secret flight from Helsinki to Moscow.

Rust saw it as a test of character. The eighteen-year-old German had never flown so far before and he reasoned that if he had the courage to fly off across the north Atlantic by himself in a tiny machine with a 160-horsepower motor, he might summon that courage later to fly into Red Square.

Seven months after the summit Rust, with scarcely fifty hours of flying time, left his home near Hamburg for the Faroe Islands. He flew on to Iceland where he spent a week, and then back via Bergen to Helsinki and ultimately into the heart of the Soviet Union.
One more aviation note: The summit secured landing rights and a U.S. foothold for then-tiny Icelandair. Ronald Reagan came bearing that license as a lagniappe for Prime Minister Steinrímur Hermannsson.

•••••

## JUST ANOTHER ARCTIC SWIM

Consider the milestones in your life, the memorable things. Your first date, maybe. A job interview or that time you got fired. Your first trip abroad. Now add this: Swimming outside in the snow on the edge of the Arctic in February.

Yes, thanks to Agnar, Mirja and I skinny-dipped on Vatnajokull in 2015, but by then we were grown up, well traveled, fully fledged. But a near-quarter century before as young world conquerors on a weekend adventure? Irresistible.

And yet, who wouldn't be wary of the touristy sound of "the Blue Lagoon?" Well:

• Way back then there just weren't enough tourists in Iceland for any tourist traps, especially in winter, and

• The French diplomat recommended it.

Hughes, the diplomat, drove us down a desolate road that cut through bare lava fields where the only life of any kind was resolute lichen clinging to rocks. A gravel parking lot and unassuming bathhouse greeted us. Some kind of huge, disconcerting heavy industry loomed immediately over the swimming area. Turned out to be a power plant, capturing free heat for Reykjavik.

No one swam when we arrived, not a single person in the lagoon, and only a lonely group of Scandinavian tourists showed up by the time we left. The water bubbled, bluish white, chemical rich, said to treat psoriasis.

Everybody loved it, whether due to the water or the utter strangeness of swimming in an air temperature below zero Celsius, I'm not sure. I am certain you never wanted to get out because of the sub-freezing run to the bathhouse.

The Blue Lagoon is different today. They've put in water park features, like the ability to swim from inside to outside immersed in warm water. Nowadays you'll require a pre-booked reservation, the luxury package running €195.

A hotel and conference center are slated for 2017, an incipient horror. Soon package groups can fly to Keflavik, shuttle to the Blue Lagoon and never see any more of the country, just like the Castros' beach resorts in Cuba.

By 2015 you could fly 26 places from Keflavik on Icelandair, Wow, SAS, Easyjet and Norwegian, mostly Scandinavian and northern European capitals, but also Bristol, Munich and Manchester, Glasgow and Seattle, Denver and Dulles. Now Lufthansa flies in summer from Frankfurt and Munich, and Delta from New York.

Less frequent contact with Europe may have put fresh ingredients at a premium in the past, but at the supermarket Bonus on a random day at the shank of winter, a teeming produce department beckons you to enjoy spaghetti squash tonight. The Pakistani restaurant Shalimar, started as result of a party given by the current owner's brother, now gets all its ingredients from the four or more daily three-hour flights to London.

Close collaboration between Icelandair and the tourism board pays off in record visitor arrival numbers (1,261,938, plus 1.46 million transit passengers in 2015) and hotel rooms (12,017 in 2014). Air Iceland flies tourists to Greenland for day trips.

Tour companies with battalions of big-tired jeeps thrive too. You will hear native Icelanders' wry commentary on "selling the Northern Lights." A driver named Sigurdur Oli Thorsteinsson, for example, professed astonishment at tour companies that "charge seven, ten thousand kronur to get in a bus, drive out of town and look in the sky."

•••••

Today tourism accounts for a full third of Iceland's foreign exchange. Suddenly the island groans under the demands of experience seekers. A law pending in summer 2016 would limit the number of days residents could rent their homes via Airbnb to 90 a year. A place called Vik í Mýrdal has rooms for 1,300 and a population of only 540. In Reykjavik they have taken to calling stores catering to tourists "puffin shops."

Nowadays Reykjavik sprawls across the rocky plain and right up to the water's edge, a bustling little city where eighteen story high rise apartment blocks ring Faxafloi bay near the harbor, 80- to 300 plus-square-meter units with frost-free parking, floor-to-ceiling windows and floor heat, so as not to impede the view with radiators.

Downtown proper still comprises just a dozen-odd blocks. The farther down main street, Laugavegur, the funkier the alternative to the tourist streets in the center with their watchmakers, leather craftsmen, carvings and knick-knacks and fashion.

More locally, the gallery DEAD, with skull-patterned hand-knitted Icelandic wool caps, sulks behind the supermarket. It's just around the corner from the Bad Taste Record Store, keeping post crash nihilism alive, offering vinyl from bands like Face the Anger, Gone Postal and Stick in the Knife.

•••••

The Monako Casino Club Bar, at 78 Laugavegur, serves beer to a dozen deaf men engaged by video slots. We cross the Icelandic/English cultural divide without speaking. Which really, it turns out, is easier.

Arnthor Hreinsson, born in January 1964, student of art from age 10, graduated from a painting course in 1986. A small man with hands you take care not to harm in shaking, Arnthor is a car buff, a comedian and a gentleman.

As we sink deeper into rounds of Viking Beer Arnthor sketches back-of-the-napkin pencil drawings of a woman feeding the whales, cars, polar bears on ice, Icelandic scenes. He mugs for the camera like Popeye, with glasses down on his nose and a stubbed out cigarette bent in his mouth. On just another winter's day in Reykjavik, we yuk it up as his friends and their beers slosh without a sound in and out of the scene on their way to the slots, a busy bistro on a frozen island, in silence.

•••••

# PART FOUR: GREENLAND

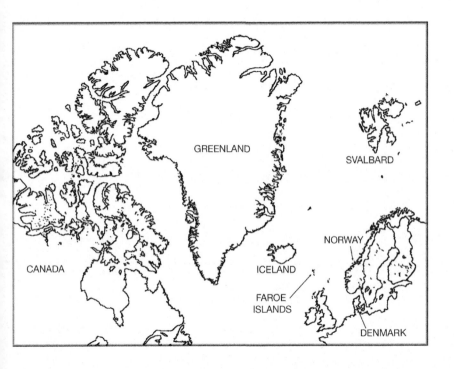

*Bill Murray*

## GETTING TO TASIILAQ

First thing we have to do, we have to find Robert.

The men smoking outside the concrete block terminal are not Robert so I ask around inside. The man behind the check-in counter might as well be collecting Arctic tumbleweeds. No flights are pending; no one is checking in.

He does not know Robert.

Together we lean over his counter to look down to the harbor. One boat is speeding away and there don't seem to be any others. He flips his palms up and shakes his head, "I think you just go down there and wait. That is your only chance."

•••••

Humans inhabit the fringe, the perimeter of Greenland not flattened by the ice cap, and I mean flattened, literally. Even with its thinning, ice reaches three kilometers deep at its thickest, pushing the bedrock into the mantle such that if the ice disappeared, the island would become an archipelago.

You can't fly to Tasiilaq, the biggest town on the eastern side of Greenland, for lack of sufficient flat space for an airstrip. So we have flown to a gravel strip called Kulusuk Airport. To get to Tasiilaq we must traverse the mouth of the Ammassalik fjord. We booked that online and all we know is, get to Kulusuk and ask for Robert.

We can see our destination twenty kilometers across the fjord behind a few icebergs and a coastline of precambrian rock thrust from the sea long before humanity, possibly even contemporaneous with the first life on Earth.

We invade and insult the silence with our prissy roll aboard carry-on bags, scraping and skipping the damned things down the rough gravel.

169

Show more respect and stand still, and the quiet closes up around you as a vehement, absolute thing.

A man from Cologne with a massive backpack walks ahead of us. He has arrived with no itinerary beyond walking for two weeks. His pack reaches up past his head, bulging with two weeks of freeze-dried food and powdered milk.

Once he walked from Ilullisat to Sisimiut in western Greenland, and that is far, far farther than from here to Tasiilaq and then clear around the island, but that time he was advised that there was no danger of polar bears and he has yet to be so advised here. His itinerary may have to be revised based on local information. Right now he plans to circumambulate Ammassalik Island. He puts great store in the advice of Robert, but none of us know how to find him.

Airport to harbor, perhaps a twenty-minute walk. No boats in sight. Either side of the gravel path, just rock and a little but not much tenacious flora. Our destination across the water is low and bare with mountains rising snow-capped, glaciers embedded toward the top. Clouds tease the ridges but do not suggest a threat of rain. In between individual icebergs, not a field, rise like several-story buildings.

It turns out that two tiny Danish-built fiberglass Poca speedboats, so low slung that the dock hides them both, bob in the sea beyond the dock. Two Greenlandic men stand down there on the shore below the dock, neither in so much as a jacket, enjoying the northern summer.

We ask, "Robert?" and the younger man, with no English, shakes his head no, "Christian." We and the backpacker, who is expecting the same ride, are at a bit of a loss until we work out, through gestures and goodwill, that Christian is here on behalf of Robert. For us, that is good.

The dock is too high for the boats, and so we scramble down onto rocks to climb aboard and Christian takes the backpacker, Mirja and me screaming across the fjord toward a similar spot on the far shore. Christian, hair stood up to a greased crown, drives standing, and stops us dead in the water alongside this iceberg, then that one, so we can take photos.

We clamber out on a rock where there is no dock at all. Christian motions without words, "up that way," and makes no move to leave the boat. So off we scramble, not having paid anybody for anything, off to find someone who wants our money. Robert, maybe.

The Inuit seldom keep individual dogs as pets, but rather tether them in groups outside in summer, and we rouse the mild attention of a pack of tethered dogs as we troop up the hill. Inuit sled dogs have two layers of fur, the inner short, like wool for insulation, and the outer longer, coarser and water repellent. That may make them hot today, but overall they are surely chillin', taking the warm season off, lounging all day except when growling and snapping over territory.

Sled dog greeting at Tasiilaq

A vehicle makes its way down the hill picking its path, for the way is gravel and bumpy. A slight girl stops to ask that we wait here, drives

171

down the road to drop some camping supplies and returns to drive us to the Red House, a tour shop and hostel run by the famous Robert.

Robert's reputation should have preceded him. Turns out in 1983, extreme explorer Robert Peroni from the Italian south Tyrol walked across the Greenland ice cap, all the way across the island at its widest point, some 1,400 kilometers, on an 88-day journey.

Now 72, Robert stands before us trim and erect, and above all relieved to find we aren't planning to stay in his hostel, for he is booked solid as he would hope to be in a very short high season. We pay him for the crossing from Kulusuk, bid farewell, and the girl drives us up the hill to the Hotel Angmagssalik.

•••••

There was a time when airline passengers celebrated successful landings. I remember applause in 1986 when my Lufthansa flight landed in Frankfurt from Moscow. I thought it was as likely for getting the bloody hell out of the Soviet Union.

We came over from Iceland today on a brand new, gleaming Air Iceland Bombardier Q400 prop plane, twenty rows two-by-two. Bustling their baby refreshment cart up and down the aisle meant actual work for the flight attendants, compared to the doorman role they play on short domestic flights.

Come time to land, the plane took on a buzz incongruent with today's humdrum air travel. In a small plane you've more of a sense of flying, and when the pilot maneuvered to dip under the clouds and between the mountains, we all craned to be the first to see icebergs, and phone cameras filled the windows. The runway at Kulusuk came up fast and we rode it right to the end lights.

About fifty of the seventy aboard were here for a day trip. Over in the morning, touch the soil, check Greenland off your list and fly back. I met a taxi driver in Reykjavik who said he did as a fifteen year old.

What did they do?

They deplaned, someone took them around the side of the terminal and they watched a man in a costume play a drum and a fat woman dance.

Some months ago he drove a man to do the same and picked him up later that day. What did they do? A drum and a dance.

•••••

## ORIGINS

For 4,000 years Inuit people have inhabited the Greenland coast. The first northern people arrived from Asia via the Bering Strait maybe 4,500 years ago, spreading west to east. In turns of adverse climate settlements died out. For centuries fluctuations in the climate-caused abandonment of individual settlements, and a culture called the Dorset people (after Cape Dorset in Canada, where artifacts were found) seems to have adapted and reoccupied this corner of the Arctic from maybe 50 BCE until about 1,000 years ago.

Around then warmer temperatures encouraged the Thule people to enter this northern region, bringing superior technology in the form of the qajak, or kayak, a skin-covered frame built to fit each hunter's body so well that you could think of it as an extension of the hunter himself, with a skin flap to pull up under the hunter's outerwear to keep him dry even if the boat took a tumble.

The Thule introduced two other technological advances: the umiak (the larger "women's boat") and the dogsled.

Since the Inuit were nomadic, the umiaq, a wider sealskin kayak, served to carry women, children and old people from one hunting ground to the next by sea, the dogsled by land.

The Thule people (so named because artifacts of their civilization were excavated from Thule in far northwest Greenland) were the Inuit's direct ancestors, overrunning and supplanting the Dorset and becoming the first to explore and settle all around the coast. In time, their culture broke apart and was replaced by the Inuit who live on the land today.

Where the Dorset primarily hunted land mammals like reindeer and musk ox, the Thule and Inuit conceived of the kayak to hunt seal, walrus, narhwal and other whales, becoming specialized in hunting on the sea. Elaborating on the Thule's work, the Inuit developed technology to further their hunting prowess, with innovations like paddles that entered the water "silently, creating the least possible wake or splash," and paddle tips inset with ivory to reduce wear from navigating in sea ice.

An Inuit golden age of hunting the vast riches of sea mammals prevailed for several hundred years until the Little Ice Age began around 1400, increasing the sea ice and limiting the ability to hunt by kayak.

Damjan Končnik with Kevin Kato write in *Greenland, The End of the World*, that "In the East Greenlandic dialect, the word for kayak hunters is interchangeable with the word for man." Right up until the late nineteenth century hunting and sealing meant the literal life and death of the community: Dead serious, survival stuff, the skill of the hunter was a matter of life and death. An unsuccessful hunt could mean death for a whole family.

Only two Greenlandic places continuously kept their kayak-based sea hunting orientation into the twentieth century - the far northwest on Baffin Bay, and the group of villages where we are now, around Ammassalik Island in barely populated east Greenland. This area of the coast was uninhabited in the Middle Ages, and most recently recolonized during the fourteenth and fifteenth centuries.

The settlements run for some 75 miles north to south, and ruins the length of them indicate houses made of alternating layers of moss and peat. A pole, probably driftwood, stood in the middle with rafters affixed, covered with branches then driftwood and turf. Seal skin would have been draped over the top and inside walls, and thin seal gut stretched across a window or two. The floor was stone.

The entrance would be dug out long and low, a cold air trap to gather the cold near the ground by the door, keeping the house relatively warmer. An ingenious way of heating.

Oral history suggests that in the eighteenth century the entire east coast supported sporadic settlements but  - whether due to tough local winters, season-long bad catches, famine or feud - in the nineteenth century the population fell so precipitously that in time the only settlement left was here on Ammassalik Island.

As far as we know Kulusuk wasn't visited by Europeans until 1884, so that about the time of Ammassalik's failing population numbers came the first European contact - just some 130-odd years ago. What came to be known as the "Women's Boat Expedition" wintered with these Inuit in 1884, having sailed around from the west coast.

The year before, Lieutenant Gustav Holm of the Danish Navy (later its commander) received orders to sail from the established Danish presence in the west around Cape Farewell, the headland at the southernmost point on the island, and back up the other side, to explore the east coast for traces of the "eastern settlement" of Norse legend.

(In error but in good faith, the Danes - and everyone else - read the Norse eastern and western settlements as representing settlements on the east and west sides of the island. In fact both the eastern and western settlements were on the west coast.)

Rounding the cape, the Holm party met east Greenlandic people who knew the people living on either side of the southern tip of the island, but no one else. Like the people of tiny Easter Island in the south Pacific, the Inuit in these settlements thought they knew everybody in the world.

175

Local Inuit handed Holm and his crew up the coast, one group to the next, and when it was time to batten down for winter of 1883, they found themselves at Ammassalik, where they counted 413 people.

While they wintered here, Lawrence Millman writes in *Last Places* that their camp "grew like a fort in Indian country; those who came to trade, or receive free baptismal rites (Christ they accepted primarily because the missionaries offered them snuff, too), stayed on for the rest of their natural lives. Angmagssalik grew so much that in 1925 eighty-one Eastlanders decided to pick up their tents and move north to less crowded and more fertile hunting grounds at the mouth of Scoresby Sound, nearly five hundred miles from their nearest neighbors."

•••••

A follow-on visit raised alarm eight years later when it discovered a population drop to just 294, so the Danes set out to stabilize life for the east Greenland Inuit, establishing a trade and mission station on the island in 1894. Twenty years later the population had grown to 599 and today Tasiilaq, population around 2,100, is the administrative capital of the eastern half of Greenland.

It may be a seat of government, with the modernity that suggests, but beyond these settlements only around 2,000 people inhabit 21,000 kilometers of shoreline on this side of the island, and after thousands of years, traditional culture runs deep. The hunter doesn't mind the clock, but rather the ancient rhythms of the ice and the wind and the tide, the temperature and visibility across the sea.

A Greenlandic catechist by the name of Johannes Hansen accompanied the Europeans on the Holm voyage, hoping to spread the Good Word to the heathens, as he described them. He found them ornery, maddening and fascinating like a train wreck.

Hansen came to convert 'em, but that doesn't mean he had to love them. He wrote that "... heathens buzzed like flies around us." He complained that one man named Alussagkât "snatched some pearls for himself" one morning, and that "these Easterlings" would "disturb (the Europeans) in their important works and fill the lounge with the bad smell of their dirty leather garments; and ... constantly run in and out of both our rooms...."

The women the expedition recruited from down the coast to accompany the expedition upset Hansen further. They were "quite irresponsible, and furthermore touchy about it, and easily offended."

"They never want to listen to my sensible advice," he wrote, "and, when I reprimand them ... they deliberately made a noise with the harmonica to avoid listening to me."

As winter dragged into the new year, familiarity bred, well, this: "How terrible and meaningless everything is which these poor people believe in and do!"

•••••

## TAKING IN TASIILAQ

The Hotel Angmagssalik commands a view over the harbor, town, icebergs and bay beyond. Behind the bay mountains rise, topped with snow fields, the centers of which are frozen in permanent ice. Patches of snow fill clefts in the hillsides and clouds skirt the peaks.

It's big, the hotel, the finest in town, our room the 38th, with more down the hall. While depicted as international standard, it is more workmanlike, fine in a Greenlandic way, by which I mean worn down some outside by the vicious climate, with aging carpet and rooms big enough for two single beds, a table, small closet and toilet.

Beside number 38 is an open-air deck, on which there are four chairs of light wood and blue cloth, one without upholstery, another having shed its back rest. Three lack substantial tears in the seat fabric.

Against the wall behind the chairs, two Mirandas and a St. Amand soft drink bottle, each over-stuffed with sufficient cigarette butts to attest to weeks of hard partying, spill their excess in a damp tobacco circle on the concrete. Either they have collected filters for many a fortnight or that was one hell of a party.

Painted dog sleds, their cargo spaces longer than a man is tall, decorate the hotel lawn. Purple lupin or its kin and fields of white and yellow wild flowers draw the eye down between the hills, and between here and the shore stand maybe two hundred brightly painted houses.

Houses built on water-shielding cement bases or on stilts over boggy ground ride down the ridges in lines along a bedrock of bare gneisses and schists. Some have smallish windows, some ample-sized and modern, all well insulated. Steep roofs. Most of the housing stock has been built in the last 35 years.

A sheltered marina holds twenty or thirty pleasure boats, more dry-docked alongside, beside which sit eight or nine stacked shipping containers from Royal Arctic, the national shipping line, and in the foreground kids run up and down a soccer pitch with roughly chalked lines.

A sailboat bobs at anchor in front of icebergs, a few substantial and many smaller, the big ones thrown up against low rocks, bare islets against which the bergs rest gleaming at the top, tending to aquamarine at the waterline. I'm guessing they'll stick around for a while. Once inside the bottleneck at the mouth of the bay, what are the odds they will soon find their way back out?

The clucking of birds and whir of machinery waft from the harbor. Tasiilaq's dramatic topography, hills rising and dropping abruptly, mutes the sounds of people and cars behind hills. Some kids play football, others beat out a riff on a 55-gallon drum.

Few roads are paved. Paths between houses and roads mark the shortest way on foot between all sorts of points, as happens on a college campus. It's haphazard. Yards aren't property. The island is your property.

Tasiilaq Town

The occasional minibus heads downhill from the hotel. People own the roads like in Africa, walking in the center, the sound of a motor enough to scurry them to the shoulder. Unlike in Africa, drivers don't lay on their horns.

If you want solitude from this world you have come to the right place. Internet? Sold by the hour, most of it spent trying to connect to the world, so that in the end you put it down and walk away.

•••••

Today is a fine day, quiet because it is Sunday, air temperature about 8C, more sun on the ground than cloud shadow. Local folks wear short sleeves. Boys might as well be living in the Caribbean as they swim down by the harbor. It is high summer.

At 1:30 the church bell rings with such determination that it gets all the tethered dogs into the act, joining in a wail. Bred from wolves, they don't bark. They howl. That church bell rings for so long I decide it must not be the church at all, but I don't know what else it might be.

The kids play football into the night, and night rambles on indefinitely, never winking entirely out.

• • • • •

## TASIILAQ TOWN

We book Robert Peroni's whale watch for the next afternoon and I walk into town, stopping at Stunk, a three-table, open-plan workshop, doors wide open to invite the fine day inside. Stunk is the project of Hans Ulriksen, a young Inuit from whom I commission a necklace for Mirja to be made from bone.

Mirja has horses, so I ask if Hans can carve a horse. Having no horses around here, Hans looks up a picture of a horse on his phone to go by, but decides it would be better to go home where he has better reference material to guide him and we agree on a time for me to return.

Whales, minke and humpback, seals, narwhals, ptarmigans, polar bears, sea fowl and reindeer... one way or the other their useful parts eventually find their way to Stunk. Here in the showroom are antlers and teeth, bones and hides.

Hans wants me to rub a section of polar bear hide draped over his chair and asks, would I like that horse from reindeer bone, or narwhal? Reindeer, I think. Now I must find local money, Danish kroner, to pay for the necklace.

Directions in Tasiilaq, it seems, are color-coded: "Go to the gray council house, left to the green kindergarten, left to the red building." In the red building I should be able to change money. There is a bank upstairs.

I find the bank but it doesn't change money. Who does? The clerk decides I should find the yellow bookshop. On the way I pass the politi station and ask a Danish cop descending a steep stairway. She fears nobody changes money.

I say the bank pointed me to the yellow bookshop. Her face lights up.

"Oh, Gerta! Maybe so. I don't know what all she gets up to in there. She sells passport photos and internet, and maybe she sells books, too."

A shambolic, tacked-onto affair with weather-beaten doors and peeling paint, Gerta's place is locked tight. According to the sign on the door Neriusaaq Boghandel opens at noon, fifteen minutes from now. I sit down to enjoy the sunshine.

A few minutes after twelve an old woman opens the door, trash bag in hand. She lives in there. She takes out the garbage and invites me in.

Gerta shuffles around, home-comfortable in gray sweatpants under a patterned blue smock. She is monochrome and stout with a saggy old bosom and a baritone voice that does not belong in that body. It is so deep, I expect that if Gerta were an American schoolchild she could use either bathroom, except in North Carolina.

No books are evident in Gerta's bookshop, though I don't make it past the front room. Coffee is on and it smells delicious. There are two tiny tables draped with cloth, perhaps for internet and coffee, tourist trinkets on offer, plus an eclectic collection of canned goods. Indian food.

Gerta does the deal, makes change, then looks up from under her eyebrows. "You can probably use dollars wherever you want, though," she rumbles.

"They take them because they know they can come to me."

*Bill Murray*

I do not learn Gerta's mysterious connection to the world beyond east Greenland.

•••••

Next morning the Mary Arctica calls, a container ship from Aalborg. Derricks swing to and fro. Tasiilaq's ship has come in.

Stunk becomes a semi-regular stop on the road to town, and I stop in just to say hello, a positive place full of bright faces, whirring and knocking and industry. This time the shop is abuzz, customers and workers, many more than before, vises, saws, the wood-cutting type and hacksaws, planing tools and a steady whine of buffing instruments I don't know the name of.

I walk in past a man sawing a narwhal tusk, trying to cut it in half. He really labors over it, a hard going, and the friction generates a heat cloud that has an unfortunate aspect of the smell of burning hair.

•••••

Heading for Robert Peroni's Red House and our whale watch, we skirt the rim of the hill. Every point A to point B involves up and down climbing, so we endeavor to avoid the valley and in so doing, way up above town, we find a secret line of sight to the sea, up over the hill behind town, and our own personal march of the icebergs.

You're always going to have to climb something around here, but this is brilliant work, this skirting thing, for it brings us right to the bottom of the Red House stairs.

Just at the top, Robert rushes over in full theatrical Italian dudgeon, and declaims, "It is cancelled!" He bites off the words. "I just found out two minutes ago! We cannot go out. It is terrible."

It is too windy, "Not here, but out there," outside the bay, and it is true that here, the clouds are gone and later a man will declare this the best weather day of the summer. In polishing the day for beauty inside the bay, the wind that drove the clouds away made waves too big out on the sea.

We take this philosophically but Robert remains wrought. He has lost a full tour, party of sixteen paying customers in a short fourteen-week season, the beginning and end of which are chancy, and here in mid full flow, a sold-out trip is cancelled.

And there is something else.

Robert's eyebrows of bushy white bob up and down and he swings his arms around the deck. "They saw polar bears in two places yesterday," he says. Over there, and, swinging, over there, pointing over the mountains, "And we have people over there camping. "Fourteen there," stab in the air, "Eleven there." His summer fortune. "And we have to bring them back."

Robert traversed Greenland on foot. A self-confident and self-reliant man, he makes sure his camping guides are too. The guides take rifles and put up a tripwire perimeter reminiscent of Svalbard, where Robert has also led an expedition, but the thing is, the politi find out about the polar bear sighting and there is nothing to be done; they must come around to all the outfitters and insist on evacuation.

Cancelling all these camping trips, with refunds, is tough. Seen from the eyes of 72-year-old, slim and fit Robert Peroni, cancelling the sixteen-person iceberg/whale run is bitter icing on a stale cake.

We peruse his shop. At least I can buy one of his books, I think, maybe that will help. But *The White Horizon*, the story of his 1400 kilometer hike, and the other three titles are only in Italian. They have been translated into German but best I can find, not into English.

In our newfound idleness, we leave Robert to steep in his woe and scramble onto a boulder to admire the icebergs. At the base of the slope just below us is a weathered metal building, sky blue to match a boat resting on its port side on dry land alongside.

Another boat, broken apart in a two-thirds/one-third configuration, lies against the rocks of a tiny inlet, where two more ships list in the water, forlorn and long abandoned. Eight yellow and red canoes lie back from the waterline opposite the abandoned ships, two camping tents pitched nearby. Farther back I count fifteen more tents and then two much bigger ones with center poles. In this direction are the chained huskies along the road where Christian dropped us off from Kulusuk.

Industrial tanks huddle in a circle on the town side of this view, and icebergs and bergy bits bob in low profile, slowly, as if asleep. On close inspection, there are a dozen and a few more out toward the middle of the bay. The water is deeper blue than the sky, and the bergs' reflections streak the water in our direction.

I can find nothing that hints of humans along the far shore, where mini-fjords disappear around bends into invisibility. Greenland is home to the world's oldest rocks; a site on the other side of the island is known to be 3.85 billion years old.

Rocks rounded by water give way to more rugged heights, snow in the crooks and dales, with tiny puffs of cloud created on the spot to hover around peaks, separating earth from clear blue.

The working ferry the *Johanna Kristina* sails in from the sea, painted red around the base with a single yellow crane and whitewashed bridge tower. The *Johanna Kristina* circles the settlements with seats for twelve, calling once a week. Today two passengers enjoy the fine afternoon at the bow of the ship.

A handsome red Air Greenland helicopter crosses in front of us. Back at the hotel they explained how charter business is good just now for the airline, as there is a National Science Foundation research station being outfitted up on the ice.

•••••

## ON THE TOWN ON THE TUNDRA

Let's look at this as an opportunity.

No brilliant scheme to replace the whale hunt occurs to either of us. We walk to a place they call the Valley of Flowers. The town cemetery is here, rows of white wooden crosses, most of them unmarked. Alongside runs a stream whose entirely clean water invites you onto your knees for a drink, and as I bring my face to the water the wind lifts a lily's bifurcated leaf in a jaunty wave hello.

The sun cuts a scythe's arc deep across the southern sky, wide and high. The brook encourages Arctic flora to happy colors, grasses and lupins and mosses and ferns, so that when I stand in the middle and regard its path as it winds to the bay, mountains wearing their snow shawls and the deepening blue of the late-day sky put me hard pressed to believe I am in Greenland.

This morning Mirja saw a building with the sign, Pizzeria. It doesn't take long to find it (or anything else), but in defiance of the opening hours posted on its door it is locked shut.

Except there are howls, shrieks from inside the building, and I mean top-of-the-lungs stuff. We investigate and, walking around the corner come upon a sign with one of the more useful words to add to your Greenlandic vocabulary, "Ammauu," and this, my similarly inclined friends, indicates a bar. Based on auditory clues though, it might mean "torture room," and really, it is only our humanitarian duty to investigate.

It is a bachelorette party. Six girls in a booth sing and shriek and sway while everyone else winces until they have played their lungs out and fall into giggling.

The lucky bride to be wears a sign I can't read, but the idea is easy enough: Give her this coin and you may kiss her hand, a larger one for a peck on the cheek, that kind of thing. Harmless, young-girl silly, a little bit of fun and a way to raise beer money.

*Bill Murray*

The poor matrimony seeker's problem is, the only patrons are a couple, then Mirja and me and Jacob Sivertsen, the son of the former mayor and a clerk at the school, who is so drunk that he blurts single words and replies to himself with "Yippee," "Uh-oh," or mad laughter. Then there is Ole, at 34 the bartender and local Casanova, and a woman down at the end of the bar with her head down on her arms, perhaps, ah, napping,

Once the wedding party shuts the hell up for a moment the man with the woman brings the excited soon-to-wed a coin and is entitled to kiss her hand. As I am the only coherent male left, I approach with a coin and learn that it buys me a peck on the matrimonial cheek.

With that, she has run the table on the coin collecting potential in this particular ammauu. So after a time they go, the imminently wed trailing a collection of crushed Tuborg cans tied to her shoe for general attention-calling and embarrassment. Which leads to the second disadvantage for the soon-to-be bride: There is only one other bar in town. Once they leave, though, Ammauu becomes a more habitable place.

We are the only Qallunaat, white people. The lady at the end of the bar continues to steal a bit of shuteye and the couple leaves after a while. Jacob wedges himself between Mirja and me. The mayor's son thinks Mirja is Scandinavian and I am Italian. Reasonable guess.

For a lifelong resident of Greenland he shows impressive knowledge of American politics, displayed thus: "Cleenton, yippee. Trump, uh oh, heee heee hee heeeee," and a recitation of presidents all the way back to "Jimmy Carter! Wheeeeee!"

Ole grants that he is in fact the town stud and contemplates his girlfriends. His hair is moussed to stand straight up in front in a fine, oily crest. Girls offer themselves to him, but his friend says go slow, he says. He may be thoughtful; he may be posturing.

In time he persuades Jacob to leave the foreigners be, by which time the roster in Ammauu is augmented by a man who admires my twenty-kroner coin, turning it over in his hands and noting that with it and just twenty more kroner he would have himself enough coin for a beer of his own. Then, in walks my friend, the Stunk carver Hans Ulriksen.

Hans pulls up a chair and joins Mirja and Ole and me at our end of the bar, not to disturb our napping friend. Hans looks tinier on his big barstool than he did this morning in his workshop. We enjoy another Tuborg or two and he invites us to his house to meet his daughter Paula and see his new acquisition, for now a secret.

Ole can't summon a taxi even though he calls all four numbers. He guesses it may be they are all drunk and have stopped driving. Instead he provides go cups and we walk a short way to a fine waterfront home.

I have read that one doesn't knock on an Inuit door, but rather walks right in. M. J. McGrath, in her fiction book *White Heat*, writes "Inuit consider ... knocking an insult, an acknowledgement that the visit might not be wholly welcome...." We bypass an awkward occasion as Hans welcomes us inside.

A young man pumps our hands at the door. He holds a bag of eight Tuborgs, wants to party, and offers to pass around his beer stash. He calls himself something like Nuuk Pjieter and Hans declares him very drunk.

Paula, five, is busy practicing handstands and persuades Mirja to join in. They share trade secrets until Paula lands near Hans and he scoops her into his arms. Nuuk Pjieter hopes somehow to coax a boat ride to Kulusuk, and after a time ambles over the hill.

There must be ten pairs of shoes at the door. Mattresses on the floor. An unexplained man lying in front of the TV and we never quite determine his familial connection. The language thing.

I think we would make the house feel cozier, warm it up, but they love it the way it is, a big, communal thing with big blank spaces. You get the idea cousins and cousins of cousins are free to come and go.

We sit around Hans's kitchen table and he explains the adzes and picks, ball peen and tack hammers, coping saws and chisels, etching knives and sandpaper, the tools of his carving trade.

His surprise? A formidable bone, red and damp, lying beside a hacksaw on the front porch. This is a polar bear humerus, the bone between the shoulder and elbow.

Hans's bloody polar bear humerus

A friend has brought him this fine gift, he says, and it is obviously a recent harvest, a fine specimen for carving dozens of tourist pendants, figurines of traditional drums, kayak necklaces, whale fins.

It is a spare way of life for the Inuit of East Greenland, no doubt about that. Hans has all the kitchen appliances, an electric kettle, a microwave, the TV in the corner, but he makes his living from the produce of the land, bones, antlers, tusks. Consider the lightning evolution from hunter gatherer to today.

•••••

## HEADING OFF WELL-MEANT ARGUMENTS

130-odd years years since first European contact, the outlying villages of Tiniteqilaaq ("the strait that runs dry at low tide"), Sermiligaaq ("the beautiful glacier fjord"), Kuummiut ("the people of the river"), and Isortoq ("the foggy sea"), are home to 118, 193, 313, and 83, respectively, and still almost every resident lives off the land.

The only exception is Kulusuk ("the chest of a black seabird"), population 277, where the land is flat enough for the airstrip. A few jobs come with that.

Each of the settlements has a central "service house," a community center offering laundry facilities, baths, a kitchen, wood, leather and metal shops, a pay telephone and a nurse. Men can come to fashion hunting tools, you can cook yourself a meal or do your daily chores, and if you are on a hunting trip you can stop to warm up in rooms to let for the night.

With no roads between towns, local transport (besides once-a-week service via the ship *Johanna Kristina*) is by kayak and umiaq and in winter, dog sleds. The airstrip came as a great leap forward in 1959. Back then Air Greenland maintained the world's largest fleet of helicopters, Sikorskys with pontoons for water landing and two engines for emergencies. The helicopter ride between Tasiilaq and Kulusk, revealing the majesty of east Greenland's mountains, is an utter thrill.

Nowadays six or eight supply ships call from Europe between June and November. By the final visit supplies enough for seven months have been laid into the big red warehouse on the pier at Tasiilaq.

•••••

If capitalism reinvents itself by creative destruction, there is little need for it in Greenland, where destruction and reinvention proceed by natural rhythms, at a pace not subdivided by hour, minute and second hands. The view from the high Arctic is constrained by nature, by the known limits of men, by what is available for a task, by recognizing what is possible.

Greenlanders eat what they catch. The Faroese persist in their grindadráp and Icelanders bristle at criticism that they eat whale or seal or horse or puffin. Newfoundlanders (who recoil at the idea of eating cute little puffins) eat seal.

Puffin, presented as a delicacy at a downtown Reykjavik restaurant, left no lasting impression. Whale meat, served in a Tasiilaq buffet, was red and dense and chewy, chewier than liver.

The island Ammassilik is named for "ammassat," the Inuit name for capelin. Small, plentiful and tasty fish that present no guile against their capture, ammassat are easily dried and stored for winter.

The most commonly served dish in the settlements around Tasiilaq is seal and seal hunting is family fun. The best family holiday still comprises a visit to a favorite hunting spot or fishing hole.

You'll find seal, protein rich for tough Arctic winters, served dried, stir-fried, roasted, as steaks or in suaasat, a seal soup with rice and onions. In older days there was seal blood soup. Lawrence Millman writes that you eat seal nose by holding the whiskers as toothpicks. To avoid greasy fingers.

Greenlanders don't just EAT seal, they consume the entire animal, not a whit to waste. Seal parts unfit for eating feed sled dogs, which are as essential to an Inuit family as your car. Before electricity, seal blubber lit the Inuit night, loaded into a carved soapstone, using cotton grass, moss or dried rabbit dung as a wick. On winter hunting trips blubber is still used this way.

While Greenland has an exception to the 2009 EU ban on sealskin imports, the ban has nevertheless hollowed out the skin business. Inuit have struggled to replace seal hunting income with fishing, but seal hunting as subsistence, for local and family food and clothing, thrives. From out here judgmentalism from an urban, temperate land - much as the Faroese feel about their grindadráp - strikes as preposterous. (Mass sealing, as we will see in Canada, well, that may be something else.)

Here caribou hide is prized for its warmth. Caribou back muscles, Alan Smutylo writes in *The Memory of Water*, carefully split, dried and twisted, make practically unbreakable sewing thread and twine. Eider duck skin and feathers are used in undergarments. "Polar bear pants, fur worn outwards, (are) highly prized," and indeed, two bear skins hang out to dry like laundry on a line near Robert Perino's Red House.

Smutylo: "Dog, wolf, and wolverine fur, being frost-resistant, were commonly used for hood and cuff lining." In the past, he writes, "A hide that got wet and dried that way got hard.... Softening was done by chewing....

Most elderly women had teeth that had been worn down to stubs by a lifetime of chewing."

•••••

## CURSES

Before we leave east Greenland I must buy a tupilak from Hans. Sitting across his work table I come obliquely to the question: "I would like the frightening thing... that mean thing that you, ah, you know...." until Hans smiles and blurts, "You want the thing we kill each other with!"

Well, yes. Exactly.

Once held to the breast of a shaman and imbued with the breath of life, a tupilak's mission was bone-evil, eat-the-entrails murder. Ritual shamanic trance-induced chants brought the tupilak to life as a monster carried to the sea and cast from kayak or umiaq with the specific mission to seek out an individual for bloody death.

191

Inuit elsewhere knew the tupilak as an invisible ghost. The tupilak as physical evil-doer was unique to east Greenland, but as tupilaks were originally composed of degradable material like animal sinew and some say, bits of human corpses, none survive.

The people of Angmassalik carved replicas to show the Christian catechist Johannes Hansen on that 1884 Danish expedition. Hansen was fascinated by shamanic practice. He described a ceremony he attended over that long winter, a shamanic (the Inuit word for shaman is Angákoq) spirit-flight:

> "They bound him in the usual way, and bent him over by tightening the bindings from the neck down around the knees. He cannot get up himself, as this is very painful for him, and his drum must, on this occasion, be able to move by itself; it then dances over and lifts him up, first by the head, so that he sits upright, and then by lifting him in the same way by his backside. Finally he gets on his feet, and then he, who is about to fly through the air, walks around on the floor for a time, whereafter he lifts himself up and floats around a bit inside the house until he finally seats himself on the drying rack beneath the ceiling, and then finally rushes straight through the roof or the wall, out into the air. Meanwhile the drum continues to dance of its own accord while the tied Angákoq flies around in the long, cold night, and gets as far away as necessary. In all this time his housemates sit in the dark, expecting his return, which sometimes happens at dawn. Even then, his drum still moves. But when he returns, he will either have been far away on the Earth or in the Heavens, on the Sun or the Moon."

The tupilak I choose at Stunk, the meanest and most foreboding, high of furrowed brow, features exaggerated, teeth grinding, a skull in the death grasp of its bony fingers, was carved from seal bone.

The fearsome tupilak

•••••

Optimists say the Inuit culture has been resilient enough to survive winters that would have undone anyone else, and they reckon that adaptability will lead them forever forward. Still, life is changing for the east Greenland Inuit, and radically.

In a land not known for such things, we live in a hotel with a considerable larder, serving beef and pork and pizza, offering (halting) internet, BBC World and the rest.

Cars and heavy trucks ply the few roads around town and Tasiilaq is resupplied by ship except in winter. Should shortages appear before the ice clears in spring, fruit, vegetables, eggs, even flowers may be brought on the short flight from Iceland.

The Inuit have moved from isolation to the internet in an instant. Uprooting an ancient way of life presents challenges like alcoholism, as with the former mayor's son. Small wonder.

An epoch of hunters has slipped between the sealskin sides of custom fitted kayaks, not just proud but intent and resolute and bound and determined to bring back food for survival, and many a family has starved in the long winters when their patriarch was lost at sea.

Now scarcely a half dozen generations from first European contact, a community of ancient bearing, heritage and oral tradition, its utter existence based on the land itself, finds its eyes off the prize and trained on the trivial, on cell phones and dating apps and beer.

While the few thousand Inuit in the east Greenland settlements carry on, 400-odd miles across the ice cap the comparatively proper cities of west Greenland bear the mixed fruit of much more direct colonial occupation. One or two of the towns almost bustle in comparison.

Greenland's capital is Nuuk, "the tip," a third of the way up the west coast; the main airport is at Kangerlussuak, a town of about 500 at the head of a fjord of the same name 200 miles north of Nuuk.

Once before, we flew to Disko Bay, a further 150 miles north of the airport. It didn't feel like a mass of humanity in the main town of Illiulisat, population 4,550, but in Greenlandic terms it surely was. We made our way straight out to a spot even more remote than Kulusuk, a tiny camp, not even a settlement, that I fear is no longer there.

•••••

## SYLVA'S CAMP AT ATAA

Imagine a gauzy coffee commercial, cozy people savoring their morning brew, steam rising in circles from their cups. In the midst of a scene like that, cradling our cups in our hands in Silva's kitchen, an iceberg broke apart with a great low rumble just offshore from Ataa camp, north of Disko Bay in west Greenland.

Boulders of ice plunged into waves around the berg, now off balance, as it rocked side to side in slow motion. Silva stoked the commotion, cursing and scurrying for his video camera (he did this more than once). He was sure someday he'd be in *National Geographic*.

•••••

Silva was captain of Ataa Holiday Camp. The tourist service down the coast in Ilulissat cheerfully recommended it, because Silva was a man of some repute in Ilulissat.

He was in year eighteen in Greenland, first as an itinerant musician from Denmark, invited up here to play hotels for a month, then three, then a year and one thing led to the next. Now he ran Travel Nature Touring Company and he was having a go at redeveloping this abandoned trading post into a tourist camp.

In 1915 Ataa boasted 59 residents: 58 Inuit and the station chief, the only Dane. They lived in six houses and three tents, with a school, the manager's house, a workshop and a storehouse for seal blubber.

Seal hunting kept Ataa alive, and that year they collected 137 barrels of seal blubber, 42 barrels of shark liver, five blue and eleven white fox skins, 70 seal skins, eight and a quarter kilos of tusks and four and a half kilos of eider down.

Nobody lives there full time. The nearest settlement today is at a place called Qertaq, thirty kilometers away.

Ataa camp sits at the base of ancient, rounded low hills of less than 1,000 meters, Precambrian gneisses finally exposed only seven or eight thousand years ago, when the ice cap most recently melted away. Ataa means "its lower part" - the base of the hills.

Mirja and I got there by speedboat. A Quicksilver 3000 Classic bounced us across choppy water under mean, lowering gray, 70 kilometers from Ilulissat north to Ataa. Its pilot, Jergen, with his broad, expansive buzz cut and ready smile, was Greenland Man.

The wind kicked up. We spied the spray of a finback whale, spun around and saw him dive, and in the spinning spotted a seal.

*Bill Murray*

Jergen pounded the Quicksilver's butt into the tiny harbor at Ataa, where Silva bobbed aboard a Zodiac, perched uncertainly and growling. He wore the only clothes we ever saw him in, Nikes and a running suit.

Silva's own hand, improbably, built the yellow plyboard breakfast and general headquarters shack where we warmed up over coffee. It perched on rocks some few meters from freezing, lapping water.

His sister Lilliana and her husband Filita were visiting from Florence, original home of all culture, and I suspect just maybe they considered Silva a bloody wide-open, straight-ahead idjit.

Loud and fifty, soft-hearted, quick to take a stand and quick to back away from it, Silva, with an impossibly full graying mustache and tousled hair, was a real piece of work, with eight bambinos - four in Italia and four in Ilulissat.

Silva shuffled across the kitchen, singing, whistling, posing, acting like supervising his sister Lilliana, who did all the cooking. What would he do when she went home?

Silva got caught up in the drama of the changing weather. We'd been there half an hour. Eyes widening, palms spread wide, he told us, "We cannot risk our lives to take you back if the weather is worse tomorrow!"

We sipped our coffee and watched him realize that since we'd just arrived he might be getting off on the wrong foot. He retreated behind his hand and allowed as how on the other hand his sister had to fly to Denmark on the same flight as us. When you can sit and watch a man think, his is a disarming guilelessness.

•••••

Mirja and I hiked up along a steep ridge to see the mouth of a glacier called Kangilerngata Sermia, forty speedboat minutes away. We traced the side of desolate Kangerdlo Bay to the north and scaled the western

196

ridge to walk back along Lake Taserssuaq. Up on the ridge Mirja played with a bird, a tiny handful of brown that followed us just for the novelty.

Mirja set out to pick mushrooms. When she found a little brown-capped thing she declared, "Greenlandic people say there are no poisonous mushrooms in Greenland and I believe them. If I die in Greenland, it is my destiny," and she ate it and she didn't die.

The world felt constrained, all gray and closed in around the edges. We walked just several meters below the cloud line that hugged the mountain, kicking tiny, bell-shaped, yellow-rimmed flowers called lavender Lapland cassiope. Truth be known, this was more dampened slog, slowed by bog and marsh, than wilderness adventure.

•••••

From the ridge you could see an old collapsed shack, fallen in on itself, from Ataa's trading post days.

"We keep it as a museum," Silva grinned.

The building next door had "119" painted on its roof. Before radar was sophisticated, the "119" marking helped U.S. pilots navigate on their way north to a Cold War DEWS base up north at Thule. It showed supply planes where to parachute in supplies.

•••••

We asked Silva for water to take on our hike and drew a stone-cold blank look of surprise. He rummaged around and came back with a bottle with Coca-Cola still rolling around inside it, and told us to take it down to the creek to wash it out and fill it up because the water here is completely clean.

When we left to hike up the hill, he promised us home-cooked caribou for dinner and there sure was, caribou and potatoes and smoked halibut, whipped up by Lilliana and Filita, and it was outstanding.

A crowd of Germans had sailed in, and we had a rollicking good time in Greenlandic, English, German, Danish and Italian. Everybody understood a little bit of what everybody else said, and there was lively Italian-style family cooking, Silva and Lilliana humming and puttering and feeling at home.

Then came an astonishing knock at the door. We all sat up to welcome three people from a boat around the bay who needed petrol. Their boat was the *Nosy Be* and that perked up Mirja and me, because Nosy Be is a resort town in Madagascar. We've never been there, but some years ago a few thousand dollars were charged to our American Express card from a resort there.

•••••

Before the end of dinner, Silva developed a mischievous grin.

"Beeel, are you tired?"

"After eight beers and caribou I will be," I reckoned.

Silva grew reticent. "Then I will suggest nothing." But he couldn't contain himself and the next thing you knew we were tearing across the bay in a speedboat with Silva behind the wheel screaming, "It's not coooollllldddd!"

It must've been 9:30, might have been ten. "Wanna see some seals?" he twinkled, and off we went, toward the mouth of a fjord called Kangerdluarssuk.

"How far is it over there, Silva?"

"Ten kilometers," he shouted. A waffling hand. "Twelve."

Glassy smooth, no chop, my thermometer read 46, but try sitting centimeters over water in air that's 46 degrees, tearing across the sea in Greenland at night. It's cold.

"We have to know the icebergs," Silva was shouting. "That one is sick ice. Cannot go close."

We trolled the coast and we didn't find any seals.

"We are worried," he told us with a twist of the mustache, maybe because he was a sage conservationist, maybe because his camp promised seal safaris.

After a good effort, Silva flat out raced back across the water, singing uproarious Italian nationalist songs then whistling Copland then humming a British march. There were no life vests. Just Silva, Mirja, me and the bare white bottom of the boat.

The south wind set in - an evil wind, pulling the wet up around the mountains behind Ataa, at the north end of the bay. Warmth whipped away on the wind.

•••••

Silva assigned us to a barracks with four rooms, each with bunk beds, a common room and a biological toilet. Nobody was there except us.

Silva came into the bunker around midnight. He would sleep there too. Eyes fired with the prospect of deals, earnestly, eye to eye, he told us of his plans for world kayak competitions and an international dive center right here, and ice golf in Ilimanaq.

•••••

## FINDING GREENLAND

Eirik Thorvaldsson, Eirik the Red, lived life in panoramic high-definition, from smallholder turned violent killer to famous explorer. After learning the violence-wracked heritage of North America's true discoverers, the gentle American reader might prefer to retain the discovery myth of the Genoan explorer Columbus. For the immediate family tree of Leif Erickson comprises serial murder, banishment and exile.

The chain of events that first led to the New World, to the northern tip of today's Newfoundland, may have begun with a bar fight. Around the year 950 the þing, the high court in Jaeder, a coastal region of southern Norway (whose most prominent town today is Stavanger), found Thorvald Asvaldsson guilty of murder and sentenced him to exile.

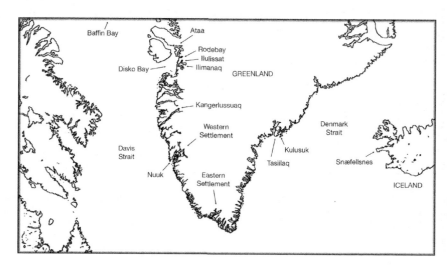

Our source, Eirik's saga, doesn't say exactly what his old man got up to that night or reveal who Thorvald killed or why. It simply says Thorvald was exiled "because of some killings." There are no details of the charges of manslaughter.

Thorvald and his son Eirik sailed to northern Iceland. Eirik grew up, married a local girl, moved south and in 980 the local Thing found him guilty of murdering Eyulf the Foul and Rafn the Duellist. He was banished from the local Thing's jurisdiction.

In two years time an argument over the loan of a religious ornament resulted in Eirik's conviction for the murder of a man by the name of Thorgest. Icelandic justice tightened the screws on Eirik, declaring him an outlaw and banishing him from the island for three years.

Now he was barred from both Norway and Iceland, and became an explorer for survival. Eirik and his family assembled a party of interested fellow brigands and determined to explore islands to the west that one Gunnbjörn Ulfsson had discovered when blown off course in the first half of the tenth century.

Eirik knew of these islands (named Gunnbjarnskerries) because the Ulfsson family lived on the Snæfellsnes peninsula in northwest Iceland like Eirik, and Eirik's wife and her sister were grandchildren of a sailor who had also been to the Gunnbjarnskerries.

We don't know where the skerries are. Perhaps they don't exist. But they were in the direction of Greenland, and the Lándnamabók, Book of the Settlements, written after Eirik's time, had sailing instructions to Greenland:

"Learned men state that from Stad in Norway it is seven days' sail west to Horn in the east of Iceland; and from Snæfellsnes, where the distance is shortest, it is four days' sea west to Greenland."

"And it is said if one sails from Bergen due west to Hvarf in Greenland that one's course will lie somewhere seventy or more miles south of Iceland."

And if one sails from Hernar in Norway?

"... one must sail a direct course west to Hvarf in Greenland, in which case one sails north of Shetland so that one sights land in clear weather only, then south of the Faroes so that the sea looks halfway up the mountainsides, then south of Iceland so that one gets sight of birds and whales from there." Makes sailing across the North Atlantic sound like negotiating the neighborhoods of a city.

Eirik and his party came upon the forbidding peaks of east Greenland, judged it best not to confront them, and sailed around to the south. Starting up the southwest coast, they picked a place to winter, and in spring moved to a preferable spot along a fjord and named it Eiriksfjord.

He returned to Iceland to recruit colonists, calling his country Greenland both because in those days the fjords really were green, and for marketing reasons, because "men might be eager to go there if the land had a good name." In 985 about 500 people set sail on 25 ships, knorrs laden with passengers and provisions including horses and cattle and sheep. Fourteen ships arrived.

And thus Eirik the triple murderer, whom we know as Eirik the Red, settled in to rule perhaps 350 hardy Icelanders on their farmsteads in two settlements on the island of Greenland.

A thousand years ago in Greenland there was nothing but room. Eirik built his farm Brattahlíð, "steep meadow," in fine pasture land and the voyage's others survivors likewise claimed land at the heads of fjords. They had reached the farthest outpost of European civilization.

Eirik's sailing coincided with climatic warming, and the settlers found willow scrub for fodder and fuel, and rowan and birch trees. Birds provided eggs, meat and feathers for insulation. Reindeer delighted the settlers from Iceland, where there were no such animals. In time, scouting to the north, the settlers found walrus and narwhal and polar bears.

The part of Iceland where Eirik had lived, at Drangar in the northwest, had been hardscrabble, and to the first settlers Greenland was a green land indeed. They appeared to have the country to themselves.

Gwyn Jones writes in *A History of the Vikings* that "when the great Atlantic voyages of discovery and exploration took place in the ninth and tenth centuries the North had neither compass nor chart."

So how did these ill-clad but fearless seamen do it? How did they slip the fetters of land and cast themselves onto the deep, the great unknown, and time and again finally scrape hull on new shores? How did Eirik's band of twice-outcast find Greenland?

To start, they used a fundamental Norse principle: Make the shortest predictable ocean passage.

## NAVIGATORS AS ROCK STARS

In Newfoundland a century and a half ago sealing captains were rock stars; Similarly, in an ancient Viking dressing room one might expect to find bowls with just the red M&Ms. People followed their careers and kept stats on their performance. Sitting around the local bar drinking mead a thousand years ago, Norse seamen might have bragged on their favorite navigators like men do today about their favorite quarterbacks.

Norse sailors shared knowledge with the Polynesians half a world away that the curve of the horizon limits islands' visibility to a distance of about 60 miles. The little island museum practically at antipodes in the Pacific, in Rapa Nui, declares that in their day, Polynesian sailors could "see" land within 32 to 48 kilometers before they could actually see it on the horizon, and within hundreds of kilometers for an archipelago. If you count that as true on either side of an island it's fair to estimate a nearly 100 kilometer greater "footprint" than an island's true size.

To the South Pacific seafarer islands set up detectable variations in wave patterns and ocean swells. Clouds formed into towering cumulus banks over mountain peaks, and the practiced eye could even detect changes in the color of the sky due to reflection off land. Floating logs, seaweed and other detritus signaled land.

The Polynesians watched sea birds. Petrels and terns flew a known distance from land and returned each night. Albatrosses tended to stay at sea, but some returned to nest in the late afternoons and in ancient times navigators studied them with a keen eye.

We know that northern explorers brought birds to release and follow to the nearest land. The Sagas tell of one Floki Vilgerdarson who set out from Norway on the first specific attempt to settle Iceland guided by three ravens with the ability to smell land and, in the legend, Floki became "Raven-Floki."

Gwyn Jones writes that 24 hours of sailing could accomplish 120 miles. For longer voyages a mariner needed to fix latitude. He could sail a fixed latitude by following the sun and the North Star, but there was a more precise method still.

An Icelander named Star-Oddi compiled detailed tables of the sun's latitude at midday for each week of the year as observed in Northern Iceland in the late 900s (coinciding nicely with Leif Erickson's purported landing in North America in 1001). How to carry such knowledge in a time when runes, most often carved in unwieldy wood or stone, ruled the day?

Perhaps there was no need. The Norse devised a before-its-time device called a bearing dial, little more than a marked stick, which would give the navigator an indication of his latitude as compared with a known place.

By holding a bearing dial level a captain could hold a course by observing the shadow cast by a stick in the center of the disc, which was notched to correspond to points on the horizon. This could set a course to a known destination but, importantly too, it could aid in returning from newly discovered lands. A Danish archeologist named C. L. Vebæk discovered half a disc of wood "marked with equidistant notches" in a convent in Narsarsuaq opposite Brattahlíð in 1948.

A cousin of the bearing dial, the sol-skuggafjöl, or "sun shadow board," was a round piece of wood sailors floated in water to insure the wood remained level. Concentric circles were drawn around a pin in the center (that could be moved up or down with the seasons, the sun being higher in the sky in summer and lower in winter). At the sun's highest point in the sky each day the shadow of the pin would fall inside or outside the circles. A practiced eye could ascertain whether the ship was too far north or south.

•••••

As we have seen, there is a phenomenon in the field of atmospheric optics that Norse sailors may also have used to move from island to island: polar mirages. Light travels in straight lines under normal atmospheric conditions, but its path is dependent on the density of the air through which it passes, which varies, so light's path may be distorted.

This can have the effect of drawing up images from beyond the horizon. An ancient navigator familiar with this phenomenon might have used it to reckon the proximity of land beyond.

From the earliest days have come reports that both Iceland and Greenland may be seen at once, and there have been a number of such reports by modern sailors when in the middle of the Denmark Strait at about 68 degrees north latitude.This phenomenon could have been used to boost a wave-wracked crew's sense of safety and well being, by relaying information from well beyond the normal horizon.

The earliest lore and some maps of the discovery of Greenland are marked by non-existent small islands, skerries. The researchers W. H. Lehn and I. I. Schroeder  suggest, "The possibility that the skerries were but distorted images of land beyond the horizon should be seriously considered." The legend of the Gunnbjorn Skerries seems to have originated in northwest Iceland, from whence the first Greenlanders sailed.

Both the Groenlendinga Saga and Eirik's Saga say that "Eirik, when banished from Iceland, sailed west to seek out the skerries seen by Gunnbjorn when he was windblown on his voyage around Iceland."

The skerries may have simply been accepted for what they probably were - predictors of land.

•••••

## GETTING TO WEST GREENLAND

Greenland is to the Kingdom of Denmark as Tahiti is to France. There's considerable home rule, with a 27-seat Parliament. Copenhagen is suzerain, maintains the courts and subsidizes prices. When we visited the only convenient access was via SAS from Copenhagen.

•••••

Approaching Greenland's gateway airport at Kangerlussuaq, you fly
across mountains of rock, covered nearly to the top with snow.
Nothing else. No people down there. not a tree. No highways. You get
around by air, ferry or dog sled. 55,000 people, all living around the
coast.

Kangerlussuaq Airport, on the Canadian side of the ice sheet, lies on a
coastal plain between bare hills alongside a sandy sluice that's also
called Kangerlussuaq, or the long fjord, 105 miles from the sea. The ice
cap is 17 miles east. Kangerlussuaq isn't a city. It's just the airport.

The oldest rocks anywhere are here and if you could get at the soil
underneath the ice cap you'd find it (they think) billions of years old.
They say the ice is so thick and heavy and it's been pressing on the
center of the island so long that the interior may be up to 360 meters
below sea level.

•••••

Northbound to Ilulissat, 25o kilometers above the Arctic Circle, we sat
in a jam-packed DeHavilland including two seats of mail. For a time we
weren't sure of getting seats.

"The mail," explained the ticket clerk, "has priority here."

Glacial lakes – tarns - skipped from the ice cap to the shore. Mineral
laden fjords turned every shade of aqua, kelp, deep blue, almost
brown. Mere meters separated deep, seductively dark blue tarns from
sluicy gray, narrow channels that wound down to Baffin Bay.

Twenty-five minutes outside Ilulissat icebergs appeared offshore. Hard
to tell how tall they were, hard to find a reference, and road number
one was nowhere. I thought of the middle of the outback, just
unedifying, useless land - here without brush, with icebergs instead.

Like Tasiilaq, none of Ilulissat had a plan. Built on an uneven, rocky promontory, it sprawled out of control (in a modest-sized way) not with roads so much as trails between boulders.

I was the only passenger on the bus into town and finally the driver stopped, turned around and wondered, "Where you want to go?" I didn't know, so I popped out where we were, at Super 1 market.

You'd be surprised what you could buy there: Tomatoes, bags of mean little onions and dull potatoes, dill and one stout yellow melon. Withered yellow and red and green bell peppers, un-bought and forlorn, apparently didn't salve the Inuit palate.

•••••

The same working freighter *Sophie Kristina* we saw in Tasiilaq sat docked, drowsy red, at harbor. Massive, appalling heaps of trash lined the docks. Maybe it was just a collection problem. Maybe snow covered the stuff most of the time. But just now trash stood as high as the dumpsters along the waterfront.

I set out up the hill toward the glacier. Now this glacier, that presses from the ice cap down the fjord to the sea, is the most prolific calving glacier outside Antarctica. They'll nod earnestly over astounding statistics, like that the amount of water frozen in the ice that's pushed out into Disko Bay every day would supply New York City for a year. And the bergs loom over town, moving and shifting with the current, changing colors with the angle of the sun. It takes over an hour to sail across the mouth of the fjord.

I swore I heard gunshots. A lone fishing boat bobbed offshore. I sat on a rock and stared. It happened again, a couple times more. I couldn't make out whether the fisherman had a rifle and what was he doing anyway, shooting fish?

Turned out those were no gunshots. They were just oxygen under pressure, escaping from the ice. Happens all the time.

Up on the hills you'd hear the sled dogs. They'd yip, and the men were a whistlin' lot. Yippin' and whistlin' and poppin'.

•••••

On rocks or wooden pallets or just debris without order, sled dogs lay sleeping, bedraggled, summering in chains. I walked home past wooden houses all shades of blue through green, and red through peach into yellow. All deep shades, all stained wood. Fish dried on wooden frames. Sometimes two dogsleds were stacked one atop the other, or three, baby-mama-papa bear style.

At dismal brown housing blocks, a couple played with their baby with a line of beer bottles up on their ledge. A frame hung over one ledge for drying fish. A huge reindeer skull and antlers, too. And on all of the balconies, the laundry. In summer, I guess, every day is laundry day in Ilulissat.

I ducked around a bucket truck and had to scoot to avoid a front-end loader. A working town. Mini-buses from the three hotels, too many taxis and bulky trucks plied the roads. Trucks with rusty brown tanks, a Volvo earth mover pounding at the roadside, paving equipment. And the cars the Politi drive, primarily for carrying their wives around town.

Ilullissat is a little bigger than you might think, maybe 4,500 good people, unkempt by background but not down at the heels. Celine Dion and Spice Girls T-shirts were here (I'm sorry), but the people owned the road.

In fact, Ilulissat was quiet and content, although you always felt the looming presence of the icebergs. The gravity of the whole place was just drawn down to the icebergs.

•••••

Icebergs on a midnight cruise from Ilulissat

About a dozen of us cruised toward the glacier under the half-an-hour-before-midnight Arctic sun. It was biting cold out there between building-sized blocks of ice.

A clumsy, gregarious Turk won over the crew. Said he was working on a magazine article about the people of the north. He'd already done Kamchatka, Alaska and Baffin Island, and meant to do Svalbard the next spring.

The crew thought they'd be famous and took us out to walk on an iceberg.

They tried to find seals.

"What do I need seals?" the Turk confided. "Other places where they don't kill 'em, they come right to you."

•••••

The sun hung fifteen degrees over the horizon at one o'clock in the morning, and then it never went down, slowly rolling to rise up again and be bright the next morning. But at that one o'clock hour, with the sun low, near horizontal, the colors of the ice changed by the minute, with crevasses deep green and purple. Like your fingerprints - no two views the same, day to day, even hour to hour. Every day forever, bergs drifted, cliffs broke off and fell and changed.

But man, right through your gloves, it was screaming bloody freezing cold.

• • • • •

## ILIMANAQ

In the new day we set sail with Hans and Edward, south across the mouth of the fjord to a settlement called Ilimanaq. The mosquitoes were so thick through the window, they blew around in the wind. As he helped us aboard, Edward put out his hand and brightly offered, "This is not guides."

We told him, "No problem." He smiled in relief and went below to brew coffee.

Steering a trawler across the mouth of a calving glacier ain't cake. You don't just point and shoot. You juke around tons of ice, most of it invisible underwater.

In 45 minutes Ilulissat had disappeared and it was just Edward, Hans, the gulls, Mirja and me and the ice. One lonely fishing dinghy bobbed out toward the open bay.

An ice-fringed blue chop kicked up under the hull and bounced our ship. The bigger icebergs were at our backs and the wind pressed down the glacier valley. Open water. We walked around the little boat to stay in the sun.

Edward and Hans. "This is not guides."

Edward, with hair, not mustache, over his lip, more or less in English, made me know he was from Christiansund, the next town of any size south of Ilulissat. He'd been to Denmark twice but wouldn't want to live there and always wanted to stay in Greenland. Watch the daily iceberg show and you'll understand why, he said.

"Is there government in Ilimanaq?" I asked.

A blank look.

I searched for another word. "Politi?"

"Maybe." Edward had never thought about it.

"How many people there?"

*Bill Murray*

Vast blankness.

"A hundert?"

"Not so much."

"What do the people do?"

"Only fishing."

Quiet for a while. Light flashed across Edward's face, followed by a rueful shake of the head. "Two-hour boat ride," he ruminated, "too far!"

He meant from the civilization of Ilulissat.

•••••

Mirja and I counted twenty-one buildings scattered up the hill, including the houses and the building by the dock and the church and I think we may have missed a few, but not many.

A leisurely walk among the houses, all pitch-roofed, up a hill to the cemetery, icebergs bobbing by, stepping through moss, lichens, spores, whatever grows closer to the ground than grass, all fiery yellow, pale green, flaky black and brown and burnt red, so thick and boggy that if you stepped just here or just there you were liable to sink half an inch, or even two inches.

At Post Kalaallitt Allakkeriviat, you could rent P.O. boxes numbers 501 to 530. There was a store (closed for lunch) and a toilet and, I guess if there was any town administration, you'd have found it there.

•••••

The Arctic Hotel Ice Rock Bar in Ilulissat is the only bar I know with an iceberg view. Ice Rock rocked in cigarette smoke, late. High summer meant something up here. Happy hour was from 22:00 to 23:00.

A drunken man pumped my hand so hard when I told him where I was from he made me glad to be American. I decided in the end he was just weary of the constant dribble of tourists from nowhere but Denmark. Sick o' Danes.

•••••

## FALLING IN WITH WILLY AND THE GERMANS

Back at Ataa we woke to hard rain. We heard it on the window overnight, in our sleeping bags on our bunk beds in the barracks with Silva. All of the tourist wonders nearby were out of the question in this weather and Silva was already scheming to pass us off onto the boatload of Germans so he wouldn't have to sail us back to Ilulissat.

And we did fall in with Willy, the captain of the German excursion, and his passengers and crew. Trouble was, they weren't bound for Ilulissat, but rather Rodebay.

When Willy came into the yellow hut for coffee, Silva set upon him. His passengers would rather be in Ilulissat than Rodebay on a day like today, wouldn't they, and Willy told Silva that he'd have to ask them, but in any event he'd take us, so Silva waved off any other complications.

•••••

By eleven we were at sea, ten of us, southbound in the rain toward Ilulissat. Willy's boat was the *Maya Qaqqaq*, from Nuuk, built for twelve, and we all sat comfortable and dry, listening to a tape of German sailing songs, three women and two men, the paying passengers, our captain Willy and his Greenlandic wife Kala (who had just had brain surgery and who slept below among the luggage), Anja the cook, and Mirja and me.

Forty-six degrees in the rain.

•••••

Dutch whalers disemboweled their catch up on the rocks of Rodebay, or "Red Bay." Just now tents perched up there on the rocks and Willy told us it was Amasat season. Amasat, a small native fish, only came here for two or three weeks, which were now ending.

Fishermen pitched tents, caught the Amasat and laid them out to dry. They're easy to catch in season. Just scoop them from the back of your boat with a net. Willy liked them fried.

We were one of three boats calling at Rodebay, joining a small passenger ship and the cargo ship *Aqipi Ittuk*, which was delivering diesel fuel. I think the three ships in the harbor doubled Rodebay's population.

Settlements like this are workmanlike places, short on aesthetics, and none really puts its best face on for the new arrival. Harbors are ringed with tanks for fuel and oil.

In Rodebay there was no river to the sea. Willy remembered that boats used to bring in the town's drinking water from ice melt, but now they had a desalination building. There was a school with six pupils. If you ever wanted cozy, you wanted it here, but space heaters and heat from oil afforded all the warmth to be had.

The roof of the Rodebay hostel was painted "H8." Rubber boots, knee high, and solid bright colored rain-breakers were the uniforms of modern Rodebay.

We dropped anchor as the radio crackled, "Maya Maya Ataa Maya," and it was Silva asking about the weather. In Ataa, his weather was "not good."

Anja prepared a fish and cucumber lunch. Bobbing around at anchor, they had a long German tête-à-tête about where to spend the night. But suddenly and above all else, excitement! A seal, dragged up on a rock, just off Rodebay town.

Willy dispatched the Zodiac off the back of the boat and we sped over to stand with a man with a knife and the seal on that rock. Four feet long, that seal was no more than a year or two old.

The Greenland seal mates in Labrador, and in summer comes over here to be killed and cut up. So we all perched on that rainy rock and watched a boy with a red Gronlandsfly cap, knee-high boots and a foot-long knife slit the seal, neck to anus, peel the skin away, slop its bowels onto the rock and cut flank and butt steaks.

A boy, a ten year old, packed the steaks in black plastic. He left spine, whiskers and feet, and the sea gradually came up and reclaimed them from the rock while we had lunch.

The seal kill at Rodebay

I don't know the disposition of this particular seal, whether the profit motive of the Europeans has seized and carried away the traditions of the Inuit of modern-day west Greenland, but the Inuit over on Ammassalik Island in Johannes Hansen's day - as with the modern-day Faroese Grindadráp - shared and shared alike.

Hansen: "The heathens share the catch with each other. The person who caught the seal just gets the head and one flipper for himself, or, if there are a particularly large number of outsiders present, the head alone. When a bundle of dried meat is brought forth, the wife of the owner splits it into as many pieces as there are people in the house, whereafter the man goes round and gives each of the men their share ... and nobody views anything as completely their own."

•••••

In the end, the touring Germans opted for a hostel in Ilulissat over a hut in Rodebay, and so about four o'clock we sailed away, skirting the shore because it was deeper there, until icebergs blocked the way.

Willy peered into the radar and he exclaimed, "Aye, there's rocks fifty centimeters below the keel!" We skirted them ever so slowly and the rain ended, and we sailed on past Ilulissat back into the mouth of the glacier.

Fantastic blue veins ran the whole way through some icebergs. Willy explained: These occur when the age-old ice cracks and water rushes in to fill the cracks. The white bergs are full of air - not dense, and the water, much denser, freezes blue. The white of the bergs is in large part due to the air trapped between snowflakes that fell thousands of years ago.

We had a go around the mouth of the glacier. Willy pointed out the pointy-topped bergs as the most dangerous. They haven't fallen over yet, their center of gravity is high, they're more unstable.

He told a gripping story about how he'd been hired some years back on this very spot to put in divers who would push around a "periscope" for a helicopter to film as the closing scene in a German movie.

He took his place and was set to put out the divers when the helicopter, inexplicably, barreled overhead and crashed upside down into the water not thirty meters in front of his boat. The divers rescued the pilot and pulled him onto the *Maya*, and "a handful of brains" of the cameraman, who, it seems, had caused the crash by hitting some forbidden switches with his foot.

In the frenzy of rescue, Willy didn't think to try to videotape it, but once he did sell a tape of a disaster at Umummaq, to Real TV, for $1,500, and he's sure he could've gotten more. An iceberg broke apart near Umummaq harbor and a dozen or more boats were swamped, though nobody, miraculously, was hurt. I thought back to Silva grabbing his video camera and cursing every time an iceberg split, always getting into place too late.

Now Willy stopped to drift as near to a berg as he dared, and went aft to dip a bucket into the water until he retrieved a bobbing basketball of ice that he picked into pieces. We all shared martinis poured over glacial ice that popped and snapped as the heat of Willy's boat freed oxygen as old as man.

"Zum Wohl!"

Three-hundred-thousand year old air popping in our glasses - The sound of Greenland.

## THE END OF NORSE GREENLAND

The Dorset people yielded to the Thule, then the Inuit. Inuit settlements died out over the centuries in bad winter or bad hunting years, save for a few thousand tenacious, remaining souls.

Over the course of hundreds of years the fearsome Norse cast their mighty presence clear across the North Atlantic from the Scandinavian peninsula to North America.

But by around 1500 the Norse had disappeared from Greenland. How did it come to pass? Once they had been invincible. At Lindisfarne they were so fearsome they caused the English theologian Alcuin to wail, "is this the beginning of the great suffering ... before the end of the world?"

They ran the Westmen off from Iceland. They founded communities in Greenland and all the way to Vinland in today's Newfoundland (we will visit the settlement site shortly). Yet they abandoned Vinland after only a few winters and for this, I think the explanation is clear enough.

Simply, Leif, son of Eirik the Red, and his band of explorers of North America, never mustered enough fellows for robust settlements and the settlements they did establish came under attack from the local Skrælings, as we will see. They were at the tenuous end of a grown-thin supply line.

But what about Greenland? What caused its demise? What ill swept down upon those once entrenched souls to consign them to their demise? Evidence suggests the Greenlanders became detached from the east. How did it come to pass?

Leif's expeditions west were probably in search of resources like wood. It was easier for the Icelanders to go to Norway for lumber than to sail around to the far side of Greenland, and in Norway there were other goods they wouldn't find in Greenland.

Kristen Seaver thinks that "wealthy and ambitious Icelanders became increasingly drawn into the orbit of Norwegian power politics and in the end appear to have lost all interest in their Greenland cousins."

She believes that the Greenlanders never stopped crossing the Davis Strait to North America for lumber. For one thing, driftwood long soaked in salt water, their only other source of wood for building, lost its bendability, becoming less worthy of use in shipbuilding than "seasoned lumber that could be made to take a proper curve."

She thinks that aside from a costly shipload all the way from Norway, the only decent-sized logs at the Greenlanders' disposal were those washed up by the sea - or those known to be available across the Davis Strait.

So without their Icelandic cousins, perhaps they did fall out of touch and orient themselves to the west. One way or another, the settlements at Brattahlíð and farther north disappeared.

Jared Diamond's theory has all the Norse Greenlanders dying after burning all their firewood. The Pulitzer prize winning author of *Guns, Germs and Steel* uses the same argument for the demise of the Mangarevans who settled Rapa Nui.

He imagines the European Greenlanders allowing their imported cattle to trample any budding replacement wood. The short growing season would have worked against tree replenishment.

Diamond blames the Norse for, unlike the Inuit, never learning how to use seal and whale oil to light and heat their homes, which would have saved burning trees. He makes a solid case that the Inuit adapted to the land more fully than the Norse, learning to make buildings, igloos, out of snow, hunting a wider variety of animals for food, using sled dogs for transportation and animal skins to stretch over boats, allowing for sea hunting of whales.

There is another possibility. Kristen Seaver: "... it was more than a coincidence that the Norse Greenland colony came to an end just when North Atlantic exploration touched it closely."

In the late fifteenth century, besides Columbus and his Caribbean adventures, business interests organized to explore the lands to the west, including shippers from Bristol, England, and Portuguese sailors. These two groups crossed paths. She concludes that some remaining Greenlanders fell in with those expeditions:

"... both circumstantial evidence and common sense suggest that the Greenlanders, who had so clearly taken active part in the North Atlantic economic community throughout the fifteenth century, had remained opportunists to the end and joined the early-sixteenth-century European surge toward North America."

Where we are headed next.

*Bill Murray*

# PART FIVE: CANADA, AND A BIT OF FRANCE IN NORTH AMERICA

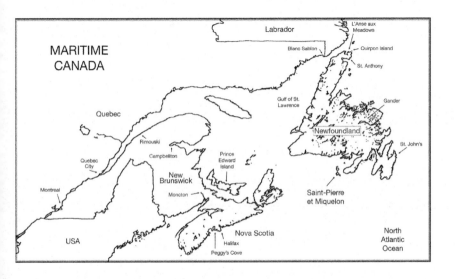

*Bill Murray*

## NIGHT TRAIN TO HALIFAX

We're off for the very northern bit of Newfoundland opposite frozen Labrador, and then just a little bit beyond, to a lighthouse turned tiny inn on the island of Quirpon near a place called L'Anse aux Meadows, the spot Leif Eriksson and his crew wintered over a thousand years ago. En route we will drop in on the fair capital of Nova Scotia, take a little spin through Newfoundland and visit the only remaining French territory in North America, the curious little exclave of Saint-Pierre. We start underground in Montreal.

There aren't many trains on the taiga. The only service to Canada's north creeps along for two days out of Winnipeg, crossing the Manitoba prairie at an average of just 28 kilometers per hour because of the track's disrepair, to a town called Churchill, on the western shore of Hudson Bay.

Rail fans will be frustrated in Atlantic Canada, too, where the only remaining passenger route is Montreal to Halifax. Branded The Ocean with a prominent logo of the lighthouse at Peggy's Cove, this is VIA Rail's overnight service from Montreal, riding up along the St. Lawrence Seaway then back down across New Brunswick to Nova Scotia and Halifax, the eastern terminus of a national rail system that stretches 3,900 miles back to Prince Rupert, tucked up under Alaska on the Pacific coast.

They queue by the down escalator, twenty people under the "Halifax" sign. A lonesome overweight man in a dirty orange T-shirt drops his very odd Hello Kitty paraphernalia around his legs and settles in beside a nun. We watch from a cafe where two women whose profiles tend toward an undisciplined horizontal enjoy poutine, a dish with French Canadian origins comprising french fries, cheese curds and gravy.

As poutine has spread across Canada and come into its own, variants have popped up, like Mexican poutine with jalapenos. These ample ladies enjoy their poutine with full-throated laughs and full-sugar Pepsis. A couple of days in Quebec's main city suggest an obesity

Bill Murray

problem, if not quite the U.S. epidemic. Perhaps poutine is contributory.

(For $14, the 200-seat harborside Hart and Thistle Gastropub in Halifax offers an egregious underutilization of lobster, Lobster Poutine Nova Scotia: Lobster morsels, cheese curds and lobster bisque topped with Bernaise. Over fries.)

By the late date I set out to reserve a train compartment, the regular sleepers were bought solid, consigning us to a room with two beds in the observation car at the back of the train, the 20th car. When I observe that we've thrown as much money at ViaRail as we can, the nice lady at check-in looks at the ticket and nods.

"Yes you have." And she stifles a smile.

The clerks (who become attendants on the train) start off on their back feet, defensive because the train is late and, they say, "in the shop." They introduce Stefan, the observation car boss, who apologizes that our sleeping compartment shares a wall with the bar, but promises he will close it down at 11:00, and in any case the bar almost never has anyone in it because the windows are higher than the tables and this is the observation car. So people take their drinks to the room in back with the big windows.

"Canada we stand on guard for thee" adorns the station wall, from the national anthem, and flags stand as honor guards around the periphery. Suburban trains deliver bustle, people hurry by and the PA booms through. Noise bounces through Montreal station and it smells of axle grease.

One end opens to underground shopping that spreads under buildings clear across Montreal. A Banque Nationale branch anchors one wall and the liquor store sells excellent padded carry-out bags.

This station is clean. Like Canada.

•••••

Across Canada, even potentially ordinary provincial airports like Winnipeg's host flights to exotic-sounding places, in Winnipeg's case jet service to Rankin Inlet and Thompson "and the most frequent flights in the Kivalliq region, courtesy of CalmAir." From Montreal, in sedate contrast, you may pick from three destinations by train: Ottawa, Toronto and Halifax.

The terminal is a cavern big and roomy with plenty of space to grow, as if there may be someday more exotic places to go. For now all the routes end with white people who talk like Minnesotans.

Time passes. It is boarding time, then it is departure time and nothing moves. Mind you, it is Monday, we have until Saturday to get to Halifax and we are here to enjoy the train, so when I wander over to the check-in stand to inquire about departure I'm just asking, but the little man who smells fresh off a cigarette break holds tight to what he knows. No information coming from this guy.

The queue at the escalator grows, and I wonder what you win standing for an hour to get to your little compartment a minute before the others. People stand in the departure lounge jammed to standing room when there are bars, restaurants and newsstands, though the Canadian newspaper business hangs close to collapse right alongside the American.

*The Globe and Mail*, "Canada's National Newspaper," (circulation 291,571 in 2013), is Canada's answer to *USA Today*, perhaps a dash more substance but heavy today on back-to-school advice, "a wonderful story about fathers," and "tips on how to sculpt your shoulders."

Good humor prevails except among the sweaty officials around the service desk, heads down and shoulders up eyeing their papers, now hoping for a 7:15 departure instead of the scheduled 6:30.

When finally we roll out from underground and into the air, crimson twilight saturates the sky behind the CN Canadian National Railroad building and the Marriott and rolling stock that reads "Alberta." Right away we are out over the St. Lawrence River, leaving Ile de Montreal parallel to a highway bridge with 79 streetlights before I lose count.

Fleeting time to enjoy the view though, because by the time the plastic flute of welcome champagne comes and goes and *The Ocean* gains speed beyond the VW and Kia dealerships on the outskirts and we have our briefing on the three steps to opening the train door in an emergency, it is dark.

They attach domed observation cars like this for crossing iconic places, up to Prince Rupert in British Columbia or over the Rocky Mountains on the train they call the *Mountaineer*. They may put on five on that route but *The Ocean* has just one, manned by our slight, prematurely graying Stefan.

Stefan is on his fourth career and proud of it. He started in photography and enjoyed taking pictures, but didn't enjoy the commercial bit, so he and his wife chucked that and taught English as a second language in Istanbul and Seoul, and they loved Istanbul so much they might retire to Turkey.

Then he tried artisanal woodworking for a time, made furniture, and now his wife has settled into teaching language immersion to first graders in Halifax, and he works *The Ocean* train.

"I'm older than I look," he explains.

The crew calls him "Steff." With well-worn, practiced humor, Steff says we will work up an appetite on the nearly train-long walk to the dining car.

There are four compartments in the observation car, two of them occupied. Our quarters has a fine panoramic picture window, a solid two and a half feet by at least five, and two armchairs yield to two single beds in an "L" shape, fixed up by Stefan while we dine. We will have to wait for morning to see if there is anything out there to justify the observation car, because as we slide through suburbs all we can see are headlights blocked at level crossings in the dark.

On the hike to the dining end of the train we pass a wrought conversation about a missing wallet. The unfortunate Mrs. Ross is quite upset. This has Mirja round-eyed and grabbing my arm, because she thinks Mrs. Ross says it is a missing woman, not a missing wallet. I can see how she might hear it that way, owing to Mirja's English as a second language and Mrs. Ross's quavering voice.

Linen napkins, plastic water cups. Little lighthouses on the glass panels that separate the tables. Sole, pork or chicken. Petty choices: risotto with this, potatoes with that, seasonal vegetables, all overcooked like you might eat at Piccadilly Cafeteria (I imagine, because I haven't eaten at Piccadilly since I was fifteen.)

The attendant waddles down the aisle sizing us up, who is sourdough and who is multigrain? His tie has a pattern of little canaries, he has lots of post cards in his breast pocket, and his belly peeks out under his uniform shirt. I pick multigrain and I'm pleased to think he approves. Served with Scottsburn beurre from Scottsburn, Nova Scotia.

We have a good look at the passengers like we can't get back in the observation car, a place not everyone cares to walk twenty cars back to experience. We find a multicultural and pleasing group, foursomes of all stripes: Asian, Indian, festive, fat. Twosomes, elderly, young, bleached. A single man listening to us surreptitiously who sucks through his straw until it slurps and furtively looks, I'm afraid, more at me than at Mirja. A Korean man too large for his seat with a diminutive pink lady, older, bored with it all.

Outside, Tim Horton's and Essos, wet streets and headlights. Tandem trucks.

*The Ocean* stops somewhere between stations for a reason obscure. Hiking back from the dining car we happen by an open door and three train workers smoking outside.

We pop out and hear about ViaRail's coming decrease in service between Montreal and Halifax from six to three days a week.

*Bill Murray*

We stand amid a near insurrection. The youngest of the three smokers expects to be fired and resents it. The oldest, with 28 years' service, "certainly hopes" his service time will save his job. Based on performance, on his caustic treatment of passengers and his loud dismay at his lot in life, this man might be the best to go.

The maritime provinces haven't the political clout of the resource-rich plains, provinces with energy resources. This service cut is a political decision that sparks widespread resentment in these late days of Stephen Harper, not only among the employees waiting for the ax, but also, it turns out, among a wide swath of the passengers.

The liberal contingent back in the lounge car castigates Harper as extra-constitutional and dictatorial, trying to explain Harper's use of an opaque Parliamentary maneuver known a prorogation to avoid a no-confidence vote in 2008, suspending the Parliament again the next year and having lost a contempt-of-Parliament vote in March of the previous year.

The venom of poisoned politics strikes me as odd in a land of calm and manners. Especially when you sit up in the bubbletop running among golf courses, deep woods and bays, with nothing but blue hair and bald spots before you.

•••••

Train travel narcotizes. The rails' rhythm induces a calm that always makes me reluctant to shake off sleep. Shortly after six a.m. I lift the window shade and the first thing I see is a sign, "Welcome to New Brunswick." All night we'd run alongside the St. Lawrence, past Quebec City where the river becomes formidable, broadening from 1,000 meters to dozens of miles in width, then east and south, leaving the river.

*The Ocean* left the St. Lawrence in the night and crossed a sylvan thumb of Quebec called the Gaspé Peninsula from Rimouski, on the St. Lawrence, inland to Campbellton, across the river Restigouche that for a time defines the Quebec/New Brunswick border. Rimouski derives

228

from the Mi'kmaq Indian "Land of the Moose," and the moose herd in the wildlife reserve has increased over fifteen years, enough to allow seasonal hunting.

From Rimouski a ship called the M/V Nordik Express sails a 1150-kilometer cargo route up the seaway and calls on the northern shore, at places like Port-Menier, named for a French chocolate-maker settler and Tête-à-la-Baleine, a town of 350 named for an island resembling a whale head.

The Nordik welcomes passengers to "Explore the villages while the crew loads and unloads the cargo." It calls in places like Kegaska, where the Nordik recommends:

- Roads of crushed clamshells
- Fish factory
- Wreck of the Brion

and La Tabatière and Baie-des-Moutons, where you can see:

- Fish and scallop factory (sea scallops)
- Robertson family foundry and cemetery

At Campbellton the fast flowing Restigouche (not to be confused with the other New Brunswick Rivers Bouctouche or Pokemouche) empties into Chaleur Bay, the largest bay, and on into the Gulf of St. Lawrence. Jacques Cartier named Chaleur Bay ("warm" in French) when he explored hereabouts in 1534. Pretty much everywhere between Montreal and the Gaspé Peninsula was named either by or for Jacques Cartier.

A 55-year-old steel truss bridge crosses the Restigouche into Campbellton, where one seven-story building dwarfs the rest. Then the usual stuff, a Sobey's Supermarket, a bank, two church steeples and alongside the bridge, a Howard Johnson's. In the center of town, visible from the train, a little man in the town's radio station sits behind glass, right there on Main Street, playing disc jockey.

When I did that a long time ago they used to put us in those display enclosures too, so you could never, oh, I don't know, lay on the floor and nap. You always had to present as respectable and that is pretty funny, looking back.

The sight of this fellow - too far away to tell if he is young or old - registers as funny, too, tending to poignant. Campbellton is small enough that working in that little studio at dawn on a Tuesday morning couldn't endow even enough celebrity to satisfy a nine-year-old boy's dreams. That is just Carl sitting in there, at work.

•••••

It must be loud to drive a train, always laying on that blasted horn at every Godforsaken rural farm track. I expect train engineers' hearing holds up right alongside heavy metal guitarists.

And then we come to run fast along Chaleur Bay between stands of trees, in August's last days just beyond full green forest sliding toward yellow. That birch trees are not predominant is just about the only difference between this part of New Brunswick and the part of Finland I know, where we have a little cabin.

The light has a northern cant, a Finnish cast. The water on the bay is still, the clouds low, and it feels like _The Ocean_ is moving to burn up some track, making up for its late start.

The bubbletop puts you above the rest of the train. At 6 a.m. (which becomes 7 at the New Brunswick border) there is no sign of anyone moving on the train, but fresh and aromatic coffee in the urn. So I sit alone with my coffee (and the marteau d'urgence, the emergency hammer), in the front seats of the bubble, watching the train spread up the track in twists and turns, 17 cars and two engines - enough metal roofs for a cinematic action adventure sword fight.

We run alongside the backsides of prim little New England bungalows with siding and decks. I wouldn't feel comfortable sitting out there with people riding by a few dozen meters away. I wonder if they just get used to it. Probably no one who rides by ever comes back to visit.

*The Ocean* left Montreal station an hour and ten minutes late, and now runs just half an hour behind. Stefan knows this because of a walkie-talkie on his hip that I could have done without. Everybody who works on the bloody train has one and needs to confer constantly.

Stefan says look in the bogs and marshes for moose, and there are usually seals visible just along this part of Chaleur Bay, but I see neither, and that holds until the very top end of Newfoundland's Great Northern Peninsula.

*The Ocean* stops and blocks a road. It is a single track, so we aren't on a siding waiting for an oncoming train to pass. I can't make out why we would stop but I have no responsibilities and refill my coffee. A different story for the drivers, for whom it is time to get to work. Damned train.

•••••

Then the train is awake and people are about. The clouds are broken and scattered. There will be no sun. Discreet little fog banks scud along close to the ground, bands of their own.

Moncton. Biggest place in New Brunswick, population 64,128. Low unemployment, call centers for UPS, Exxon, Fairmont Hotels and others, and Moncton Center, the Canadian air traffic control facility that handles flights after they arrive from over the Atlantic.

A small cluster of mid-rises in the center, a five-story, a seven, two eights, a ten-story Crown Plaza and one bona-fide twenty-floor building with the corporate logo of Assumption Life. A mast with microwave links, shopping on one side of the station and an open, weedy field on the other side of the train.

Plenty of time to get out, stretch and admire all the parking lots. One couldn't-be-anything-but-government building flies a Canadian flag.

Moncton looks built inside itself in a northern way, walled off from the winter cold - and you can just about feel the gaunt bleakness of winter, snow drifting across empty parking lots in afternoon half light.

Leaving Moncton we are invited by advertising to enjoy "K945.CA, Today's Best Music." The St. Bernard's Roman Catholic Church looks ancient - and French Fries Plus does not.

•••••

By this time they have done lectures in the bubbletop, Steff and a man from Parks Canada who came aboard at Rogerstown and left at Moncton. Lobsters and lobster traps, the Acadians, and a general piece about Canadian parks during which I learn that 35 beaver pelts used to get you a shotgun and ten, a gallon of whiskey. This during a stretch of straight-line track, marsh and sphagnum bog (where curious, carnivorous pitcher plants grow) and birch trees only cut back a couple of meters from the train.

I love these north woods. Calm, deep and welcoming, you feel you could stroll about all day without the thick air, free from being sucked and bloodied by leeches, infected by ticks, stung by wasps or hornets or yellow jackets or killed by snakes, all circumstances that might befall back home.

You get the idea that in the woods of New Brunswick you won't be fated to wander forever across the taiga, as you might along the Trans-Siberian Railway. But the Canadian north woods does compete with Siberia in one respect - mosquitoes, the infernal "itikkas" like we say in Finland, mosquitoes with such heft they land with perceptible weight.

Where Campbellton marks the beginning of the province, Moncton means goodbye. Leaving the north woods of New Brunswick, *The Ocean* begins its traverse of Nova Scotia to the much more maritime Halifax.

•••••

In time, people press in again on the empty woods, a few houses then business parks and industry and the heavy infrastructure of Halifax, bridges and cranes and steel. As we gather ourselves up and file off the train, Mrs. Ross continues her missing wallet testimony, morose before a sympathetic ViaRail employee, going over details, her voice still wavering.

•••••

**FORGOTTEN HISTORY**

Beautiful maidens and wildflowers fragrant o'er the moor grace few pages of Nova Scotia's history. A town brought up on hard work, Halifax has a history of hard luck. Some of it is other peoples' hard luck, it is true, but that only helps so much.

In September 1998 Swissair Flight 111 fell into Margaret's Bay just outside town, about five miles out in the ocean. Private fishing boats, the Coast Guard and then the Halifax military bases responded, but the plane had broken up on impact and all 229 passengers were lost. There are two memorials out along the bay.

After the crash, Ian Shaw, a Swiss national who last saw his daughter Stephanie when he drove her to the Geneva airport, moved from Switzerland to the tourist village of Peggy's Cove and built a restaurant called Shaw's Landing to be near his deceased daughter. Shaw's Landing only recently closed, Shaw presumably having finally worked through his loss.

As in the Swissair tragedy, when the *Titanic* sank in April 1912, ships were dispatched from Halifax to recover bodies, since Halifax, then as now, was the nearest big port with continental rail connections.

The *Mackay-Bennet*, a Halifax-based steamer normally used for laying communications cable, led the recovery effort. Two days after the sinking she set out with a cargo of coffins and canvas bags, an undertaker and a preacher.

Peggy's Cove

Over the next four weeks two ships from Halifax followed, the *Minia* and the *CGS Montmagny*. Together they and the *SS Algerine*, sailing from St. John's, Newfoundland, recovered over three hundred bodies. Some were buried at sea, but 209 bodies returned to the Halifax shore.

Just 59 were sent away to their families. The rest, including the *Titanic*'s unidentifiable and unclaimed victims, were buried in Halifax, and local businesses donated bouquets of lilies. The Maritime Museum on Halifax's waterfront has an extensive *Titanic* exhibit - complete with deck chair.

Haligonians couldn't have imagined it, but after the *Titanic* an even more horrific tragedy lay five years down the road, and this was all Halifax's own. In 1917 Halifax harbor fell victim to the greatest conflagration of the Great War. I don't know if it's just me, but polling people I know, it sounds like nobody else knew about the largest man made explosion before Hiroshima either.

Deck chair from the *Titanic*

## CONFLAGRATION

Halifax is a mid-rise city, but if it aspires to more, it might not take kindly to my saying so. Pardon. An attractive, purposeful, working town with a population just under a million, it hosts 200,000 cruise ship passengers a year and some 40 percent of Canada's defense assets. Nova Scotia is the world's largest exporter of Christmas trees and lobster, although Mirja makes a run at eating all the lobster in Halifax before it can be sold abroad.

It doesn't look like a place afflicted. Perched on two rocky shores, Halifax and it's sister city Dartmouth across the water enjoy refuge from Atlantic storms, set back from the ocean. Still further back, the Bedford Basin affords a strategic ice-free port, invaluable in wartime.

Because it has one of the world's deepest and most protected harbors, Halifax prospered in wartime, providing men and materiel from the War of 1812 through to the onset of World War 1.

Canada entered the Great War in 1914 as a colony when Britain declared war on Germany. Canadians were just about unanimous in support. Halifax boomed, and harbor traffic rose to seventeen million tons a year from just two.

By 1917 businesses were bursting. Industry struggled to keep up with demand. A quarter of the men in Halifax were serving overseas. Foreshadowing the U.S. experience in World War Two, women took jobs formerly thought of as men's work. Women's suffrage came to Canada in 1918, two years ahead of the United States.

The first regular, systematic convoy of war materiel from Canada left Sydney, Nova Scotia's easternmost harbor, on 24 June, 1917. By October as many as 36 supply ships were assembled for each convoy.

The Maritime Museum maps out a typical convoy: Two corvettes out front and one on each flank, trailed by five ships abreast, typically freighters with deck cargo of tanks, trucks and tankers, other freighters with aircraft, maybe a heavy lift ship with locomotives, sailing alongside rescue ships and an oiler with fuel for the corvettes. A destroyer carrying the escort force commander brought up the rear.

Convoy traffic moved from Sydney to Halifax during winter, owing to Halifax's back bay. The basin, with a surface area of six and a half square miles, jammed up with ships in winter.

•••••

By autumn 1917, a jittery uncertainty hung over the twin cities Halifax and Dartmouth; it had for months. The Canadians dragged submarine nets across the harbor each night against U-boats.

Thursday, 6 December: The *SS Imo*, an empty Norwegian relief ship in transit from Rotterdam bound for New York to load civilian relief supplies, was keen to sail at first light.

Coal for its boilers arrived too late the day before, trapping the ship in the Bedford Basin behind the submarine nets overnight. The *Imo* had to bide its time one more night. The Norwegian captain, Hakaan From, stormed about the ship, livid.

The submarine nets prevented the French ship *Mont Blanc*, arriving from New York, from sailing into the harbor to join up with an assembling convoy. Laden with war supplies, it stood at anchor outside the nets overnight.

There was a time just four years before, when a munitions ship like the Mont Blanc wouldn't have been allowed into the back bay. But with the outbreak of the war, control of the harbor transferred to the British Admiralty and they, considerably more detatched, allowed munitions ships in.

The *Mont Blanc* carried a fearsome load - 5.8 million pounds of picric acid, 200 tons of TNT, ten tons of guncotton and 35 tons of benzol, a high-octane gasoline, stacked in drums across her decks.

Picric acid was a relic of the time, an explosive chemical compound used in artillery shells by the Allies. It was less stable than TNT, which largely replaced it for war applications between the World Wars.

So worried had been the New York port authority when loading the incendiary *Mont Blanc* that before putting the cargo aboard they lined its holds with wood secured by non-sparking copper nails, and stevedores wore cloth over their boots.

Now both ships, the *Imo* leaving the Bedford Basin and the *Mont Blanc* coming in, were intent on making time, and Halifax became ground zero in its own unique horror.

Riding high in the water, the empty and impatient *Imo* was ready to move. Captain From, having sailed twice through Halifax before, felt familiar enough with the harbor to drive the *Imo* to its limits.

The Narrows is the smallest space between Bedford Basin and the twin cities of Halifax and Dartmouth. Scarcely two thousand feet wide, it is precisely where the *Imo* and *Mont Blanc* collided.

Benzol spilled from the drums onto the deck of the *Mont Blanc*. Fires broke out. The smoke was so thick the crew couldn't tell if it was the benzol or the picric acid that was burning, but every sailor realized it didn't matter. All too aware of what was to come, they bailed frantically for shore, for safety. Townspeople, unaware of the *Mont Blanc*'s deadly cargo, gathered at the waterfront to watch the flames engulf the ships.

Halifax's fire crews raced to the waterfront in their horse-drawn wagons and the fire chief arrived aboard the town's only combustion-engine fire truck. He and most of the town's fire brigade were incinerated.

When the big blast came it laid bare two square kilometers. The *Mont Blanc* became the most potent bomb exploded until Hiroshima. The windows in most of Halifax's houses were blown into their inhabitants' faces.

The *Mont Blanc* heaved into the air and rained fire back down on the town. Its big gun landed two kilometers away. Rocks sucked up from the sea floor fell onto the town as deadly shrapnel.

So terrific was the blast that it created a tsunami. Water drained from the Narrows, then flooded back in across the opposite, Dartmouth, shore, where a Mi'kmaq Indian settlement washed entirely away, just disappeared.

The town burned. Home heating in those days came predominately from coal and wood stoves, most of which were stoked and burning on a December day. The heaters overturned, setting further fires.

At nightfall a blizzard closed over the bay, the worst in years, with temperatures plunging to 10 or 15 degrees fahrenheit. People with no shelter who survived the blast died in place, trapped, frozen in the blizzard.

Halifax reeled. Worry spread that the naval artillery stores at the Wellington barracks would explode (they didn't). Dazed and traumatized victims, many with their clothes and even skin burned right off, stumbled through the storm like zombies.

Rumors. Halifax was being bombed by the Luftstreitkräfte, the World War 1 German air force. How did they get their Fokkers all the way over here!? No, it was a naval bombardment. Some thought Halifax's unique hell came from German zeppelins.

Some people were lucky, if only by comparison. People told of being lifted up and deposited up to a mile from where they lived. In the end, as many as 9,000 people lost their homes, some 6,000 were injured, many horrendously, and 2,000 were dead.

•••••

## SNAPSHOT, HALIFAX

Halifax, Nova Scotia

You can't grow up in Halifax without knowing everything about the explosion. It simply can't be done, A downtown furniture maker tells us. Not long ago he petitioned for and was granted rights to cut down a maple tree under the McKay bridge built across the narrows, just about where the blast occurred.

A 22-inch maple, with the growth rate at one inch equals five years, it would have been ten years old in 1917, the year of the disaster and, sure enough, it has a seared ring near its center. He will market it to the cognizant community.

To stand and survey Halifax harbor, to regard the little drumlin Georges Island across the way and its lighthouse on the hill, and consider that all this water went away, sucked out beyond the harbor by the explosion before plunging back in and sweeping away much of Halifax and the Mi'kmaqs on the opposite shore, that will make you shudder.

• • • • •

Clouds reach to the edge of shore and not beyond; the breeze arrives fresh off the water. Raindrops on my laptop screen. There is precious little sunlight. Chilly on this balcony, wet deck chairs, but a fine St. Ambroise Ale Noire À L'Avoine oatmeal stout from Montreal at my side, for Canada produces fine craft breweries. The original Alexander Keith brewery building just across the way (est'd 1820) has finally given it up, now making its brew outside town and owned by Labatt.

Canada is sparse. There is ample space along the long airport road for city planners to pick and designate "new business area." Anywhere along here they would like. On the road in, certain trees still display tentative, new leaves on 9 June. A cruise ship lies in harbor on our arrival around 3:00 but when it sees us it sets sail by 4:00. Thank you.

We watch regular helicopter patrols, turning low and easy circles around both sides of the harbor. I can only guess it is because Canada's biggest military base on the east coast is here and even a peaceful land needs somewhere to practice its helicopter pilots.

No bustle. Sweatshirts and anoraks. 58 degrees in summer. Unfailingly agreeable people, more than their share of whom are unaccountably from Alberta. United States, don't take it as America North. Canada is its own place.

One thing it's got that the U.S.A. ain't got, as we're about to find out, it's only a couple miles from France.

What do you say we go and have a look?

• • • • •

*Bill Murray*

## FRANCE IN NORTH AMERICA:
## SAINT-PIERRE ET MIQUELON

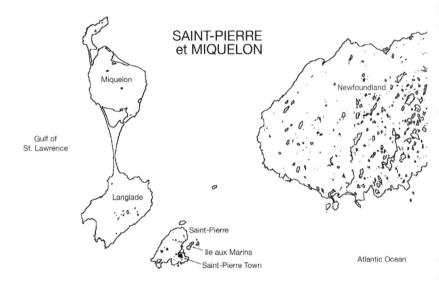

Suppose France had won the colonial battle royale for the New World. Would America now have a natural ally in the alternative universe Parisian hub of world business, all of us speaking Français, la langue du monde, anchored to the thriving economic powerhouse on continental Europe's western shore?

It didn't work out that way, and today, within sight of Newfoundland, one tiny archipelagic husk rises from the sea, an unsure, tentative vestige of French colonialism in North America, a tiny territory called Saint-Pierre et Miquelon.

Just 93 square miles of spare, rocky islands, the firmly Francophone territoire d'outre-mer (overseas territory) comprises Saint-Pierre, where just about everybody lives, and the two larger islands Langarde and Miquelon, joined at low tide and populated principally by a few vacation homes and 624 people.

Ride sharing with the mail

As with Air Greenland, on Air Saint-Pierre people compete with the mail for seats. There is a lot of mail today, the entire left side of the plane. All but the front four rows of an ATR turboprop are filled with canvas covered mail bags, and the front galley is jammed full too. That leaves room for 21 passengers among 44 seats.

I can't recall ever having to call a taxi at an international airport, but they are good enough to hang a phone on the terminal wall for you to do so. He wants five Euros for the ride. That is correct; surrounded by Canada and 2,350 miles from Brest, the closest landfall in continental France, he wants Euros.

My conjured vision of a grand Place Charles DeGaulle isn't quite so grand in reality, not to denigrate. La Place is dominated by the post office on the waterfront and a happy tourism office with bright little displays in the windows. Scarcely a two-minute walk away, the Hotel Robert, a former police barracks, is a throwback, a tiny reminder that once, personal honor trumped personal gratification.

I must sign a pledge, a strip of paper by which I testify that "I (fill in your name), pledge that we will not smoke in our hotel room." With a space to sign and date at the bottom.

We live in an annex, down the stairs, across the street and back up the stairs, with fine blonde hardwood floors and two big picture windows overlooking a tiny waterfront promenade and green public space, common "saline sheds" for fishermen, and I can see a bit of the airport control tower across the harbor.

The park's picnic tables and benches are a fine place to pop across (cars yield to people) with your morning coffee. Trees still budding on the 12th of June, yellow wild flowers and thistle all sway in the breeze on a rare, almost cloudless Sunday morning.

Besides the little ferry that runs fifteen or twenty at a time over and back from Ile Aux Marins, Fishermen's Island, a zodiac laden with prospective whale watchers is the busiest ship in the harbor, tethered sailboats and Hobie Cats bobbing in its wake. In side-by-side dry slips the *P'Tit Saint-Pierre* sits under repair beside a smaller sailboat that ran into a problem just beginning a solo trans-Atlantic crossing causing a "famous German sailor," a woman surnamed Joshka, an extended, unintended Saint-Pierre vacation. The parts for her ship must be summoned from abroad.

Bicycles make more sense than cars, but Saint-Pierre is full of boxy Renaults. Just the same, none of them drive very fast and Saint-Pierre town is one of those places with short stubby blocks built all in a huddle down at the water, buildings right up on the road so drivers must slow at every block to check around them. Pedestrians rule; cars defer.

•••••

Frederic Dotte drives up in fashionably torn jeans and a colorful horizontal-striped sweater, a journalist perhaps curious who would be curious about Saint-Pierre. He has agreed to show us around.

French through and through with a good command of English, he is far too good to us, meeting us at Place Charles DeGaulle, taking us to a lookout point at the top of the island, the radio and TV studios where he works, posing for pictures out front with his work satchel, glasses pushed up on top of his head, showing off his island, freely spending time with strangers.

As it happens, his wife is away enjoying a weekend with friends on Langlade, the southern island in the Langlade/Grande Miquelon duo just over Saint-Pierre Island's spine to the west. Her absence serendipitously affords us a chance at some of Fred's time, aside from his fielding regular calls from his sixteen-year-old son and chauffeuring around his daughter.

Fred works as a presenter at Saint-Pierre et Miquelon Première radio and TV, where they employ 87, making it the biggest private employer on the island, although it is a curious hybrid, a government institution dependent on profit, as opposed to say, the hospital, which employs more but not for profit. (Subsidies are everywhere. Construction industry workers get some pay in the non-construction season, which runs much of the year.)

"Winter is hard here," Fred says. A simple fact. But he and his family have stuck it out for six years. Now with an eighteen-year-old daughter at school back in France and their younger kids here, he and his wife plan two more years on the island. They will return when it is time for their boy to go to college.

They own a home in southern France, a little town toward Switzerland. To get here they swapped jobs with a Saint-Pierrais journalist who rented their house in France, but they also bought a house here. They're not overly expensive, he thinks, certainly cheaper than in France. €150,000 will buy you 1,500 square meters.

Architecture is a jumble, buildings built right on top of one another in that waterfront clapboard style you see in sand-scoured communities here clear across the continent to the Pacific northwest coast.

Part because it's built for winter, part because everybody knows where everything is, Saint-Pierre merchants don't fancy up their storefronts. It's hard to tell if shops are open, sometimes hard to tell if they are even shops.

Some have display windows but some only offer a door to the street. If you have business somewhere you'll find it. In a place Saint-Pierre's size it won't take long.

It is not quite high season (high and short, running from July maybe into September), so no one bothers to open on Sunday. Everybody knows it who lives here, and there are no tourists liable to pop in and buy something. When we leave we must arrange a taxi to the airport in advance because "sometimes on Sunday everybody disappears."

•••••

Today is the first day of the Euro 2016 soccer tournament, as 24 European national teams face off across France. The French national team opens the tournament in the Stade de France, the site of suicide bombings the night of the Bataclan shootings the November before.

France is seized with apprehension this week but terror is the last thought here, and we settle in at the Bar Le Rustique among high-spirited men with "bucket beer," a scheme in which five tiny Heinekens are served in an ice bucket for the price of four.

The match starts at 21:00 in France, 17:00 here, for they have tacked on an extra hour of time zone beyond Nova Scotia's extra hour beyond east coast time, helping the Saint-Pierrais feel closer to home.

They shout. They scream. They chew their nails. They sweat the minutiae until in the 89th minute the home team thrills the island with a 2-1 victory over pesky, persistent Romania. Most incongruent, and not a little poignant to see full-throated table-pounding nationalism in such an unlikely place, so isolated from France.

•••••

France stations 23 marines here and a ship to enforce the peace, but there is only light crime, says Fred. Kids smoke dope, no hard drugs to speak of. His biggest worry, that of all Saint-Pierrais parents, he thinks, is probably alcohol.

There are eleven jail cells. Unlike in the Faroes, they don't send their big criminals back to the motherland. That would be too far. We're part of France, okay, but we're also stock born on this rock and it is a long way to France.

There was a celebrated murder last summer. Murders happen once in a while, more often that out in the Faroes, and maybe these islanders are inured by proximity to a big land mass, people coming and going from Halifax and St. John's especially, and Montreal and Toronto besides, so while any murder is riveting, it doesn't cause the reflexive shock that Piddy's did in Torshavn.

Last year, after a first date, a young woman declined a second. The jilted took a gun to the house where she lived with her family and her father, in intervening, ended up dead. Not that everyone isn't well known in a community of 6,000, but this man was a singer known and loved. The case had a huge impact like in Torshavn, but it brought no suspense, only sadness, for once the young gunman shot the singer he turned the gun on himself.

•••••

Little problems loom larger in little places. Take the trash, for example. Where to put it? Landfilling is not a good option because these islands are mostly rock and what's not rock tends to freeze in the long winters, making digging a problem.

Saint-Pierre has always burned its trash. Just put it in a big pile and set it alight. All of it, even batteries and tires. When the wind isn't right everybody in town can tell that's not healthy. Besides, burning trash isn't legal in France and we're part of France here don't you forget, so a solution has had to be found and that solution is recycling.

A still gleaming new recycling center seeks to minimize trash by composting, grinding glass bottles into material to resurface roads and breaking down cardboard into bedding for livestock. But ultimately there will still be trash.

What to do with it? Canada won't buy it (although it buys trash from the Americans, I hear, which piques some Saint-Pierrais), so in the end Saint-Pierre's hard core trash will sail all the way to France.

Trouble is, these tiny islands have to check with big, looming Canada (an uncommon characterization of Canada, that) before everything they do. Which sets up a love/hate thing. On the other hand, with the bounty of Canada so nearby, in Fred's words, "you have no poor here."

Saint-Pierre is a member in good standing of a club of islands like British St. Helena and Chilean Rapa Nui, places ruled by constraint, the overarching sense that you may have enough, but you will never have plenty. With Canada in literal line of sight, whatever you need, if you can wait a bit, you can get it.

Perhaps being accustomed to scarcity shapes the work ethic. For example, there is no apparent reason they must, but here on Saint-Pierre the boulangeries only bake a certain amount of bread a day.

People become regular patrons of their bakery and place orders in advance for their baguettes, not exactly like, but similar to having your favorite skerpikjøt provider in the Faroes. The result: If you haven't ordered for yourself and you don't get there in time, you may find yourself out of luck in search of fresh bread.

•••••

**A DAY IN THE LIFE OF ONE TINY ISLAND**

Beatrice and her husband, who declines to share his name but who has a bit of meteorite he wants us all to rub for good luck, come from Alberta, Harper country. Beatrice clucks and shakes her head. Says the only thing worse than Harper is this young man Trudeau.

We have come to sit with them at a café after failing to visit the Musée Heritage (next open four days from today with a new exhibit - the perils of missing high season) and the souvenir store (why would they be open at 4:00 on a Friday?).

Down the street Bar Le Baratin has the distinct benefit of being open, even if it stinks of cigarettes. It nestles into a row of buildings in general disrepair, several blocks off the waterfront, all of their paint wind-flaked, garden plots grown wild all around, yellow flowers wagging in the wind. Bar Le Baratin is a purple concrete block with a string of lights coiled around at the top that at night must be lovely, or at least, notable. A stab at flair.

Five patrons, smaller men, Basques, are local remnants of Portuguese fishermen who sailed from the Azores in the fifteenth century. A bartender and his boys and the soccer match. Nobody at the bar, all of us gathered around the big screen, the bartender too, the boys rooting for Russie to upset Angleterre, so as to bring an easier victory for the home team playing 2,650 miles away.

Calm. Smiles. Contentment.

There goes a girl on a bike. I've seen her before somewhere. Of course you have. You've seen everybody before, in one day. She was the bartender where Fred took us, the Bat Bar, Bar La Chauve Souris.

•••••

Twilight at 11 p.m. Raised voices, anger in the building across the way. Far above a jet powers out over the Atlantic. Here at the Hotel Robert we live above the dining room of L' Atelier Gourmand, where we regularly dine. One night we are the last diners.

You know the easy command a chef has on his home turf, in his toke and double-breasted cook's coat, serving a flaming entrée perhaps, or bowing low over your menu to confide a secret of his kitchen? That bluff and commanding stature is threatened when seconds after taking our leave, a leather-jacketed version of the same person climbs onto a scooter to whine off into the island.

His consigliere, the waiter, leaves his suit coat inside the restaurant too in favor of his leather jacket and leaves the premises himself, no sooner than we can walk upstairs. I mean, two minutes.

•••••

## THE GHOST ISLAND OF ILE AUX MARINS

We take the ferry a short way outside the harbor, the air fresh out on the water. Lighthouses and remnants of lighthouses are several, and collectively picturesque.

No one lives on Ile aux Marins (Fishermen's Island) year round anymore, but on a pretty day like today workmen hammer at the roofs of a handful of second homes making them ready for summer. A fine old repurposed home alongside the dock serves snacks and beer. Someone has rigged up wi-fi, making it a gathering point. A girl does her homework; a couple of tourists peck at their phones.

A mere slip of land, the island covers 50 hectares. 1,700 meters long, its width doesn't exceed 700 meters; the narrowest point is a scant 100. The island serves as a barrier against storms, a natural breakwater for Saint-Pierre's harbor.

We set out along the sodden foot path out to the highest point, Cape Beaudry, 35 meters above the sea with a view to Newfoundland.

With a boom in cod fishing in the middle of the nineteenth century, the Saint-Pierre harbor grew overfull. The search for new space led to the settlement on the then lÎle aux Chiens, renamed in 1931 as lle aux Marins, which began as a drying ground for fish.

Fishermen gutted their catch, cut off the fishes' heads, removed their backbones, cleaned them. On sunny days, cod were spread on flat rocks, drying grounds, with the flesh side up. They stacked them up at night in anticipation of bad weather. Women salted and dried them. In 1862, a hundred children worked alongside the women.

From 1860, the drying grounds were divided and sold in parcels, each with space for a house, a vegetable garden, a drying ground, a fishing shed (called a saline) and a slipway for boats. Once Ile aux Marins had a population of 700.

One of several lighthouses on Ile Aux Marins

The village faced the harbor and Saint-Pierre town. Two main rows of 200 wooden houses were built, separated by drying grounds, lined up close together for protection against the wind and to optimize space. They protected the gardens from the formidable winds with strong fences and each house had a gravity-fed cistern that collected groundwater.

•••••

_Bill Murray_

In winter cod leave these shores for the Grand Banks, where the Labrador current mixes with the Gulf Stream to create what was once the richest fishing ground in the world. The short fishing season, May to September, afforded little margin for error. No fisherman got rich. The selling price always favored the traders.

Around 1920 the French company Là Morue Française built an artificial fish drying machine to circumvent bad weather and to improve yield, but it burned to the rocks in 1938 and was never rebuilt. A fishery crisis had thus begun and the population declined. In the early twentieth century the islands had 500 dories. In the 1980s, there were about 30 left.

It is a tale of depopulation and desertion like in the outer Faroese isles. We will talk about the disastrous decline of cod fishing in the Grand Banks later, in Newfoundland, but in the end, cod fishing was the only reason for people to stay on the island. Year after year the population decreased as the catch declined until the final exodus in the 1960s. Only twenty families remained in 1962.

A family of fishermen once lived in the little Télétchéa house. We can still see and poke around at the remains of the electrification system installed on the island in 1961. The network of electric poles was powered by an undersea cable connected to the power plant in Saint-Pierre.

The miracle of electricity improved the daily life of those twenty families still present on the island but a boat entering the harbor damaged the cable and the whole system gave out a few months later.

With the rehabilitation of the island in the 1980's, some summer homes are now equipped with solar panels for light. Others have kept the old traditional lamps.

In early spring 1931 the 398-foot, 3865-ton _Transpacific_ raised anchor and left Canada with eleven passengers and cargo but problems developed with its radar. The captain radioed to St. Pierre for a tech to look at the radar but the ship snagged on the Marie-Rose reef, next to Trehouart cove off Ile aux Marins.

In the shallow water there was no danger of sinking and a farewell dinner was held onboard. Once the ship was abandoned some 70 ships of all sizes visited the *Transpacific* overnight. The captain returned next day to reboard, to pump fuel off the ship, but the looters prevented his boarding until the ship had been picked clean.

As a result the ship's cutlery and furniture, compass, wheel and bell, found their way into fishermen's homes across St. Pierre, while other homes enjoyed their own jukeboxes, and riding mowers decorated boulder-strewn lawns.

We wander around the bow of the *Transpacific*, rusting in repose across the shore. You can walk right up and kick it.

•••••

## PROSPECTS

Colonial ownership of the archipelago swung between France and England something like nine times, sometimes violently, but from 1816 the territory has remained French, so that in two weeks Saint-Pierre et Miquelon will celebrate the 200th anniversary of uninterrupted French sovereignty.

There had been talk of Prime Minister Manuel Valls visiting to mark the occasion. They used a spate of strikes across mainland France (when aren't there French strikes in summer?) as an excuse for postponement, but the real business of a Valls visit would have been to announce agreement on a €300 million port development deal.

A trans-shipment hub for container ships has been on the drawing board for some years, promising to provide 180 permanent jobs by 2020. Based on Saint-Pierre's history, trans-shipment would be an area of Pierrais expertise.

*Bill Murray*

Al Capone had an operation here during the Prohibition Era, as Canadian whiskey and French wines moved through the islands in bulk. The Tourisme office can fix you up with a guided Prohibition walking tour.

Alas, the time was not right for a visit by Prime Minister Valls. That transport deal still awaits government approval.

•••••

Saint-Pierre is one of those places like, say, Zanzibar or Paraguay, where everybody's waiting for something to happen and nothing ever does. The port project, or a sustained drive for tourism - one of those ought to be the next big thing.

A trading port is too big-dollars for ordinary people to facilitate; that's out of their hands. The gradual birth of tourism is one of those pesky things, nobody puts out tables to make a Parisian-style café until tourists come, and no tourists come until there are cafés. If I were a merchant I wouldn't venture to invest too far out in front of the curve. In 2015 there were just 130 guest rooms in Saint-Pierre.

Then there is the weather. The one English speaker in the little shop on Ile aux Marins lamented that oh, it was so horrible last year. "It was only one-month season here" for tourists. I read that in 1985, flights to Saint-Pierre were grounded by fog for 23 days in the high-season month of July.

When tourists come, there isn't a lot on. We meet an older Newfoundland couple, standing damp in wet-weather gear in the hotel lobby. The gentleman observes that,

"We've just come from a boat tour."

What did you see?

"Rocks and short trees."

There are experiences to be had, though not for the thrill-seeking, tour-guided crowd. Up at the viewpoint at the top of Saint-Pierre you can see across to Langlade and Miquelon and Newfoundland beyond. A woman, batting down her skirt in the wind, arrives with her dog, smiles and points at her field glasses. Maybe whales, she hopes.

•••••

Fred Dotte was born in January of 1968. Over lobster at L' Atelier Gourmand, we get to talking about the upheaval in the U.S. and back in France at the time of his birth, a thing he has only read about in school books.

It was tough then; it is tough now. Sixty people are born here every year; when they grow up to eighteen, forty of them leave and there is still a struggle to find jobs for the remaining twenty. One solution is the port deal, but the more logical, local, practical thing is increased, everyday, on the ground tourism, because part of what holds Saint-Pierre back is just getting here.

Next year car ferries will ply two routes to Newfoundland. Up to now potential visitors park their cars in lots over there and catch passenger-only service. Maybe more will come if they can bring their cars.

Some of the problem comes from this side though, from the island, Fred thinks. The attitude of some is to take their French patrimony, put it in their pocket and say, we're from here and you are not. Darker stories of cousins marrying cousins are covered up with Appalachian verve. It is the way of insular places.

Air Saint-Pierre operates a fleet of two ATRs and a Cessna. All its international flights go to Canada and there is no other scheduled service.

If you live here, Fred explains that you can get your car on and off the island via a weekly French-government-subsidized transport ship from

*Bill Murray*

Halifax, but it's hardly convenient. You must surrender your car down at the dock for some days or a week in customs before departure.

• • • • •

What to make of this place? Tiny, tenacious, windy and foggy, lobster huge and cheap. It may not be exactly pointless for France to have Saint-Pierre, but it sure is lots of trouble. Our questions for Fred boil down to this: France puts in way more than they get out of this relationship. Why? What makes it worth it?

Fred thinks that first, because France owns it, they have invested French nationalism in it and it is here. They can't just give it back.

Second, up until, say, twenty years ago there were imposing domes up on the hills that all but announced spying on Canada and the U.S.

And finally, and this is new, France may perhaps suddenly, after two hundred years, see a way to use Saint-Pierre to become a stakeholder in the coming Arctic trade wars. Somewhere deep within the Institut Français des Relations Internationales back in Paris, someone must be working on this tonight.

• • • • •

## NEWFOUNDLAND

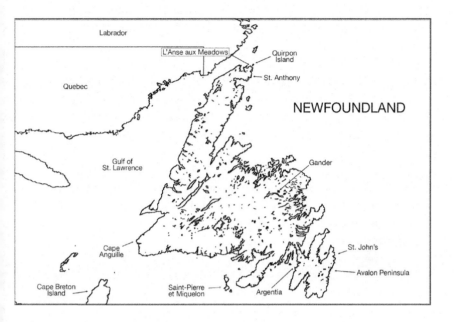

We humans feel pain but fail to appreciate its absence. There are solid, evolutionary, survival-dependent reasons to prioritize pain - flee that sabre-toothed tiger, and fast! - but how much fuller life would be if we could celebrate time spent pain free. And what do you know, here is an island full of people who do just that. Welcome to "The Rock."

Newfoundland marches to the beat of its own drummer, or at least to the ticking of its own clock. An hour and a half ahead of the U.S. east coast, the island they call "The Rock" is an island alone. No one shares Newfoundland Standard Time, which is a half hour ahead of the rest of Atlantic Canada and a half hour behind Saint-Pierre et Miquelon.

At 400,000 square kilometers, Newfoundland and Labrador comprise a province triple the size of the other maritime provinces of Nova Scotia, New Brunswick and Prince Edward Island combined. Newfoundland is the sixteenth largest island in the world, larger than Iceland, or Cuba.

*Bill Murray*

A twenty-minute ride from St John's three main streets, Cape Spear is hardly 1,650 miles from Ireland. In this far eastern perch, St. John's is a hybrid of the working towns of Greenland that put their industrial sides forward and the larger coastal towns farther south in Nova Scotia and New England.

The St. John's working harbor dominates the tiny sheltered bay along Water Street, the oldest commercial street in North America, dating to the early 1500s. Two important streets parallel Water Street away from shore, Duckworth Street and Queen's Road, and that, really, is St. John's.

Except in the precise center, Duckworth dominates commerce with Water Street nearly at water level, a harder, grittier block toward the water. The Toronto Dominion bank dominates the skyline the way banks do.

The place we're staying has a proper entrance on Duckworth Street, a long commercial street housing the courts, bookstores, a Tim Horton's and ethnic food enough to feed the world. On ethnic food St. John's punches far above its weight.

They've put us in a room in the back of the hotel. It faces Water Street at ground level, feet from the road, with a closeup view of the harbor, immediately across from a fleet of dangerous looking tanks that will surely do us in if they're the type to explode.

I imagine dock smells, rope, sawdust and tar, fish, petrol and turpentine, but we are sealed against the weather and the traffic noise.

•••••

The climate is not the best. When you visit St. John's it will rain, but the day we arrive is gorgeous, just about cloudless, belying its reputation that St. John's is made of fog. Sunshine ignites the colors of the jelly bean houses, as they've taken a civic fancy to calling the rows of gaily painted wooden Victorian style houses built after the Great Fire of 1892. It's cold, though, even in summer.

The bane of this Avalon peninsula is the wind. When not from the southwest via the jet stream, it sweeps down as an express from Greenland. Unlike Iceland and even Svalbard, which are touched by the Gulf Stream, Newfoundland's coast is subject to the Labrador current from the north. St. John's finds itself in the path of icebergs while south of the latitude of Paris. Even with the air temperature in the 40s the wind will slice you up.

After one seductive afternoon of sun, we will never see as far as 500 meters again; the tamped down hues of fog and rain set in with determination. Signs on the buildings caution "beware of falling snow and ice," a hint at the real weather around here.

•••••

We are sitting in a restaurant, talking with a man who calls himself Chico. He gushes about his love of camping, moaning about the brevity of the season. May to October is best. This May there were warm days, he says, highs in the 20s. Well, not many, though. His first camping trip was 24 May, which is a "pre-summer" holiday here. His favorite camping spot is Dildo, 80 kilometers up the road.

Dildo? Really? Is Carlos trying to get a rise out of us? Of course he is, and there is lots more. The Newfoundland & Labrador Travel Reference Map is a playground of flamboyant cartography.

Here are Bare Need, Baking Kettle Pond and Blow Me Down (which has somehow come to mean "a place with steep bluffs."). Welcome to Butter Pot Hill, Cape Onion, Come By Chance, Cranky Point, Ha Ha Bay (there are five), Happy Adventure, and Indian Tickle, a tickle being a narrow inlet to the sea in which water runs opposite the tide, sometimes even drawing in icebergs.

See also Jerry's Nose, Joe Batts Arm and Pinch Gut Point.

•••••

259

*Bill Murray*

## ONLY ONE SUNNY DAY, NO EXCEPTIONS

Everybody has come out to bask on that first, sunshiny day.

The crusty, balding stalwarts of the Royal Canadian Legion fill the town from across the country to debate by-laws and elect officers, to show the wife a good time and test out that new hip replacement all in one go. Banners and berets, sashes with ribbons and medals fill the streets, even a marching band with someone still hardy enough to march inside a tuba.

They spill out of George Street, the locally famous concentration of debauchery, restaurants and bars, where touts invite you to get "Screeched In," a transaction by which they'll call you an honorary Newfie if you gulp their booze, then kiss a fish.

Traffic stands down in good-natured deference for the old guys. We fall in with two men in berets who have peeled off from their wives for a pint of locally-brewed Iceberg lager down at the Celtic Hearth pub. Men have come not just from across the land, they say, but from Germany and even New Zealand and one man from Australia.

They comport themselves with earned honor. One old soldier gives me a Prince Edward Island lapel pin he has a pocket full of and says it is the friendliest province in Canada. I'd like to believe it, I say, but it would be hard to top the hospitality right here in St. John's. Just come and give us a try, he says.

These two old war horses must have just come from a remembrance, for, eyes misty and each embellishing the other's words, they relive for our benefit the bloody battle and desperate fight for survival at Blaumont-Hamel on the first day of the battle of the Somme, its centennial imminent on July 1, when 801 Canadians of the Newfoundland Regiment went in and only 68 came out alive.

Older Newfoundlanders tend toward considering themselves Newfoundlanders first and Canadians second. It was just in 1949 that a referendum bound Newfoundland to Canada, prior to which it had been a British colony after a brief period as an independent British dominion. At the height of the war some 100,000 Americans lived and worked in Newfoundland and many hoped the colony would become part of America.

And then, uh oh, the vets realize how long they've been away. Wide eyed, making haste, they flee to find the old ladies.

• • • • •

Fun while it lasts, the warmth and sunshine, but the next afternoon down at a used bookstore called Afterwords, the heater rumbles right here in mid-June and wet coats reinforce the natural musk of old books. Rain overfills the gutters, slaps against the pavement and slings itself at the plate glass.

The proprietor, upturned nose above a popped collar in some Victorian conceit, says he reads from the very poetry book Mirja buys for six dollars, prompting us to ask if he'd rather keep it. No, he'd rather sell it, he mumbles. How riveting could his marble-mouthed readings be?

Heaters chug inside restaurants up and down Duckworth and George Streets. Newfoundland cuisine is cod, cod, cod a hundred ways. Cod baked, battered, broiled and fried, cod en papillote, confit of cod, cod roasted and poached. Lapland does this with its reindeer.

A recent law, a thunderclap of sensible governance, will give cadres of regulatory officials in Ottawa palpitations. Restauranteurs may now buy what food they wish from whomever they want - meaning right off the boat. Your lobster claws may still be twitching.

Then there is fried bologna, "Newfie steak." The local paper says that if the rest of Canada shared Newfoundlanders' bologna fervor the country would consume 141.1 million kilograms of the stuff each year.

Poutine, dastardly poutine. "Shed Party," made from Lamb's spiced rum, bologna gravy, caramelized onions, pork sausage and green peas. You may plead for poutine as comfort food here in the cold and the fog and the wind, but you may not claim it promotes good health. Still, in a pub on the 13th of June, heater ablaze and rain pounding the roof, you can make a fine case for poutine's home food attraction.

## BIG PERSONALITIES, BIG PROBLEMS

Newfoundland has always had room for big personalities. Even so, imagine some wild-eyed zealot named Guglielmo sailing into town (in 1901) with a cargo of kites and hydrogen balloons and hydrogen gas and making straight for an abandoned hospital for fever and diphtheria.

This was Guglielmo Marconi, who hauled his kit up Signal Hill. With aerial wires attached, kites raised (and torn away by the wind), balloons floated (and torn away by the wind), reduced to using an improvised telephone receiver, mouth agape and ears straining, he finally heard the three dots that signified "S" in Morse Code.

Marconi proved that for reasons obscure and unproven at the time, signals would travel not only at distance but also around the curvature of the earth. He proved they would propagate all the way across the Atlantic, in this case, 3,425 kilometers (2,128 miles) back to a headland in Cornwall called Poldhu, where in old photos, the transmitting antennae he set up, a 200-foot circle of 24 200-foot masts, look as other-worldly as Stonehenge.

By 1907 trans-Atlantic service was available for public use. In 1909 Marconi won the Nobel Prize for physics.

•••••

You like St. John's the minute you drive in. A hippie town. Piercings and peasant dresses, muscle cars and used bookshops. A kind of north/south bookend to Key West.

In Key West it's the occasional hurricane. Here maybe five times a year the city just shuts down completely in snow. The rest of the city behind Duckworth Street rises sharply onto a hill and when it's slick enough everything not secured slides straight down, so when a storm comes everybody just stays home.

This is the grim physical expression of Newfoundland that flies in the face of all these winning smiles: Limits. Northern constraints. St. John's is no brash, can-do American town.

Port cities' wide harbors invite in guests, their front doors flung open to the world. But access to St. John's is boa-constricted, the sea visible only for a scant thousand feet through the Narrows, just a notch between the dramatic not-quite-mountain called Signal Hill after Marconi and the opposite perch of Fort Amherst.

On the inland side of the Narrows, ships are marvelously protected; the hills on either side of the notch run effective interference, sparing St. John's waterfront the fury of the sea.

That is good because St. John's, and Newfoundland and Labrador more generally, have had their share of superlative calamities. Some places have all the luck, and others just aren't destined to have an easy go of things. In Canada, the farther east you go, the greater the tales of woe, and Newfoundland is as far as you can go.

In Canada's deadliest natural disaster, a water borne fury spread without warning across Newfoundland in September 1775. The squid catch was late that summer, so untold numbers of fishing boats were at sea when hurricane waters rose twenty feet higher than normal in Conception Bay, killing 300 men at a stroke. Tales are told that the sole survivor at sea was a boy who sailors tied to a ship's mast. Total casualties numbered over 4,000.

In 1846, a fire in a cabinetmaker's workshop fed on closely built wooden buildings, consuming 2,000. Another in 1892, this one they call The Great Fire, left 13,000 homeless.

The 1929 Grand Banks earthquake caused Canada's largest submarine landslide, snapping twelve trans-Atlantic underwater cables, and kicked up a tsunami that killed 28 along Newfoundland's coast.

Maritime Canada's meanest tragedy tore St. John's families apart; just outside this hotel window on Water Street, the human aspect of a terrible tragedy played out as families thronged the telegraph office, demanding news of their men caught on the ice outside the Narrows.

• • • • •

## THE 1914 NEWFOUNDLAND SEALING DISASTER

> "O hear us, when we cry to Thee
> For those in peril on the sea."

A century ago St. John's was a vital, bustling hub of maritime commerce, Water Street its beating heart. As the closest North American landfall to Europe, a concentration of trans-Atlantic communication cables came ashore here. St. John's anchored the most bountiful cod fishing grounds in the world. But the sea provided bounty far beyond fish.

Clubbing helpless baby seals may not strike you as the most manly activity, but take a look at Newfoundland's climate, its isolation, and then at the benefits of swiling, as they called seal hunting on the ice:

> • Seal meat is nutrient-rich food in a land where coaxing food from the ground presents a perennial challenge.

> • Seal hides make fine boots.

> • After flensing (separating the fat), seal fat makes soap, margarine and lipstick, and in the old days powered the lamps that drove away the long winter darkness.

The rest of the seal, the dogs would take care of. Like the Inuit, Newfoundlanders knew how to use every bit of nature's scant provision.

In late summer ice forms between Canada and Greenland in Baffin Bay, far to the north of the sealing grounds. The Labrador current moves the young ice south and with the coming of winter it grows into ten-foot blocks the aquamarine color of sea water, save for edges made white and jagged by constant grinding against other ice.

Off the Labrador coast, most of the way to Newfoundland, the ice freezes into vast, miles-long sheets that jostle, crack and re-form, and arrive off Newfoundland covered with gravel from scrapes against land. The job of the swiler was to walk across this ice field for miles, searching for seals.

Harp seals follow an ancient migratory cycle between the Arctic and the Grand Banks, a shallow part of the continental shelf off Newfoundland. In early March harp seal mothers climb onto the ice pans, give birth to their pups and abandon them, so that each year hundreds of thousands of newborn seals would lay helpless when the swilers approached.

The swiling ships sailed through the Narrows north into the ice field each March. It was St. John's biggest event of the year. Swiling became a sort of national sport, with statistics compiled like the number of pelts taken in a season and the career lifetime hauls of "jowlers'," or successful swiling captains.

No other country's commercial fleets systematically sailed into ice floes. No other country even had a dedicated sealing fleet. Successful St. John's captains became swashbuckling national heroes, in demand as pilots for polar excursions.

The swiling trade exploded over the course of the 1800s. From 140 vessels in 1804, by the middle of the century 13,000 men collected half a million pelts in a season lasting only weeks.

It was brutal, brutal business, a coming of age, a test of manhood for country boys from all across The Rock. Men and boys converged on St. John's, the younger ones exaggerating their age. If selected they would be pelted, pounded and battered by snow, hail and ice; every year some would be crushed in the floes.

Jenny Higgins writes in *Perished: The 1914 Newfoundland Seal Hunt Disaster,* that "A typical pay would have probably been between $30 and $40, that would have been for about six or seven weeks of very hard physical labour, severe deprivation, little food, and basically putting your life at risk."

It was for their families' survival. "It really is a story about men who are putting themselves in harm's way to put food on the table," says Higgins.

•••••

Twenty-nine- year-old Wes Kean sailed as Captain of the *SS Newfoundland.* The aging, wood-hulled ship, in its 42nd year, was by now one of the smaller swiling ships in the fleet, without a wireless or a steel hull, but Wes, an unfledged, still aspiring captain, had a name to make so he would take what he could get.

Wes's father, a former cabinet minister and Tory government representative named Abram Kean, sailed in command of the *Stephano*, the most powerful ship in the swiling fleet. Some called the *Stephano* the finest ice-breaker in the world.

At 59, Old Man Kean was a sealing legend, prohibition advocate and a strict Methodist. A sailing superstition discouraged launching a mission on a Friday. Abe Kean always launched on Friday. The kind of man he was.

Even while working for rival companies, Wes and Abe Kean had arranged a discreet signal in the event one found seals. In *Death on the Ice: The Great Newfoundland Sealing Disaster of 1914*, Cassie Brown writes that:

"Wesbury, me b'y," the Old Man said, "Kape as handy to me as you can, an' when we reach the swiles I'll let ye know be raisin' the after derrick. Now when ye see the after derrick ris, ye'll know we're in the fat."

Even before, there was talk of a disastrous season. The ice was too tight for the ships to work, they said. Wes had no time for such talk, only a reputation to make. To become a big league "jowler," he had to get out on that ice.

On 30 March, Captain Abram Kean initiated his signal to Wes by raising his ship's aft derrick (a wooden crane). Wes saw the signal but the *Newfoundland* was already jammed into ice a half dozen miles away. His ship's lack of a steel hull prevented him from breaking through in the direction of his father and the seals.

Wes Kean sent his men on foot across the ice toward his father's ship. He expected his men would spend that night aboard the *Stephano* after a day of hard swiling. Trouble was, a mighty storm was coming on.

Already at 6 a.m. the sun was veiled and there were "twin reflections of yellowish light, like minor suns, one on either side." The older sailors knew these as foreboding "sun hounds," formed from ice crystals flying out ahead of a storm.

All these sailing men were firm believers in superstition, unlike Old Man Kean who was a firm believer in Jesus Christ. Like Faroese and Icelanders, they knew damned well that evil spirits existed. Spirits living along the coast, called Jack-o-lanterns, they said, shined false lights to lure ships to their destruction.

Plus, fate was fate. The sea would claim its due of victims and if a man was marked for death, well, nothing could be done.

A total of 166 men set out that morning from Wes Kean's ship but sensing the storm, 34 turned back, to catcalls and shouts of "cowards!" A fair number of those who turned back were elders who knew more weather lore than the boys, aphorisms like "If the wind come from the east, 'tis good for neither man nor beast.".

The 132 of Wes Kean's swilers who didn't turn back spent two nights stranded in a blizzard on the ice. Seventy-seven didn't come back alive.

After a four-hour hike across tough ice they reached and boarded the *Stephano* in late morning, weather coming on fast. Captain Abe searched the skies, fortified the *Newfoundland*'s sailors with hard tack and tea, and turned them back out on the ice in under an hour.

Cooks on all the ships worked only for the officers, who enjoyed, among other delicacies, fresh beef. The rank and file lived on hard tack (as made by the swiling fleet, oval three inch flour cakes) or food they'd brought for the time before the hunt had taken seals. So far that had meant eight days of little to eat besides hard tack, and counting.

Early in any year's harvest, blood and grease would cover the rough planking laid down on the ships' decks as protection against the sailors' hob-nailed boots. Before long even new swilers "learned to eat the warm, fresh hearts cut still beating from seal carcasses." But so far this year, for more than a week now, it was only hard tack and tea.

Old Man Kean's orders might as well have been the Firm Law of God, not only on his ship but across the whole fleet. When he turned Wes's men back onto the ice the Old Man told the sailors to walk back to their own ship, harvesting a field of pelts the *Stephano* had left earlier. Abram Kean foresaw no problems.

Grumbling broke out, but the Old Man convinced George Tuff, the leader of the men on the ice, that he and his men had an easy walk to back to his son's ship, considered them safe and put them out of his mind.

"They'll be ahl rate," he thought.

Wes grew uneasy with the worsening of the storm, in the absence of his crew.

St. John's was (still is) compact with most commerce conducted on foot, but early on Monday, 30 March, Water Street emptied out as snow, Cassie Brown writes, "... was beginning to choke the streets ... Business came to a halt. Streetcars tried to plow through snowdrifts, bogged down, and could not be moved. People deserted the shops and the streets and let winter have full sway." Clear across The Rock the fear of wives and mothers curdled into fright and rose with the howl of the wind.

The enduring, infuriating frustration is that Wes Kean and the Old Man each assumed the other had Tuff and his men. Wes was sure his father had kept them aboard the *Stephano* and Abe assumed they followed his orders to return to Wes and the *Newfoundland*. Neither sent out a search party.

Sure in their own assumptions, neither Wes nor Abram sounded their whistles so that as the blizzard closed in the men on the ice could hear in what direction to walk. And because Wes Kean had no wireless (the owners had removed it the week before as an unnecessary expense) there was no way for father or son or to be sure.

The sealers were a hundred miles north of St. John's when the first flakes fell. Wes Kean's brother (and the Old Man's eldest son) Joe commanded another swiling vessel, the *Florizel*. He sounded his ships's whistle to summon his men back from the ice. Tuff's men, the *Newfoundland*'s men, would spend the next two nights on the ice.

Messages to look out for each other's crew were flashed between Wes's brother Joe and the Old Man, but Wes had neither wireless nor, in the closing weather, sight of his brother in the *Florizel* or his father in the *Stephano*.

Once there were 400 wooden swiling ships. Larger steel-hulled steamers reduced the fleet to only twenty by 1914. As a result the ships were spaced more widely around the ice. It was harder to see from ship to ship.

Captain Abe, his ship with its mighty steel hull, steamed away to the north in search of seals, further confusing the *Newfoundland*'s ice-bound sailors as to their position relative to their ship.

Finally becoming blinded by blowing snow, the men raced through snowdrifts and over the ice, struggling in ever more desperate search of the *Newfoundland*. At dark they built what shelter they could from loose ice. They split into three watches and each built windbreaks from the ice, against which they would spend the first night, but the progress of the storm moved winds from the east around to the north, rendering only the best built windbreak effective by morning.

•••••

With morning's light the men who could tried to walk on, hearts pounding just to stay alive. Consumed by violent, shivering convulsions, they searched each others' eyes and found only stark, open terror. Their predicament, they were sure, meant that they were doomed.

Some died frozen in a posture of prayer. Stephen Donovan died on his feet and froze standing. One father and son were found frozen in an embrace, a pose captured in a memorial statue. Each man died in his own intimate way, stilled by the ice.

Survivors lost arms, legs and feet. Tom Dawson survived with the help of his friend John Howlett. Exhausted, his legs and feet frozen, Dawson lay on the ice to die but Howlett found the strength to collect bodies and stack them around Dawson as a miserable windbreak.

Delirious men walked into the water and drowned. Some were pulled out by their fellows but quickly froze to death. Men were found after the storm so frozen to the ice they had to be chipped free.

•••••

In the morning Wes Kean spotted what was left of his men through his spy-glass. He signaled other ships. The SS *Bellaventure*, his brother's ship the *Florizel* and Captain Abe's *Stephano* responded as best they could.

Two men helped Cecil Mouland to the *Bellaventure*, his brother Ralph alongside on a stretcher. Mouland saw a seal. He pleaded, "Turn 'im over and put yer knife in 'is heart." They lowered Cecil to the carcass where he drank the warm blood of the dead seal. Mouland, the last survivor, died in 1978.

Of the 77 who died, 69 bodies were found.

As news of the disaster spread family members besieged the telegraph office, gathering with the dread of knowing there must be few survivors. Crowds grew until Water Street was impassable.

Funeral parlors ran out of caskets. In the basement of the Seamen's Academy, doctors thawed bodies and pulled those frozen together apart.

All of Newfoundland wept. Some of the men's bodies rode home in trains they could never afford in life.

•••••

At the inquiry neither Kean was found guilty of anything more serious than "errors of judgement." Ships were henceforth required to carry additional safety equipment and  from now on, a wireless. The *Newfoundland*'s owner's counsel testified "The safety of the crew was not thought of at all, or it (the wireless) would not have been removed...."

Cassie Brown's *Death on the Ice* is among the most read Newfoundland books of all time and has been used in the province's schools since its publication.  At the time the sealing disaster was the worst calamity in the nation's history, though that would hold only for the next three and a half years, until Halifax.

Abe Kean hunted seals for twenty more years. In 1934 he brought back what they reckoned was his millionth pelt, for which he was awarded the Order of the British Empire for being the most lethal killer of seals in history.

•••••

## SOME QUALITY TIME IN THE RAIN

"St. Johner" can't be right. St. Johnsian? St. Johnite? What do you call a St. John's resident? A Townie, it turns out. It means either native-born, or someone who has come from a Newfoundland village to the main town. In Rock-think, there is no one beyond the island.

Bullets of rain sling themselves into the door of the Ship Pub, away from the determined fun purveyors on George Street, entrance to the side, across the street from the Fog Off clothing store. The storm rumbles outside while we hear about the life of Beth Twillingate, not born a Townie. She started life as a fisherman's daughter. St. John's is a big city to her and a fine and comfortable home, she says as she serves up Iceberg beers.

She answers a cell phone on the bar.

"No. No, I'm a bartender. In. St. John's.

In Newfoundland."

A woman she'd never seen before was in here not twenty minutes ago and left the phone. We wonder if she has just caused a divorce. The chill makes that humor wry, not sardonic.

She plays music from the Halifax band Hillsburn, a song with the refrain, "I killed Billy but Billy wouldn't die." On the relative culinary merits of the local wildlife, caribou, says she, is more gamey than moose. And Newfie steak is just fine.

A retired railroadman in a red jacket, a regular named Melvin, recalls the good old days when he worked the stretch of line from Argentia to St. John's. He remembers the days when the trains would leave Port aux Basques with five locomotives to carry 140 rail cars up the grades in the interior, but now there is no rail line in the province, and toward the end of his working days he helped to pull up the narrow gauge rail he worked all his life. They sold it to Chile for their coal mines.

Rain pounds the pavement when the door opens. Here is Martin, a philosophy doctoral candidate, who helps us all handicap the prospects of the coming end of Western civilization, beginning with the then-imminent Brexit and followed by the elections of Donald Trump and Marine Le Pen, and then the collapse of the EU. It sounds just possible.

The whales ought to be here in ten days, two weeks, and they will bring tourist dollars. Things are looking up. Hard to imagine how they couldn't be after the howling wind and spitting showers of the night before. We won't be here, but by Saturday they're looking for nineteen degrees, proper basking weather again. Trouble is, it's only Tuesday.

•••••

## GANDER

There is an odd place, a working artifact, two hundred miles up the road, a twenty-four-hour airport, forever stocked and ready for any calamity. It stretches across land that otherwise would surely lie vacant on the rocks and bog, alongside a warren of unremarkable low buildings at a former military airfield.

The buildings comprise Gander Oceanic Control, the busiest oceanic air traffic control center in the world. Looking east on a map of the sky, a box labeled Gander OACC stretches across watery space to 30 degrees west longitude where it is met by its counterpart, "Shanwick OACC" that will take you into European airspace.

Gander airfield fashions itself as the "airlines' lifeboat," available to handle any incident that may afflict incoming aircraft - mechanical, navigational, atmospheric-related, unruly passengers, hijackings, bomb scares. Gander can help.

When the order came to ground all air transportation in the U.S. at 9:45 a.m. on 11 September, 2001, some 4,546 aircraft scrambled for a place to land. About 400 more planes were inbound, most en route from Europe. Canada took in 250, in the maritimes at St. John's and

Stephenville in Newfoundland, Moncton in New Brunswick, Halifax and Gander.

Thirty-eight commercial jets bound for the United States diverted to Gander and deposited 6,595 people from all over the world in a piney woods town of 10,000 people, a few traffic lights and one high school.

When it was built as a joint military base for the U.S., England and Canada, Gander's was the biggest airport in the world, with runways so huge it was designated as an east coast abort landing site for the Space Shuttle. Even today, twenty percent of business jets flying the North Atlantic stop at Gander.

It had been an air hub for decades so Gander field felt it could handle the 9/11 planes, if just. In the end they parked some of them on the second runway.

In pre-jet days they kitted out Gander as a refueling stop for shorter range trans-Atlantic flights. More than 20,000 planes built in the U.S. refueled at Gander on the way to war in Europe. Gander served as a staging point for anti-U-boat flights.

Before the rise of the jet engine and the decline of Gander in the 1960s, the West Germans opened a consulate, better to accommodate Cold War East German Asylum seekers. The shortest way from Berlin to freedom was through Gander.

In 2001, there was room to stack all that grounded metal around the airport, but could the citizens of the town cope with a two-thirds increase in population in the course of a single warm September day?

They could. They met the deplaning passengers with bagged lunches. They filled their prescriptions for free. They processed the passengers as they left the 38 flights, making sure the Red Cross knew where each passenger would stay. They unplugged all the televisions and they hung "out of order" signs over the airport telephones to keep passengers moving. The telephone company Newtel put tables of telephones on the sidewalk outside its office so passengers could call home for free. Gander's school bus drivers were on strike, but in light of events they rallied to carry their unexpected guests to shelters in Gander and nearby towns.

Kevin O'Brien, a pharmacy owner, coordinated the other pharmacists as they called countries around the world to determine medication and dosage for all passengers requiring prescriptions - and filled them for free. Pharmacies donated toiletries and 4,000 toothbrushes.

On September 11th Mirja and I were in Ulan Ude, the capital of Buryatia, east of Lake Baikal in Siberia. Surrounded by Russians and lacking in the Russian language, we experienced bewilderment, but nothing like the hothouse of rumors that swept the stranded passengers.

*"Have you heard? Seven planes hijacked! The towers of the Trade Center have collapsed! The Pentagon and the White House have been hit! More than 10,000 people are dead! The president has gone into a hidden nuclear bunker!"*

•••••

Gander is but one aerial manifestation of Newfoundland's geographic proximity to Europe. Air Canada runs the shortest scheduled trans-Atlantic flight from St. John's to London Heathrow each summer, at 2,300 miles and five hours eastbound.

Back in 1918, the first trans-Atlantic crossing ever left from St. John's Lester's Field on 15 June, in pursuit of a £10,000 prize offered by the *Daily Mail*. Two British airmen flew sixteen hours 27 minutes carrying 197 letters, the first air mail, 15-1/2 years after the Wright brothers' first powered flight.

When John Alcock and Arthur Whitten-Brown landed in a field near Clifden in Ireland reports said their converted World War 1 Vickers-Vimy biplane landed "behind the Marconi wireless station at Derrigimlagh," known for our very own Marconi of Signal Hill fame's efforts 18 years before.)

*Bill Murray*

## TO QUIRPON ISLAND

Quirpon is a foggy a wisp of nothing, a nub, a windswept bit of bog off the northern tip of Newfoundland atop of the Great Northern Peninsula, across the Strait of Belle Isle from Labrador. It stretches about six and one-half kilometers to its northern headland, which is the direction you will walk coming from the mainland. At the northern tip of Quirpon (pronounced to rhyme with "harpoon"), overlooking "Iceberg Alley," on the highest point on the cape, they built the Cape Bauld lighthouse 240 feet above the sea.

A contract was let in 1880 for $4,775. "Owing to unexpected difficulties in the carrying out of the contract" the light was not lit until 15 August, 1884. Its light could be seen for up to eighteen miles.

Early wooden lighthouses like the one at Cape Bauld burned down more often that you'd think, for a couple of good reasons. First, since they were usually the tallest thing for miles lighthouses drew lightning and sometimes burst into flames.

(Benjamin Franklin was aware of the problem, having written a poem as a twelve-year-old about a tragedy at a lighthouse off Boston Harbor, which subsequently nearly burned down twice. Franklin, he of the kite and the thunderstorm, invented the lightning rod but clergy held up such protection for more than twenty years on the grounds that mere men should not presume to avert the stroke of heaven.)

Another reason: Before electricity the keeper kept the fire lit with constantly burning - and combustible - whale oil, way up in the sky at the top of sometimes rickety wooden stairs. Too often oil and wood didn't mix. (Rhode Island's first lighthouse burnt down at age four in 1753.) And thus early lighthouses saved sailors at peril of lighthouse keepers.

I can find no record that the wooden Cape Bauld met a fiery death before it was replaced in 1907 with a cast iron and concrete tower. The current octagonal concrete tower was built alongside the older one in 1961.

(Crashing against rocks wasn't the only way a ship might meet its end. In swiling lore down toward St. John's, evil spirits called Jack-o-lanterns shone false lights to lure ships to their destruction. Up this way it was said that early scavengers called "wreckers" - or "mooncussers" - for a bright moon served as a ship's best navigation aide in the absence of lighthouses, haunted dangerous shores. Legends say that they would tie lanterns to animals, walking them on the beach to lure sailors off course.

Radar, radio beacons and GPS ultimately put most lighthouse keepers out of business, but Cape Bauld Light remains lit. It runs by automation maintained by the Canadian government.

Every once in a while a man flies in from the Federal Bureau of Lighthouses or some such, to make sure the old Cape Bauld lighthouse still works. There used to be a foghorn until it broke. They came and took it out.

In the 1990s Canada began to divest itself of its lighthouse properties, and in 1998 Ed English, who used to work in the Newfoundland and Labrador tourism department, bought the top part of Quirpon Island (except for the lighthouse itself and an out building), including the old lighthouse keeper's residences, at a blind auction.

By the looks of him, nearly twenty years ago he must have been just a kid on a lark. Said he was headed out on vacation one day after the bid when he got a call, "you own a lighthouse."

Shouldn't be here right now, he says. Should be tending his 52 new condos in Cornerbrook. Or his new lighthouse all the way down at the other end of Newfoundland, 400 miles south to Cape Anguille.

But it has been a late spring, the season a little slow getting going, so he has come up to give a hand, get his Quirpon project up and running. Up here the season only opened a couple weeks ago, at the beginning of June.

*Bill Murray*

I called Judy, who handles reservations, back in April. "Is it spring yet?" I asked.

She said, "it was minus ten last night. There's not as much snow as there was, though."

**IFFY ARRIVAL**

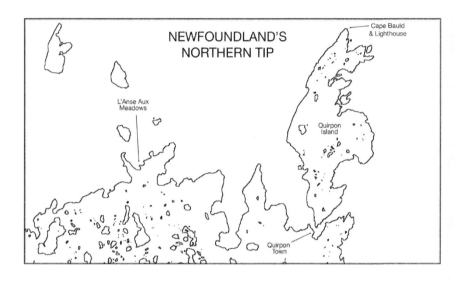

NEWFOUNDLAND'S NORTHERN TIP

We don't mean to visit Labrador and in the end we narrowly avoid it but for a while a night in Goose Bay looks likely. When we board the little Provincial Airlines deHavilland DHC-8-100 in St. John's, there is a "weather alert" and as of takeoff, we can't land in St. Anthony's because of fog. If the same prevails once we've flown up the coast we will fly on to Blanc Sablon in Quebec, across the Bay of Belle Isle, then up to Goose Bay.

Sounds like an adventure. The crew's assurances and cheerful expectation can not be disproven. We are soothed by sandwiches served by the first attendant, trailed by a second who dangles styrofoam cups between her fingers, mustard packets in one, mayo in the other.

278

In the end the weather clears, at least enough for the pilot to make out the airstrip.

•••••

Sequoia is a white huskie with an albino watery blue eye that a man named Angus adopted in northern Labrador. She and Angus have been been partners for twelve years. They come to meet us at the airport and drive us an hour to the dock in Quirpon town. Before long, Angus will leave for northern Labrador to guide tours up there. Among the prettiest places on the planet, he says.

On the ride up, Angus declares it is capelin weather. It's wet and humid when these small fish (20-25 centimeters), go out in their blaze of collective glory, throwing themselves on the beach to be gathered by the scoop in buckets. Like they do with Amasat in Greenland.

To lay down these highways across bog, it is necessary to scrape down to firm foundation and in the process untold rich black earth gets thrown up along the roadside.

The Newfoundlander is not one to pass up an opportunity and as such individual "private" garden plots have sprung up in the rich, excavated earth between the road and the larches just budding here in mid-June, fenced off and bolstered with beached capelin and livestock manure. It's "crown land" out here mostly and the government doesn't seem to mind.

We run alongside balsam fir, black spruce, birch and aspen trees, all of modest height and shaped by wind. They have lately moved the tree line back from the road, collisions with moose having become so frequent that residents admire the beasts' beauty less than they grow weary of their nuisance.

Moose were only introduced at Gander Bay in 1878 but today figure in almost 700 road accidents each year. In many, the moose battles the vehicle to a deadly draw. After twenty years of driving past Beware the

Moose signs in Finland, today I spy my first, ruminating in peace on the road to Quirpon Island.

Cloudberries, much loved for jam across Scandinavia, grow wild all along the route, into a tiny town called St. Lunaire-Griquet where New England saltbox houses ring a natural harbor, and then right into tiny Quirpon town. Locally called "bake apple," cloudberries *may* be the vines of Vinland, Leif Ericksson's arrival point in North America which we will see in a few days time, but Angus is skeptical.

He asks why they would name Vinland after golden, round cloudberries when the Vikings knew full well what cloudberries looked like, and real grapes too, having sailed down the Volga to the Black Sea, and around Portugal. And in Vinland, grapes *can* grow. Angus proved it by planting some vines around the company's other lighthouse down south. Who knows, he wonders, whether the climate was different enough around the year 1000 for wild grape vines to flourish?

•••••

When we arrive at the dock two men, Brian and Ed, have their heads down, deep into some construction project with electric sanders and metal grating, inventing some kind of better mooring for the shuttle boat.

Quoia the huskie jumps into the boat and rests her paws on the bow as Angus steers us across to the island. The sea is roiling today. Sometimes it is possible to sail right out into the sea and around to put guests in near the lighthouse on Quirpon's northern tip. Today we take the shortest route from town to the southern tip, across a route that the island protects from the sea. In this event the island's more or less trusty Polaris Ranger ATV is available to carry guests to the lighthouse.

Now, the island is just shy of seven kilometers long, today's landing spot is at the southern tip and the lighthouse perches on the Strait of Belle Isle facing Labrador, close enough to the cliff to fall off the far end of Quirpon Island at fifty paces. Yet Angus calls the walk between the two places five and a half kilometers.

Angus makes the case for us to hike; it is gorgeous, he tells us, and we are game. Once we see the condition of the ATV track we surmise that they always make that case, because every trip by vehicle digs ruts further into the bog. The ATV spins its tires and ventures ever farther out, ever widening the track, meaning more work for the three men out here, Angus and Brian and Ed, who have to lay a lattice of planks across the tracks.

Sizing up my brand new hiking boots back on the mainland, they dismissed them as useful as a saddle on a cow, assigning me a pair of Wellingtons instead, and I systematically proceed to grind the flesh off both heels and both sides of both ankles over the next five and one half kilometers of Viking-inspired hiking bravado. I believe that were Angus's buddies there to elbow in the ribs once we disappear over the first ridge, he surely would have.

Hiking across Quirpon Island with Quoia

Quoia comes with Mirja and me to the lighthouse, and she minds us, rather than the other way around. She runs ahead thirty meters, stops and spins, and waits for us to catch up.

This is tundra, there are no trees and the wind blasts across the island from the direction of Labrador, due north. Exposed rocks turned vertical betray some frightening event in Quirpon's distant geological past.

Out in mid island we stop on a bluff of clefts and gullies to watch a bob of seals down near the rocks, watching for diving gannets because Angus says diving gannets mean whales. I suppose the walk takes a couple hours and a little more but time isn't terribly important once here, and when we arrive at the Lighthouse the ladies tell us there's a fridge full of beers, just help yourself, and I am happy to dig in to several cold Iceberg beers, from the Qidi Vidi brewery in St. John's.

•••••

**DINING WITH DARLENE**

Wind rattling the windows, we sit before the locally famous Jiggs dinner: Roast beef and carrots with potatoes, puréed turnips and dressing, each served from ice cream scoops, and gravy from a gravy boat for every two people.

I believe it may be served every night. Learn one thing, learn it well.

The kitchen crew of Marilyn, Mariah and Madonna prepare breakfast, dinner in two seatings, and keep the kettle on for visitors. They serve tonight's meal, repair to the back and we dine, strangers at the common table.

Stooped and graying Reiner and his wife Ellen from Kitchener. Two German girls, one pregnant. A young woman and her consort, neither terribly fetching, whose names are never revealed because they never say a single word except "hi." Nor do they make eye contact. Ever.

Showing a natural disfluency with politesse, Darlene, a formidable woman who gives her chair disquiet, regales us with tales of her extensive travels to Myanmar, Sossusvlei and Maccu Pichu. She makes sure we know of her extreme devotion to photography and shares a blow by blow of her fall getting into the boat earlier today.

Rapacious with our little group's time, she lectures with apodictic certainty on the state of Canadian politics while the table prefers a much more politically vegetarian conversation. Ellen stares at her scoop of turnip.

Sometimes klatches of strangers provoke stimulating conversation, but often there is a Darlene. I'd like to advise her that if one is convinced she is the smartest person in the room, she will find greater mental challenge by changing rooms. Alas, here there is a shortage of rooms.

So I take my own advice and find an early opportunity to track down the boys in the back. Angus and Ed and Brian are downing beers, TV on, sound down. This is a small house, this inn, once the lighthouse keeper's residence alone, and the boys sit atop one another, furniture and belongings in a jumble, a rumpled, strewn-about place far more lived in than the anodyne common space.

Time worn jokes about needing to get around to some remodeling. You have to close the door to the hallway to open the door to the toilet, which is full of toothbrushes.

These men provide all the brawn on Quirpon Island, the laboring face of Ed's lighthouse business. Ed, the leader, lanky and craggy with long teeth and a formidable Newfie accent, folds himself into his chair. Brian, the quiet one, is charged with running the ATV up and back across the island, not an inconsiderable task.

Angus, the great outdoorsman, says they dress to be out all day every morning, because they never know quite what chore will have to be gotten up to, and the wind is blistering and he guesses maybe 250 icebergs arrive each year, having sailed the 1,600-odd kilometers from

Greenland (The *Titanic*'s fateful berg drifted in this same way down the Labrador current from Baffin Bay south of here). And after another day out amid the wet and the wind and the icebergs, Angus is simply and openly baffled why we would ever want to go back to St. John's.

I want to hear stories, but they are in their home space and I don't begrudge them their private time.

So: Squeeze down the hallway to the kitchen, gaze at the gale through the window, then look around this tiny kitchen in this modest building. Consider the even more modest one in which we stay. These two buildings, when full, hold 22 max. I must surmise that Marilyn, Mariah and Madonna spend an indoor life constrained. We make the short walk back to the building where we've been given a bed.

Thinking back to walking the sodden earth, Quoia leading us through blowing bitter wind across the island, honestly, the Jiggs dinner (named for a local comic strip character) was sweeter in anticipation. If only just.

• • • • •

The north Atlantic throws itself against boulders offshore. The wind tears the door from my hands and throws it full open against the porch rails. The whole Earth is swallowed up in wintry Atlantic gray; surf kicks up aqua where it dashes against rocks.

Icy bits form into striations offshore. They call them growlers, no more than five meters across, say, the size of a grand piano or less. It is foggy and wet and windy, a mausey day in Newfoundlandese.

The wind comes beeline straight from the north, utterly icy with air temperature around six. The lighthouse tip of the island is shrouded in fog and either the Cape Bauld Light station works better at distance or at night, or the need for lighthouses is overrated because here underneath it, it suggests all the power of a table lamp.

Since we leave our outdoor shoes at the door of both buildings, in short order we learn shoe sleuthing, through which one can tell on entry whether the dire Darlene is in the house.

They've made a run at making the front, common room into a "family room" in the outbuilding, with two couches, an arm chair, low tables and chairs, throw pillows, books and puzzles, this and that for the kids - none of whom, mercifully, are here at present - and coffee and a small fridge in the anteroom.

It's a good try but without the unifying element of, say, a fireplace or a wood stove, people keep to their quarters. Which suits me well as I enjoy the common room all to myself, riffling through the books on the shelves, titles like *The Newfoundland and Labrador Book of Everything* and *Confederation: Deciding Newfoundland's Future 1934 to 1949* by James K. Hiller.

Out the side window the lighthouse keeper's house and the lighthouse proper, done up in red and white, compliment the Canadian flag being systematically torn to shreds by the wind. In wind like this, how long can a flag last?

The Arctic and Angmagssaliq Hotels in Greenland offer iceberg views. The common room here on Quirpon will not be outdone, and I have the march of the icebergs all to myself.

•••••

Most with a vague mental map of Canada imagine its eastern extent somewhere near the mouth of the Gulf of St. Lawrence, that storied and stately entrée to the St. Lawrence Seaway, the gateway to Quebec and Montreal. You must sail 800 miles further east to Belle Isle, the little island between Quirpon and Labrador.

•••••

Cape Bauld Lighthouse and Its Keeper's House

In the morning, in the moments the fog lifts, you can see across to Labrador, a brooding presence with snowy patches across the way, the other part of this province that extends nearly 1,200 more miles north. Between Labrador and Quirpon a tabular iceberg approaches, over a hundred meters across, perhaps the size of an oil rig, closing on the island. "Lotsa water in that one," Ed observes.

When the fog pulls back the icebergs gain character and definition, changing through gray and white toward blue and aqua. Birthed as a mighty litter far to the north, but now fully fledged, they march solitary this far from calving. In the relative way of icebergs, this one's approach is not so fast, and we will not be around to watch it come crashing against the shore.

Hugs around when it is time to go. Mariah and Madonna pose for photos with the two German girls to whom their Newfie patois is utterly impenetrable. They have been persuaded by Angus of the superior excellence of walking the five and one half kilometers back to the dock and the three of them leave together. An impressive exhibition of fortitude for the pregnant lady.

We judge that the juice in the second glass isn't worth the squeeze and politely decline to revel in the same retreat by foot. Brian is charged with driving us up to the other end of the island in the Polaris Ranger.

And so we begin, lurching forward and back from the lighthouse end of the island to the Quirpon town end because after the momentous (Angus's word) storm of the other night the sea still hasn't calmed down enough to take the boat into the open sea to the lighthouse side of the island.

Brian is an agreeable fellow with matching gray beard and hair under a knit skull cap, a green anorak, yellow gloves. Everybody wears gloves, it's that cold in June. In his touch-and-go comprehensible accent, he readily agrees that the path is a fresh challenge every day. At select spots, every day means driving farther afield onto the bog, to get 'round the ruts, mate.

A mighty little machine, the Polaris, pulling the three of us up close to vertical when necessary, over the planks they've laid across the bog, even across the most egregious ruts. Until it doesn't, of course, and we slide near fatally sideways and sink in the mud.

Little crises are de rigueur in places like this and who could tell wide-eyed travel stories otherwise? Our right rear wheel, over which I sit, is firmly and defiantly planted in a hole and spinning up a haboob of mud.

In all such calamities the good guys are ultimately extricated and so we are, but it is comforting to know that Ed is waiting at the other end with a bespoke motorboat crossing for us, rather than fearing a race against time as well as mud.

We pile out to lighten the load and not dig us in deeper. Drama and considerable mechanical thunder follow, foul-smelling blue engine-straining smoke and roiling of moss and mud bog, and eventually

Brian makes things right, just like you know he will, and no one even gets over-muddy. Back in the civilization of the outpost of St. John's I will have to scrub the salt water's high-water mark off my brand-new hiking boots. Hardly the definition of hardship.

Straining to mount Quirpon's final southern crest, we can see Ed and Angus and Quoia (the non-canines dressed in bright reflective jumpsuits) down by the shore. Brian radios in and Ed radios back, "Look for a Minke, I can't see it no more but it's near," and shortly Brian points "Dair tis!"

"Dass da closest I ever seen a Minke to shore, dat is," says Brian, and it is close, bobbing and feeding just meters from shore. So close, we see fish jump out of the water in the flight of their lives. Thrilling, the island's first whale sighting of the season.

Brian, Angus, Ed, Mirja and I, and Quoia too, jump into the boat and motor across to the mainland.

When word reaches the lighthouse Darlene will not be pleased that she, her publicly elaborated photography techniques and her raft of 43-pound lenses have missed the whale. Down with the boys at the dock, the thought brings quiet smiles all around.

•••••

## L'ANSE AUX MEADOWS

Funny thing about humans. The stakes are never so high a little hocus-pocus can't help. It seems the more we lay on the line, the more we are willing to countenance a little conjuring.

Because come on now, wearing your lucky cuff links, or dancing your little good luck jig, how could that hurt, really? Everybody deploys crossed fingers once in a while - just a harmless little attempt to sway fate.

So consider the medieval mariner, slighted and sequestered, hard-pressed and gaunt, prey to the caprice of wind and wave, confined below decks on a sailing ship. If the captain - and the sea - don't get the respect they demand, they will impose it.

The sailor finds solace in ritual. You get the idea he rather enjoys the taboo:

> • If the ship's bell rings of its own accord the ship is doomed.

> • Flowers are for funerals, not welcome aboard ship.

> • Don't bring bananas on board, or you won't catch any fish.

> • Don't set sail on Fridays. In Norse myth that was the day evil witches gathered.

Helge Ingstad, whom we are about to meet, wrote:

"The Norsemen firmly believed in terrible sea trolls …. And those who sailed far out on the high seas might be confronted with the greatest danger of all: they risked sailing over the edge of the world, only to plunge into the great abyss."

If they fell short of the abyss, what did they find when they sailed farther than ever before? Fortunate men like Eirik the Red found safe harbors and terrain hospitable enough to scratch out a life beyond the reach of Norwegian kings.

No men found untold riches. More likely came calamity, hardship, deprivation. Life on an ancient sailing ship was, in Henning Mankell's allusion, "a flimsy branch over an abyss." Yet they came, and the boundary of the world pushed ever farther west.

•••••

## THAT LAST LEAP

Eirik the Red established the farthest-west Norse colonies, all the way over to the far side of Greenland, but Eirik's story still doesn't get us quite to North America. Enter Bjarni Herjólfsson, an Icelander, a merchant and master of his own ship.

Herjólfsson traded in the triangle between Iceland, Ireland and Norway, and wintered odd years with his father Herjólf, in Iceland. He arrived there to shock in the winter of 985, for his father had disappeared. He'd followed Eirik to Greenland.

Herjólfsson sailed again at once, this time really reaching for the abyss. Battered by wind, engulfed in fog, he and his crew drifted day after day sailing blind, at the mercy of storm and tide.

At last the fog lifted over a low, wooded, foreign land. On the wind - with a prayer - reckoning by sun and stars, by the grace of Odin or God or their own sailing prowess, they fled and found their way back to Greenland, a harrowing tale to tell.

From the Greenlanders' Saga: "Bjarni now repaired to his father's and gave up seafaring, and was with his father so long as Herjólf lived." Sounds like Bjarni was freaked out.

Bjarni's odyssey made for distraction over mead around the fire back in Greenland, but at Brattahlíð the men were up to their ears in clearing and building, scratching out the settling of a new land. Fifteen years passed before Leif, son of Eirik, sought the land that Bjarni described.

•••••

The Greenlanders' Saga imagined Leif straight from central casting, "big and strong, of striking appearance, shrewd, and in every respect a temperate, fair-dealing man, wise, and an outstanding leader."

This paragon of rectitude and leader of men packed his attributes, a crew of 35 and set sail, northbound. Scarcely 200 miles north of the Western Settlement the current Greenlandic town of Sisimiut marks the departure point for the narrowest crossing of the Davis Strait, a couple hundred more miles to Baffin Island, north of Labrador.

Towering cliffs and mountains run up and down the Baffin Island coast, so crossing here, the sailors weren't out of sight of land for long. They turned south at the new continent, and the Labrador current held Leif's ship on a firm southerly course toward ever better weather, with Labrador, Newfoundland and the Gulf of St. Lawrence now before them.

At first they found nothing good - just rocks and glaciers and icebergs, so Leif named the place Helluland, or "Slab Land," after the icebergs. Farther south they found "vast forests inland from sandy beaches," and called this Markland, or "Forest Land." Kirsten A. Seaver, in *The Frozen Echo*, presumes this was the southernmost hundred miles or so of Labrador.

Rounding southern Labrador Leif and his men found land on both sides, Labrador to starboard and Belle Isle to port. From Belle Isle they would see Cape Bauld on our Quirpon Island, just 30 kilometers away. Through this gap between Labrador and Newfoundland's northern peninsula, the expedition sailed a short while more.

Coming ashore four or five miles west of Quirpon on a cape of broad sweep extending back toward Labrador, the men stood on a fine sandy beach, long and level and made to order for hauling up and dismembering whales. With stiff winds and sight lines to the occasional iceberg, for all the distance the sailors had come this must have felt familiar, chill of the wind on their faces right down to their sodden shoes.

Squishing around the marsh exploring the new land one day, a crew member named Tyrker went missing for several hours, returning just as Leif assembled a search party. Said Tyrker, "I have not been much further off, but still I have something new to tell of; I found vines and grapes," and thus was the legend of Vinland born.

But were they really grapes? Angus on Quirpon has grown grapes at Cape Anguille, farther south in Newfoundland, so we know they *can* grow here. Or, in the writing of the sagas, Tyrker's discovery could have become conflated with one made elsewhere on the expedition.

Here is what Kirsten Seaver thinks: "The Vinland sagas were written over two hundred years after the events they tell about, and the accounts of these early voyages show the writers grappling with descriptions of places they had never seen and for which they had no maps."

Except that there *are* maps, two in fact. The first, reputed to be a fifteenth century copy of a thirteenth century original, surfaced in 1957. It suggested Vinlandia was visited in the eleventh century by "companions Bjarni and Leif Eiriksson."

The scion of the Mellon banking family, a racehorse breeder named Paul Mellon, bought and donated the map to Yale University, his alma mater. Eight years of rigorous authenticity-testing later, Yale cheekily put the eleven-by-sixteen inch map on display on 10 October, 1965 - the eve of Columbus Day.

Doubts surfaced immediately. The map contained chemicals uninvented at the time of its purported creation. The Latin æ ligature in the map's text may not have made its way to the Norse by the time the map was said to have been drawn. Still, the parchment appears to date from the fifteenth century as claimed, and the argument remains unsettled.

Mellon's map is augmented by another, said to date from 1570. The original survives no more, but the Danish Royal Library has a copy dating from the next century. The Skálholt map of Norse discoveries, named for an Icelandic seminary town and drawn by a young teacher there, correctly depicts Norway, then to the west the Faroes, Iceland, Greenland and finally, a peninsula labeled "Promonterium

Vinlandiae." It fixes the northern tip of Vinland at roughly the same latitude as the southern coast of Ireland.

Mythology withered with the dawn of literacy. Oral history gave way to written facts no longer embroidered with each retelling. The bard and the troubadour yielded to the scribe and the scientist. In this case, with the Skálholt map in hand, to the wet and muddy archeologist.

•••••

## FINDING THE RUINS

Helge Marcus Ingstad's life spanned three centuries, 1899 to 2001. A wunderkind Norwegian lawyer in his twenties, he chucked it all to live with a native tribe as a trapper in Canada. He studied the history of the north. He became a governor in east Greenland, then governor of Svalbard, where he met his wife Anne-Stine. They were married in 1941 and settled back in Oslo, where Helge developed a following writing about his travels.

Book research drew the Ingstads to search for Vinland. They set off for the United States because the science of the day suggested that a bit of coal found in a gathering hall at Sandnes, Greenland (a place similar to the ruins he ultimately found) was anthracite from Rhode Island.

When it was determined to have come from England instead, the Ingstads took their search north, to maritime Canada. For successive summers Helge and Anne-Stine sailed up and down Newfoundland's west coast. It never ended, visiting these villages. Just mind-numbing, repetitive, wearying wet work.

Finally, in the summer of 1960 the Ingstads called at a village on the northernmost tip of Newfoundland. They arrived by ship because there were no roads. Just thirteen families lived here, reminiscent of Gásadalur, way back in the Faroes.

Everywhere they sailed they asked the same tired and practiced question. Did anyone know of any "strange, rectangular turf ridges?"

For no special reason, on this particular smudge of nondescript, sodden shoreline, a place like endless others, they met a man, George Decker, "the most prominent man in the village." And he did.

From Anne-Stine Ingstad's diary:

> "We hadn't been on land but a few minutes before we saw a small group of people come walking along the shore. A little yellow dog ran in front, followed by a man who looked to be in his 60s. He waved to us with his stick and yelled out something or other. Behind him followed a crowd of children of all ages. This was the first time I met the man who was to become our best friend in all the years to follow, George Decker. His whole stature radiated personality and authority. At first glance he appeared rough, with his weather-beaten face and dark stubble. But in his deep brown eyes shone warmth and humor, and he was quick to smile."

Helge Ingstad wrote, "Decker took me west of the village to a beautiful place with lots of grass and a small creek and some mounds in the tall grass. It was very clear that this was a very, very old site. There were remains of sod walls. Fishermen assumed it was an old Indian site. But Indians didn't use that kind of buildings, sod houses."

The name of this spot of wind-blown turf almost 400 miles north of St. John's as the crow flies, is L'Anse aux Meadows. Farley Mowat, the grand old man of Canadian adventure writing, calls this a distortion of the French L'Anse aux Méduses, or Jellyfish Bay.

The Ingstads spent that winter arranging an excavation to be led by Anne-Stine, now an archaeologist at the University of Oslo. It started the next summer and continued seven years.

Experts from Toronto and Trondheim collaborated to fix charcoal from the L'Anse blacksmith's furnace as dating from 975 to 1020. The excavation revealed three stone and sod halls, five workshops, iron nails and decorative baubles consistent with the period. By 1961 they had authentic archaeological evidence. The Ingstads had found Vinland.

•••••

## THE WORLD THAT LEIF BUILT

The team unearthed sod-and-timber proof of settlement, halls built to sleep more men than back home. The only same-sized buildings back east were found at þings or Viking military slave-camps like Dublin.

Where a concentration of halls existed, at Þhingvellir in Iceland for example, they sprawled across the landscape spread up to a kilometer apart, surrounded by fields and outbuildings. Here the entire encampment lay tight against itself suggesting a foreboding, garrison mentality, uneasy disquiet in an alien land.

They built three halls between two bogs at the back of the beach near what they call today Black Duck Brook. Each had room outside for storage of turf, what wood they found, drying fish. A smaller fourth area centered on an open-ended hut with a furnace for iron working, and a kiln to produce charcoal needed for ironworks.

•••••

L'Anse aux Meadows is a UNESCO World Heritage and Canadian National Historic Site. Parks Canada has assembled replica buildings alongside the ruins, with detail right down to spare blocks of peat for roof repair, turf squares stacked fifteen high like bags of pine bark or potting soil on pallets at the garden center.

On a Wednesday in June, before summer has taken hold, smoke rises from a chimney in the main hall. There are four fireplaces the length of the building, fires for illumination and cooking, iron kettles for boiling stews.

The scent of wood smoke makes me eager to step inside. Here is immediate, well-insulated, welcome warmth. You may shed your winter wear and you will be surprised how roomy the interior space, much taller than a man. Any Danes among the explorers, here they could find their hygge, some respite, mental salve for the hardship of life on the edge.

An elaborate lattice weaves across the ceiling. The walls are extravagantly hung with ropes - coils and coils of line - as befits a sailor's colony. Against the back wall the length of the building run benches wide enough for sleeping, benches and the wall all lined with skins.

L'Anse aux Meadows was no mere summer camp. It took twelve Parks Canada workers six months to craft the outdoor museum. Birgitta Linderoth Wallace, author of *Westward Vikings*, reckons that is comparable to sixty explorers working for two months of summer, or six weeks for ninety men.

She writes, "For the posts bearing the roofs of the three halls, 86 tall trees had to be felled and dressed plus those needed for the roof beams ... at least 1,500 cubic metres of sod were cut for the walls and roofs." Buildings meant to withstand winter.

Maybe the Vinland voyages explored further south in summer. And maybe, as colder weather returned, so the men returned to L'Anse to celebrate Christmas, embellish tales of their exploits and mainly, stay warm. The excavations unearthed a soapstone spindle whorl that suggests spinning, possibly weaving. Perhaps the explorers brought bags of unspun wool, a worthwhile way to keep hands busy over the tedious winter.

•••••

Leif's exploration of Vinland lasted through winter but less than a year. The party returned to Greenland with a rich cargo of lumber and grapes (the latter perhaps in a liquid form), and found with a shock that Erik the Red was dead. Leif took up the mantle of leadership in Greenland, and his brother Thorvald sailed back to Vinland.

Thorvald led a crew of thirty using Leif's ship and sailing instructions. They found the L'Anse camp, and shortly thereafter they found the "skrælings," local people unlike the Inuit in Greenland. These were Native Americans, "short in height with threatening features and tangled hair on their heads." The word skrælings is translated as "small people" by scholars, "screeching wretches" by the more flamboyant.

Leif's first group of explorers, who built their settlement in tight formation, had been right to do so. The Greenlanders' first encounter with other people did not go well.

One day Thorvald's men came upon nine strangers sheltered under upside-down skin boats and the Norse killed all but one. The escapee returned next day primed for vengeance. The men saw countless canoes advancing from the sea, and Thorvald exclaimed: "We will put out the battle-skreen, and defend ourselves as well as we can."

Battened down, the men withstood the skrælings' attack unharmed except, calamitously, for Thorvald: As the skrælings fled he wailed, "I have gotten a wound under the arm, for an arrow fled between the edge of the ship and the shield, in under my arm, and here is the arrow, and it will prove a mortal wound to me."

Thorvald Eiriksson became the first European buried in the New World and, dispirited, the Greenlanders soon departed for home. According to Linderoth Wallace, "the next expedition to Vinland is said to have been mounted for the explicit purpose of bringing his body back to Greenland."

A clash on a subsequent expedition killed two more would be settlers. The Sagas tell us that the explorers realized "despite everything the land had to offer there, they would be under constant threat of attack from its prior inhabitants." The Vinland settlement effort stalled.

Perhaps the explorers recognized all along they didn't have the numbers for permanent colonization. Maybe the realistic among them never planned more than temporary missions to this continent-sized storehouse of supplies.

Had they intended a sustained occupation there would have been a church and a cemetery, but there were none. The explorers never farmed the fields. There was neither barn nor byre for cattle, no corral or fold for sheep.

Amid carpentry waste archaeologists found three butternuts, a tree never known to grow in Newfoundland, its range from southern Quebec to northern Arkansas. Their presence suggests the explorers traveled at least as far as New Brunswick, more than 400 miles to the southwest.

Down there food may have grown wild, for "that unsown crops also abound ... we have ascertained not from fabulous reports but from the trustworthy relations of the Danes," wrote a German chronicler in the 1070s.

Nowadays most everyone agrees the Vinland of the Sagas was a land and not a single, specific site like L'Anse aux Meadows. Vinland perhaps comprised an area from L'Anse along the Newfoundland coast south to Nova Scotia, down the St. Lawrence to present-day Quebec City where the river narrows, then up the opposite coast in a grand arc along Newfoundland, New Brunswick, Quebec and Labrador back to L'Anse. Which also helps to explain the grapes.

•••••

**THE MODERN VIEW**

Today is as fine a day as we will see in northern Newfoundland, no sun but no rain and a fresh, steady, penetrating wind. Hardscrabble ground, uneven, firm enough if you are deft, but step off the rocks and you will sink to your boot tops in the bog.

Helge Ingstad wrote of a Norse "will of iron and a character able to endure privation and pain without a murmur," and he must surely be right. Standing out by Black Duck Brook dressed in snug twenty-first century down clothing, I can not summon to mind the impossible hardship of men dressed in skins and bad footwear who sailed from

Greenland in the cold and the wet dodging icebergs, serrating wind and jostling seas.

A foot bridge crosses the brook leading away from the museum toward the ruins. A modest few visitors pick our way up and down the paths. The original shelters, slumped back to Earth, now present as mounds, the effect a gently dimpled plain. Plaques identify the dimples: Huts and halls, the boat shed, the forge, the carpentry shop, storage, the smithy.

Twenty people make a ring around the Parks Canada man in ranger-wear, who is fit to the place, kind of wild and outdoorsy like a pirate. He spins tales with a performer's twinkle; his audience is all in. Sometimes he must raise his voice if the wind kicks up, bearing down across the Gulf of St. Lawrence from Labrador.

But walk away, find your own place, stand still, and the sounds slide away. Trifling waves come to shore too far away to hear. The cinematic clash of icebergs proceeds in acoustic stealth, distant enough not to disturb the quiet. Seabirds' calls soar away on the wind and we are left only with the benign rustling of the tall grass.

We stand by the brook. Helge Ingstad wrote in the 1960s, that "There is salmon in Black Duck Brook, we caught them with our bare hands." George Decker's grandfather told him there was considerable forest here in his younger days, but from the brook to the shoreline to Labrador this morning I am hard pressed to find a single tree.

The fog clears across the strait and Labrador emerges, brooding. Wisps of fog play up its cliff sides, snowy patches running up onshore. A peculiar lopsided iceberg, too heavy to bob, has come with us from Quirpon.

In the course of an hour the fog recedes, pulling with it more character and definition from the icebergs, moving their surfaces from amorphous gray through bland white, in the end striking out toward the flamboyance of blue and aqua.

*Bill Murray*

The original European explorers stared hard into this view, wind burning their faces and blowing their beards as they ended their era of discovery one thousand years ago. Five hundred years before the European voyages that got all the good press, here at the end of their long road stood a mottled and murderous clan of northmen.

I imagine the view today is much as it was then. Expansive but spare, open to possibilities and full of challenge, but also of promise. Two virgin continents awaiting the hand of European man. Leif's scruffy battalion left that promise for others to fulfill, but he and his rough-hewn men, standing here on this earth wild and untamed, they had found the future.

•••••

*Out in the Cold*

*Bill Murray*

## ACKNOWLEDGEMENTS

I am indebted to many who gave of their time, experience and kindness for this book. In particular I thank the Parisian photographer and author Léo Delafontaine, who kindly shared his experience of weeks spent in Barentsburg. Mark Sabbatini, the editor of the *Icepeople* newspaper in Longyearbyen, dodged too-frequent avalanches to share his time, wisdom and newspaperman's editing knowhow. In Torshavn, the Faroese diplomat Gunnar Holm-Jacobsen provided valuable guidance, and he and his wife Sigga welcomed us into their home with real warmth and hospitality. I met Icelandic author and philanthropist Hrafn Jökulsson 25 years ago and would know little about Iceland - or have met Iceland's president - without him. Frederic Dotte, a presenter at Saint-Pierre et Miquelon Première radio and TV, gave freely of his time and helped me understand his adopted island. My old friend Bobby Long provided patience, fact-checking and solid advice. And as ever, the biggest thanks to my wife Mirja, who for nearly a quarter century has shared with me the joy of obscure travel.

*Bill Murray*

**SOURCES AND ADDITIONAL READING**

**SVALBARD:**

"Arctic blast can harm your body in an instant:" http://www.wusa9.com/news/health/arctic-blast-can-harm-your-body-in-an-instant/285243616

*Arctic Dreams* by Barry Lopez

"Berry pickers from Finland worry industry:" http://sverigesradio.se/sida/artikel.aspx?programid=2054&artikel=4661960

*The Bradt Guide to Svalbard* by Andreas Umbreit

"Byrd Antarctic Expedition II 1933-35:" http://www.south-pole.com/p0000108.htm

"Cold and Body:" http://manfredkaiser.com/?s=cold+and+body

"Confrontations between humans and polar bears in Svalbard:" http://www.polarresearch.net/index.php/polar/article/viewFile/6881/7714

*The Consolations of the Forest: Alone in a Cabin on the Siberian Taiga* by Sylvain Tesson

"Denmark doesn't treat its prisoners like prisoners — and it's good for everyone:" https://www.washingtonpost.com/posteverything/wp/2016/02/02/denmark-doesnt-treat-its-prisoners-like-prisoners-and-its-good-for-everyone/?utm_term=.2c6d13634192

"Detailed Discussion of Polar Bears and the Laws Governing Them in the Five Arctic States:" https://www.animallaw.info/article/detailed-discussion-polar-bears-and-laws-governing-them-five-arctic-states#id-13

"Eclipses And The Moon's Nodes:" http://astrologyclub.org/eclipses-and-the-moons-nodes/

*Bill Murray*

"The Effects of Extreme Cold:" http://www.allianz-assistance.ca/en/
help-for-customers/travel-advice/during-your-trip/the-effects-of-
extreme-cold.aspx

"Effects of the Extreme Cold on the Human Body:" http://
www.inchr.com/effects-of-the-extreme-cold-on-the-human-body/

"Five awful things extreme cold does to the human body" by Daniel
Martins: https://www.theweathernetwork.com/news/articles/five-
awful-things-extreme-cold-does-to-the-human-body/43834/

"Fridtjof Nansen, Man of many facets:" http://www.mnc.net/norway/
Nansen.htm

"Friluftsliv:" https://en.wikipedia.org/wiki/Freedom_to_roam

"Futhark: Mysterious Ancient Runic Alphabet of Northern Europe:"
http://www.ancient-origins.net/artifacts-ancient-writings/futhark-
mysterious-ancient-runic-alphabet-northern-europe-003250

*Generous Betrayal* by Unni Wikan

*Girl at War* by Sara Nović

"How Eddington demonstrated that Einstein was right" by Kash
Farooq: https://thethoughtstash.wordpress.com/2011/01/03/how-
eddington-demonstrated-that-einstein-was-right/

"How Humans Deal With And Survive Extreme Cold:" http://
www.coolantarctica.com/Antarctica%20fact%20file/science/
cold_humans.php

"How Politics Shaped General Relativity" by David Kaiser: http://
www.nytimes.com/2015/11/08/opinion/how-politics-shaped-general-
relativity.html

*Icepeople*: http://icepeople.net

*Islands Beyond the Horizon, The Life of Twenty of the World's Most Remote Places* by Roger Lovegrove

List of countries by refugee population: https://en.wikipedia.org/wiki/List_of_countries_by_refugee_population#cite_ref-nor_8-0

"How Humans Deal With And Survive Extreme Cold:" http://www.coolantarctica.com/Antarctica%20fact%20file/science/cold_humans.php

"How Many Polar Bears Are There in Svalbard?" https://thornews.com/2014/10/22/how-many-polar-bears-are-there-in-svalbard/

"How Wonder Works" by Jesse Prinz: https://aeon.co/essays/why-wonder-is-the-most-human-of-all-emotions

"March 20 eclipse and the Saros" by Fred Espenak: http://earthsky.org/space/march-20-eclipse-and-the-saros

"Norwegian mass killer Breivik to sue to end prison isolation" by Gwladys Fouche and Terje Solsvik: http://www.businessinsider.com/r-norwegian-mass-killer-breivik-to-sue-to-end-prison-isolation-2015-10

"Migration policy promotes foreigner inequality in the workforce:" http://yle.fi/uutiset/osasto/news/study_migration_policy_promotes_foreigner_inequality_in_the_workforce/7721007

*New York Review of Books*, March 5 2015, Hugh Eakin on Unni Wikan

"Norway Offers Migrants a Lesson in How to Treat Women:" http://www.nytimes.com/2015/12/20/world/europe/norway-offers-migrants-a-lesson-in-how-to-treat-women.html

"Norway to disarm its police force after officers ordered to carry guns for just one year:" http://www.independent.co.uk/news/world/europe/

*Bill Murray*

norway-to-disarm-its-police-force-after-officers-ordered-to-carry-guns-just-one-year-a6844946.html

"Norway's capital wants to ban cars from its city center, once and for all:" http://qz.com/527833/norways-capital-wants-to-ban-cars-from-its-city-center-once-and-for-all/

"Norwegian Air resumes Svalbard flights despite strike:" http://icepeople.net/2015/03/09/norwegian-air-resumes-svalbard-flights-despite-strike/#more-356

*Norwegian Folk Tales* by P. Chr. Asbjørnsen & Jørgen Moe

"Norwegian Police Will No Longer Carry the Guns They Don't Use:" http://foreignpolicy.com/2016/02/01/norwegian-police-will-no-longer-carry-the-guns-they-dont-use/

"The Norwegian Town Where the Sun Doesn't Rise by Kari Leibowitz:" http://www.theatlantic.com/health/archive/2015/07/the-norwegian-town-where-the-sun-doesnt-rise/396746/

"On Not Totally Seeing a Total Solar Eclipse" by Lavinia Greenlaw in the March 28, 2015 *New Yorker* magazine: http://www.newyorker.com/tech/elements/faroe-islands-2015-total-solar-eclipse

"Polar Bear Mauls Svalbard Tourist:" http://www.outsideonline.com/1962186/polar-bear-mauls-svalbard-tourist

"Polar Bears in Svalbard:" http://kho.unis.no/doc/Polar_bears_Svalbard.pdf

"Polar bears in Svalbard in good condition – so far:" http://www.npolar.no/en/news/2015/12-23-counting-of-polar-bears-in-svalbard.html

Polar Bears International: http://www.polarbearsinternational.org/

"Ramadan Fasting: Muslims In Arctic Look For Guidance On How To Fast In Darkness:" http://www.huffingtonpost.ca/2012/07/24/muslims-in-arctic-look-fo_n_1697528.html

"Reports from March 20th's Total Solar Eclipse:" http://www.skyandtelescope.com/astronomy-news/observing-news/reports-march-20-total-solar-eclipse-032020153/

*The Scramble for the Arctic, Ownership, Exploitation and Conflict in the Far North* by Richard Sale and Eugene Potapov

"The Search for Eclipses as Perfect as Earth's:" http://nautil.us/blog/the-search-for-eclipses-as-perfect-as-earths

*Skyfaring by* Mark Vanhoenacker

Slooh.com: http://Slooh.com

"Solar Eclipses for Beginners" by Fred Espenak: http://www.mreclipse.com/Special/SEprimer.html

"A Soviet Ghost Town in the Arctic Circle, Pyramiden Stands Alone" by Rachel Nuwer: http://www.smithsonianmag.com/travel/soviet-ghost-town-arctic-circle-pyramiden-stands-alone-180951429/?no-ist

"Svalbard - Climate change, resources and ownership" by Maartje Tubbesing: http://www1.american.edu/ted/ICE/svalbard.html

"Svalbard eclipse prompts warnings:" http://www.newsinenglish.no/2015/01/22/svalbard-eclipse-prompts-warnings/

"Svalbard, Tourism's Final Frontier:" http://www.ft.com/intl/cms/s/2/afcda94a-018c-11e6-99cb-83242733f755.html

Svalbard population statistics: https://www.ssb.no/en/befolkning/statistikker/befsvalbard/halvaar/2015-09-24?fane=tabell&sort=nummer&tabell=240632

"Thai Seasonal Migrants Working for the Finnish Wild Berry Industry" by Pekka Rantanen: https://isaconf.confex.com/isaconf/wc2014/webprogram/Paper67646.html

"The Total Solar Eclipse of 2015:" https://live.slooh.com/stadium/live/the-total-solar-eclipse-of-2015

*Totality, Eclipses of the Sun* by Mark Littman, Ken Willcox & Fred Espinak

"Trapped to Pick Berries in Finland: The Many Forms of Labour Trafficking:" http://humantraffickingcenter.org/posts-by-htc-associates/trapped-to-pick-berries-in-finland-the-many-forms-of-labour-trafficking/

VisitNorway.com: https://www.visitnorway.com/

*The Wayfinders* by Wade Davis

"What Effect Does Extreme Cold Have on the Human Body?:" http://www.bbc.com/future/story/20140107-what-extreme-cold-does-to-human

*World of the Polar Bear* by Peter Scott, Thor Larsen

**THE FAROE ISLANDS:**

*The Baltic, a New History of the Region and Its People* by Alan Palmer

"The Best Lamb Is Fermented by Sea Air:" https://munchies.vice.com/en/articles/the-best-lamb-is-fermented-by-sea-air

*The Brendan Voyage* by Tim Severin

"Early Norse Navigation Tools:" http://tigerprints.clemson.edu/cgi/viewcontent.cgi?article=1045&context=lib_pres

"Eight Things Americans Should Know about the Danish (and Nordic) Welfare Stake:" http://suffragio.org/2015/10/14/eight-things-americans-should-know-about-the-danish-and-nordic-welfare-state/

"Exploitation of Aquatic Systems and The Emergence of Commercial Fishing:" http://www.academia.edu/15690210/Exploitation_of_Aquatic_Systems_and_The_Emergence_of_Commercial_Fishing

Faroe Business Report 2010: http://fbr.nordixis.co/_fbr10/FBR10_lores.pdf

"The Faroe Islands: Options for Independence" by Maria Ackrén PhD Candidate Åbo Akademi University Åbo, Finland: Island Studies Journal, Vol. 1, No. 2, 2006, pp. 223-238 http://www.islandstudies.ca/sites/vre2.upei.ca.islandstudies.ca/files/u2/ISJ-1-2-2006-Ackren-article.pdf

"The Faroe Islands' Security Policy in a Process of Devolution:" http://www.academia.edu/3536917/The_Faroe_Islands_Security_Policy_in_a_Process_of_Devolution

"Faroe Islands: Vagar Airport records biggest ever passenger numbers:" http://www.icenews.is/2015/01/13/faroe-islands-vagar-airport-records-biggest-ever passenger-numbers/

*Faroe, the Emergence of a Nation*, by West, John F. (1972). London, C. Hurst; New York, P. S. Eriksson.

"Faroese (Føroyskt):" http://www.omniglot.com/writing/faroese.htm

"Faroese independence movement:" https://en.wikipedia.org/wiki/Faroese_independence_movement

Global Peat Resources by Country: http://www.peatsociety.org/peatlands-and-peat/global-peat-resources-country

Bill Murray

*The Good Hope* by William Heinesen

"Grindadráp, Out of our backyard" by Kevin McGwin: http://arcticjournal.com/culture/2279/out-our-backyard

*Harvest* by Jim Crace

"Infield-Outfield Systems — characteristics and development in different climatic environments" by SOFUS CHRISTIANSEN: https://tidsskrift.dk/index.php/geografisktidsskrift/article/view/6739/12835

*The Last Refuge* by Craig Robertson

*Liberal, Harsh Denmark* by Hugh Eakin in The New York Review of Books, Volume LXIII, Number 4, March 10, 2016

Mapping Megan: http://http://www.mappingmegan.com/

*The New Tsar* by Steven Lee Myers

*1913* by Charles Emerson

Nólsoy: https://issuu.com/visittorshavn/docs/nolsoy_faldari_en

"The Official Gateway to the Faroe Islands:" http://www.faroeislands.fo/

*An Outline History of Denmark* by Helge Seidelin Jacobsen

*The Old Man and His Sons* by Heðin Brú

"On Not Totally Seeing a Total Solar Eclipse" by <u>Lavinia Greenlaw</u>: http://www.newyorker.com/tech/elements/faroe-islands-2015-total-solar-eclipse

*An Outline History of Denmark* by helge Seidelin Jacobsen

*The Physical Environment of the Faeroe Islands* edited by G.K. Rutherford

*Pilot Whaling in the Faroe Islands* by Joan Pauli Joensen, 2009

"Russia Threatens Danish Warships with Nuclear Weapons:" http://www.newsweek.com/russia-targets-danish-warships-nuclear-weapons-315928

*The Sleepwalkers* by Christopher Clark

"Solidarity and Sharing" (Grindadráp): http://www.whaling.fo/en/communal/solidarity-and-sharing/

*To Copenhagen a Fleet, The British Pre-emptive Seizure of the Danish-Norwegian Navy, 1807* by Hans Christian Bjerg in the International Journal of Naval History, August 2008, Volume 7 Number 2

"Total Solar Eclipse of 2245 May 26:" http://eclipsewise.com/solar/SEgmap/2201-2300/SE2245May26Tgmap.html

"The Tree Farm" by Cal Flyn: https://granta.com/the-tree-farm/

*True North* by Gavin Francis

*Windswept Dawn* by William Heinesen

*A World Lit Only by Fire* by William Manchester

"Yes, I butcher whales. What's all the fuss about?" by Heri Joensen: http://www.spectator.co.uk/2016/09/in-the-faroe-islands-we-butcher-whales-heres-why/

"You Provide Sustenance For Yourself With What Is Available To You" by Elin Brimheim Heinesen: http://heinesen.info/wp/blog/2014/11/21/you-provide-sustenance-for-yourself-with-what-is-available-to-you/

## ICELAND:

"Adam Smith: Selected Philosophical Writings:" https://www.amazon.com/Adam-Smith-Selected-Philosophical-Philosophy/dp/1845400011/

"Air Travel Crisis Deepens as Europe Fears Wider Impact" by Steven Erlanger and Jack Ewing: http://www.nytimes.com/2010/04/18/world/europe/18ash.html

*The Almost Nearly Perfect People, The Truth About the Nordic People* by Michael Booth

"Aluminum Smelting By-Products:" http://www.shashikallada.com/aluminium-smelting-by-products/

*Atlantic* by Simon Winchester

"Construction of a pagan temple to begin in Reykjavík next month:" http://icelandmag.visir.is/article/construction-a-pagan-temple-begin-reykjavik-next-month

"The day Iceland's women went on strike" by Kirstie Brewer: http://www.bbc.com/news/magazine-34602822

"The Discovery of Iceland" by Kristin Axelsdottir: http://www.viking.no/e/info-sheets/iceland/iceland.htm

"Elf lobby blocks Iceland road project:" https://www.theguardian.com/world/2013/dec/22/elf-lobby-iceland-road-project

"Elton John performs at Icelandic birthday party:" http://icelandreview.com/news/2007/01/22/elton-john-performs-icelandic-birthday-party

"Elves delay Iceland road-building project: http://www.icenews.is/2014/01/01/elves-delay-iceland-road-building-project/

*Extreme Geohazards* by the European Science Foundation

"Financial crisis: Full statement by Iceland's prime minister Geir Haarde:" http://www.telegraph.co.uk/news/worldnews/europe/iceland/3147806/Financial-crisis-Full-statement-by-Icelands-prime-minister-Geir-Haarde.html

*Fire: Nature and Culture* by Stephen J Pyne

*Iceland* by Roger K. Sandness and Charles F. Gritzner

"Iceland, from the Observatory of Economic Complexity:" http://atlas.media.mit.edu/en/profile/country/isl/

"Iceland plans Airbnb restrictions amid tourism explosion" by Caroline Davies: https://www.theguardian.com/world/2016/may/30/iceland-plans-airbnb-restrictions-amid-tourism-explosion

"Iceland Ranks High on World Atheist List:" http://icelandreview.com/news/2012/08/13/iceland-ranks-high-world-atheist-list

"Iceland: Where one in 10 people will publish a book" by Rosie Goldsmith: http://www.bbc.com/news/magazine-24399599

"Iceland's Financial Crisis" by Iceland Chamber of Commerce: http://vi.is/files/1350175258Icelandic+Financial+Crisis.pdf

"The Icelandic Althing - Dawn of Parliamentary Democracy" by Jesse Byock: http://www.viking.ucla.edu/publications/articles/icelandic_allthing.pdf

"Icelandic Scorn Poles, A Look At Historical Witchcraft Of Scandinavia:" https://theroadtohel.wordpress.com/2014/06/04/2180/

"Icelandic Volcano Caused Historic Famine In Egypt, Study Shows:" https://www.sciencedaily.com/releases/2006/11/061121232204.htm

*Independent People* by Haldor Laxness

"Interview with Hilmar Örn Hilmarsson of the Ásatrúarfélagið, Part Two:" http://www.norsemyth.org/2011/06/interview-with-hilmar-orn-hilmarsson-of_30.html

*Island on Fire* by Alexandra Witze & Jeff Kanipe

*Íslendingabók*: http://www.vsnrweb-publications.org.uk/Text %20Series/IslKr.pdf

"Letter from Iceland:" http://www.ft.com/intl/cms/s/0/66c87994-aec1-11dd-b621-000077b07658.html

*Meltdown Iceland* by Roger Boyes

"Moral Hazard in Iceland:" http://www.huffingtonpost.com/iris-lee/moral-hazard-in-iceland_b_457531.html

*Nazistar* by Hrafn Jökulsson

The Norse Mythology Blog: http://www.norsemyth.org/

*The Northern Lights* by Lucy Jago

*Reagan at Reykjavik, Forty-Eight Hours that Ended the Cold War* by Ken Adelman

*The Rise of Iceland's Heathens* by Fiona Zublin: http://www.ozy.com/fast-forward/the-rise-of-icelands-heathens/73711

*The Saga of Hord*

*Stories of the Vikings* by Mary Macgregor

"The Strange Lake Nyos $CO_2$ Gas Disaster:" http://www.massey.ac.nz/~trauma/issues/2011-1/fomine.htm

Thingvellir: http://www3.gettysburg.edu/~cfee/
MedievalNorthAtlantic/Thingvellir/

Thingvellir History: http://www.thingvellir.is/history.aspx

"Tourism in Iceland in Figures:" http://www.ferdamalastofa.is/static/
files/ferdamalastofa/Frettamyndir/2015/mai/tourism-in-iceland-in-
figures_15.pdf

*Visitors to Ancient America*, William F. McNeil

"Volcanic Eruptions: Science And Risk Management" by <u>Bente Lilja
Bye</u>: http://www.science20.com/planetbye/
volcanic_eruptions_science_and_risk_management-79456

*Why Iceland? How One of the World's Smallest Countries Became the
Meltdown's Biggest Casualty* by Ásgeir Jónsson

"Why Iceland Is Building a Temple to Its Pagan Gods:" http://
www.thedailybeast.com/articles/2015/02/05/why-iceland-is-building-
a-temple-to-its-pagan-gods.html


**GREENLAND:**

*The Age of the Vikings* by Anders Winroth

*Ammassalik, East Greenland - end or persistence of an isolate?
Anthropological and demographical study on change* by Joëlle Robert-
Lamblin

*The Arctic, The Complete Story* by Richard Sale

*Collapse* by Jared Diamond

*Crowds and Power* by Elias Canetti

Bill Murray

"Cultural adaptation, compounding vulnerabilities and conjunctures in Norse Greenland:" http://www.pubpdf.com/pub/22371594/Cultural-adaptation-compounding-vulnerabilities-and-conjunctures-in-Norse-Greenland

*Eskimos and Explorers* by Wendell H. Oswalt

*The Frozen Echo, Greenland and the Exploration of North America ca A.D. 1000-1500* by Kirsten A. Seaver

*Greenland, The End of the World* by Damjan Končnik with Kevin Kato

*A History of the Vikings* by Gwyn Jones

*Last Places* by Lawrence Millman
*The Magnetic North* by Sara Wheeler

*The Man Who Ate His Boots, the Tragic History of the Search for the Northwest Passage* by Anthony Brandt

"Mead and the Vikings" by Paul Lewandowski: http://warontherocks.com/2016/01/mead-and-the-vikings/

*The Memory of Water* by Allen Smutlyo

*North to the Night, A Year in the Arctic Ice* by Alvah Simon

*Polar Mirages as Aids to Norse Navigation* by W. H. Lehn and I. I. Schroeder

Tangling with Tupilaks by Lawrence Millman: http://grapevine.is/travel/2013/08/06/tangling-with-tupilaks/

*This Cold Heaven, Seven Seasons in Greenland* by Gretel Ehrlich

Viking Cultures: http://ecuip.lib.uchicago.edu/diglib/science/cultural_astronomy/cultures_vikings-2.html

Viking Navigation: http://ecuip.lib.uchicago.edu/diglib/science/cultural_astronomy/cultures_vikings-2.html

*Vikings* by Tracey Ann Schofield

*Visitors to Ancient America: The Evidence for European and Asian Presence in America Prior to Columbus* by WIlliam F. McNeil

*White Heat* by M. J. McGrath


**CANADA:**

*A Voyage Long and Strange: On the Trail of Vikings, Conquistadors, Lost Colonists, and Other Adventurers in Early America* by <u>Tony Horwitz</u>

*Ancient Site in Newfoundland Offers Clues to Vikings in America* by John Noble Wilford: http://www.nytimes.com/learning/teachers/featured_articles/20000509tuesday.html

*Blizzard of Glass* by Sally M. Walker

*Brilliant Beacons: A History of the American Lighthouse* by Eric Jay Dolin

"Cape Bauld, Newfoundland:" http://www.lighthousefriends.com/light.asp?ID=1268

"Cod Make a Comeback:" https://www.newscientist.com/article/dn27867-cod-make-a-comeback-thanks-to-strict-cuts-in-fishing/

"The collapse of the cod fishery of the grand banks:" http://www.sjsu.edu/faculty/watkins/grandbanks.htm

*Crossroads of the World* by Roderick B. Goff

*Curse of the Narrows* by Laura M. MacDonald

*Bill Murray*

*The Day the World Came to Town, 9/11 in Gander, Newfoundland* by Jim Defede

*Death on the Ice* by Cassie Brown and Harold Harwood

*Doyle's Almanac of Newfoundland 2016*

*Even Scientists Act Superstitious at Sea* by Erica Cirino: http://nautil.us/blog/even-scientists-act-superstitious-at-sea

*Fate is the Hunter* by Ernest K. Gann

"Gander Airport, Our History:" http://www.ganderairport.com/about-giaa/history-growth/

"The Grand Banks: Where Have All the Cod Gone?" https://www.nps.gov/olym/learn/education/upload/The-Grand-Banks-Collapse.pdf

"Hunting the origins of 'Newfie Steak'" by Tobias Romaniuk: http://www.thetelegram.com/Living/2012-04-04/article-2946865/Hunting-the-origins-of-&lsquoNewfie-Steak&rsquo/1

"The Labrador Gale of 1885:" http://ngb.chebucto.org/Articles/dis-labrador-gale-1885.shtml

*Left to Die: The Story of the SS Newfoundland Sealing Disaster* by Gary Collins

"A Long Weekend in France without Leaving North America (Really!)" by Saul Gitlin: http://www.huffingtonpost.com/saul-gitlin/a-long-weekend-in-france-without-leaving-north-america-really_b_7992924.html

"The Newfoundland Disaster by Robert Cuff:" http://www.seethesites.ca/media/43905/the%20newfoundland%20disaster%20of%201914%20_2_.pdf

"Newfoundland's 1914 sealing disaster:" http://www.canadashistory.ca/Magazine/Online-Extension/Articles/Newfoundland-s-1914-Sealing-Disaster

*Perished: The 1914 Newfoundland Seal Hunt Disaster* by Jenny Higgins

"The 1914 Sealing Disaster:" http://www.heritage.nf.ca/articles/politics/sealing-disaster-1914.php

"The 1914 sealing disaster: 100 years later:" http://www.cbc.ca/news/canada/newfoundland-labrador/the-1914-sealing-disaster-100-years-later-1.2591837

"The North and the great Canadian lie" by Scott Gilmore: http://www.macleans.ca/politics/the-north-and-the-great-canadian-lie/

*The Sea and Civilization* by Lincoln Paine

*Seafaring Superstitions & Marine Myth Rituals Explored*: https://dtmag.com/thelibrary/seafaring-superstitions-marine-myth-rituals-explored/

*Shattered City, the Halifax Explosion and the Road to Recovery* by Janet F. Kitz

*The Story of Newfoundland* by Frederick Edwin Smith

*Superstitions and the Sea* by Cindy Vallar: http://www.cindyvallar.com/superstitions.html

*Superstitions, Portents, Omens, Jinx, Taboos in the Sailing World*: http://www.snipetoday.org/articles/exchange-of-views/item/1360-superstitions-portents-omens-jinx-taboos-in-the-sailing-world

*Taboos of the Yorkshire Trawlermen who Fished the Arctic Waters* by Dr. Alec Gill MBE: https://www.hull.ac.uk/php/cetag/5bseadal.htm

*Theatre of Fish* by John Gimlette

"To the Lighthouse" by Nathaniel Rick in *New York Review of Books*, May 26, 2016

"The Transpacific:" http://www.vos.noaa.gov/MWL/fall_03/transpacific.shtml

"The Vinland and Skálholt maps:" http://bigthink.com/strange-maps/433-plotting-vineland-the-skalholt-map

"The Vinland Map:" http://archives.chicagotribune.com/1965/10/11/page/32/article/map-proves-norse-explored-america

*The Vinland Sagas, The Norse Discovery Of America* by Anonymous and Magnus Magnusson, Penguin Classics

## ABOUT THE AUTHOR

Bill Murray has visited 120 countries and territories from Albania to Zimbabwe. His other books are: *Common Sense and Whiskey*, a collection of off-the-beaten-path stories, and *Visiting Chernobyl, A Considered Guide for Travelers*, a quick, accessible introduction to the worst nuclear accident in history, written for both aspiring visitors and armchair travelers. Audiobook versions of both are available, narrated by the author.

•••••

Bill and his wife Mirja maintain the photo web site EarthPhotos.com, featuring 20,000+ photos from around the world. They live on a horse farm in the southern Appalachian mountains of Georgia, U.S.A.

Blog: commonsenseandwhiskey.com
Twitter: @BMurrayWriter